Is It Love
or
Is It Addiction?

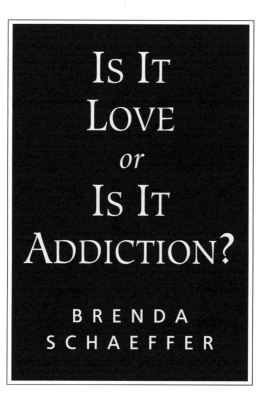

IS IT
LOVE
or
IS IT
ADDICTION?

B R E N D A
S C H A E F F E R

THIRD EDITION

HAZELDEN®

Hazelden
Center City, Minnesota 55012
hazelden.org

Library of Congress Cataloging-in-Publication Data
Schaeffer, Brenda.
  Is it love or is it addiction? / Brenda Schaeffer.—3rd ed.
  p. cm.
  Includes bibliographical references and index.
  ISBN 978-1-59285-733-3 (softcover)
  1. Relationship addiction. 2. Love. I. Title.
RC552.R44S34 2009
158.2—dc22
                                                          2009004685

Editor's note
The vignettes in this book are composites of actual situations and persons. Those who wrote the autobiographies have given their permission and are real, although the names and some identifying events have been modified for purposes of confidentiality. Some names and events have been created by the author for illustrative purposes only. Any resemblance to specific persons, living or dead, or to specific events, is entirely coincidental.

This publication is not intended as a substitute for the advice of health care professionals.

        13 12   3 4 5 6

Cover design by Mary Ann Smith
Interior design by Will H. Powers
Typesetting by Madeline Berglund

I dedicate the third edition to Dr. Barton Knapp, whose friendship, wisdom, and wit inspire me deeply; to my children, Heidi and Gordy, that they may know healthy love; to my father, Ralph Furtman, in gratitude for his steadfast support and caring; to my mother, Bernice Furtman, in acknowledgment of her permission to be all that I can be. May the souls of Bart and my parents know a peace they so deserve.

A good book is a supple and yielding thing. It is meant to be argued with, challenged, marked up. It is a battle ground for ideas and should show some evidence of a fight or at least some preliminary skirmishes. It is good for igniting minds. It is not the be-all and end-all of a balanced and productive life, but it can touch off needed thoughts and action.

NORMAN COUSINS, Human Options

Contents

Preface

I am excited to present the third edition of *Is It Love or Is It Addiction?*—not because anything from the first two editions has been invalidated, but because there is so much fresh information to prop up what I have said in earlier editions. In some ways this is a totally new book, and so it should be, as the study of addictive love continues to develop and a new generation of lovers presents itself. New brain research and imaging now support that our attachments, attractions, and sexual drives are unique and how they can be used to self-medicate some obscure need within us. Technology has changed the way we relate to love, sex, and romance, whether for good or bad. And pending scientific research is providing evidence that, indeed, love makes the world go 'round.

When this book was first published in 1987, the idea of love, romance, and sex as addictions was new and quite controversial. There were few places where people suffering with love addiction could go and be taken seriously. Some addiction specialists and clinicians questioned whether a *process* such as sex, love, or romance (as opposed to a *substance* such as cocaine or nicotine) could be addicting at all.

Today, there are more professionals taking these process addictions seriously, there are inpatient and outpatient programs for them, and there are viable training programs that help therapists work with them. And because of the public attention sex addiction is now getting, the proliferation of books about it, and the organization of professionals behind it, sex addiction has become well known.

Just as the study and science of addictive love has evolved over the past twenty years, so, too, has my experience and knowledge of the subject. I gave my first lecture on addictive love in the early 1980s. I had been invited by a local treatment center to give an evening lecture. It was a blustery, cold evening with blizzard warnings out, and I almost cancelled. But considering that some might already be on their way to the lecture, I decided it was important to be there. When I arrived, I was amazed to find an auditorium overflowing with people. Some who had made the harsh journey out that night had to listen and watch from a cafeteria monitor. The title of my presentation was "Love and Other Addictions."

The first edition of this book grew directly from that lecture. Its phenomenal success was as surprising to me as the number of people who turned out for that first lecture. The audiences of both told me I was talking about something important to them. Although the professional community was still grappling with the concept of process addictions, the readers understood love as an addiction because they were living it.

The first two editions of this book used the term *love addiction* to discuss the myriad problems people encounter in their love relationships. Yet over the years, the readers of this book and my therapy clients taught me that I was indirectly addressing three different, often overlapping, kinds of process addictions—love, romance, and sex. It was time for the language of this book to catch up with this development. This third edition uses the umbrella term *addictive love* and the categories "love addiction," "romance addiction," and "sex addiction." *Love addiction* will refer to the enmeshed attachments we form with other people. Much of what I wrote about in my first two editions refers to this. *Romance addiction* will refer to the unhealthy attachment to the sensations that being in love produces, and *sex addiction* will refer to the uncontrollable attachment to sexual activity. This edition speaks to all three.

One wish I have for you, the reader, is that through this book you pick up one new insight that can help you or someone you care about enjoy and protect the human gifts of sex, love, and romance. If you do, I have done my job.

Acknowledgments

A book begins as a creative thought in its author's mind. The road from idea to publication is a long and sometimes arduous one. From the onset, my road contained many supportive people whom I wish to gratefully acknowledge. I wish to thank Muriel James, Jean Clarke, and Patricia Dunn for encouraging me to write, and my brother, Michael Furtman, along with Dr. Bart Knapp and Lynnell Mickelsen, for their critical review of the first draft. Their honesty and encouragement are deeply appreciated. I wish to thank Pam Miller for her creative editing. Nancy Barrett, my typist, deserves special thanks for miraculously transposing any handwritten words into legible type. Thanks, also, to my agent, Vicky Lansky, for her enthusiastic support of my manuscript, and to my secretary, Jan Johannes, for working odd hours to meet deadlines.

I wish to extend grateful appreciation to those at Hazelden who believed in and encouraged the publishing of the first edition of this book—Jim Heaslip, Beth Milligan, and Pat Benson. Thanks, too, to editors Judy Delaney and Brian Lynch, who took the time to care about my perceptions.

Thanks to the Rev. Fred W. Hutchinson for his spiritual guidance and support. A very special thank-you to my children, Heidi and Gordy, for their loving acceptance of me and the time it took to write this book.

I would be remiss if I did not mention those who contributed their thoughts to the second edition. Heartfelt thanks go to Peter R. Richards, Patrick Carnes, Jennifer Schneider, Sally Stevens, Christina Storbeck, Mark Laaser, Helen Palmer, Jacquelyn Small, Bart Knapp, Homer Mittelstadt, Barry McKee, Jerry Buckanaga, and Linda Star Wolf. Special thanks go to Hazelden editors Steve Lehman and Dan

Odegard, who understand the importance of the written word.

I wish to thank Cathy Broberg, editor of the third edition, for her diligence and skill in blending the new with the old while maintaining the integrity of the original work.

Beyond that, I want to thank my canine pal, Sage, who patiently sat by my desk and insisted I take walks in the woods at predictable times, and to nature for providing the pristine setting I write in.

To the men and women who, over the years, opened your hearts to me and kept them open, thank you. To those who opened and then closed them, I thank you, too. There are important lessons in it all.

I am, perhaps, most grateful to the clients who took the time to live and validate the theory I write about, especially those who wrote their stories so others can experience hope. Thank you.

The following publishers have generously given permission to use quotations from copyrighted works: Page 159: from *The Prophet* by Kahlil Gibran, copyright 1923, renewed 1951 by Administrators C.T.A. of Kahlil Gibran Estate, and Mary G. Gibran. Reprinted with permission of Alfred A. Knopf, Inc. Page 175: from *Scripts People Live* by Claude Steiner, copyright 1974, as printed in a handout at an International Transactional Analysis Association (ITAA) conference. Reprinted with permission of the author. Pages 168, 183: from *The Bridge Across Forever* by Richard Bach, copyright 1984. Reprinted with permission of the author. Pages vii, 185: from *Human Options* by Norman Cousins, copyright 1981. Reprinted with permission of W. W. Norton and Company, Inc. Page 185: from *The Velveteen Rabbit* by Margery Williams, copyright 1975. Reprinted with permission of Doubleday. Page 10: from *Love and Addiction* by Stanton Peele, with Archie Brodsky, copyright 1975. Reprinted with permission of Taplinger Publishing Co., Inc. Pages 7, 40, 160, 173: from *The Art of Loving* by Erich Fromm, copyright 1956. Reprinted with permission of Harper and Row.

Introduction

People everywhere are struggling to have more meaningful relationships. I have met men struggling to change cultural habits that shame them for being vulnerable, or that tell them it is healthy and macho to act in sexually addictive ways. I have met women struggling to call attention to our cultural endorsement of unhealthy dependencies, romantic illusions, and sex as a consumer product. In my travels around the world, I have heard scores of relationship stories from people of diverse cultural backgrounds. And everywhere, women and men are confused about what is healthy, mature, interdependent love and what is compulsive, dependent, addictive, immature love. I have been reminded how many people hold back their love because of being wounded by a parent, friend, partner, society, or cultural group. People desperately want yet fear intimate relationships. The result is loneliness, isolation, pain, violence, and more betrayal.

So, is it love, or is it addiction? The answer is that it is probably a little of both. In that regard, this book is for *anyone* wanting to improve important love relationships, whether they are with children, parents, friends, peers, siblings, partners, or lovers. You do not need to be a love addict to recognize the warning signs. *Addictive love* is an inclusive term in that it includes men and women, both heterosexual and homosexual, some of whom have been referred to as "addicts" and "co-addicts," "codependents," and "love avoidant." It is for the single and the coupled. Addictive love may or may not include a romantic high or sexual addiction.

In truth, sometimes a love relationship feels good, and sometimes it feels bad. Often a person does not understand why. In spite of the proliferation of self-help books on the subject, love relationships

1

remain a profound mystery: Why do we have certain attractions? Why do we continue to want relationships even after a devastating loss? What is it about a relationship that is so powerful that we fear commitment? Am I staying in a relationship for the right or wrong reason? Why is transforming our love life so important? Am I in love or in addiction? These questions are universal and deserve answers.

As a psychotherapist, I'm asked to help others ease their emotional pain. I'm reminded over and over again how basic is the need for love. In spite of the bereavement we feel when a loved one dies or a relationship ends, we seem determined to keep loving. Why? Is it because we are compelled to fill some mysterious inner need? Are we using love to avoid the bombardment of stress that contemporary life produces? Are we responding to a deeper need to connect soul to soul? Or is it because we believe at some level that true, deep love is the only constant we can count on in this somewhat perilous life?

The problems in love relationships stem not from the nature of love. True love is life-giving. It is an expansive, nourishing energy that knows no limits. It does not injure, it heals. Problems arise from the fear that originates in a violation of trust. Such violations make it difficult to be vulnerable to love again. In the wake of such violations, we become guarded. The result is relationships that have more drama than intimacy. Being in a relationship that is floundering can be like having a pain in the neck or an aggravating headache. And, when we are sick, we lose ourselves. Our capacity for creative living gets sapped as we instead focus on our pain. We become driven to find relief from that pain, seeking quick fixes in the form of substances, people, and processes outside of ourselves. Obsessive illnesses and addictions often result. When the attachment is to a person, romantic highs, or sex, it can become addictive love.

Almost everyone has addictive tendencies. We know that we can become addicted to alcohol and other drugs and that we have excellent programs to treat those addictions. There are other things and behaviors that we can become dependent on or obsessed with to the point that they can hamper our lives as well, but they are not always recognized or addressed. This list includes food, exercise, spending, sugar, sex, gambling, video games, work, the Internet, television, love objects, romance, drama, pain, chronic illness, and even religion. Perhaps you recognize an obsession of your own among them. If you do, be kind to yourself. We live in a world that provides hundreds more experiences than our parents had. We are constantly bombarded with more information than we can possibly take in and process. We have more demands on our time. We hear threatening news each day that perpetuates fear. And, in the midst of this, we are expected to live our love relationships well, if not perfectly. I used to say that a love relationship is like a hundred-piece puzzle, and we are lucky if we have 20 or 30 percent of the pieces. Now, with the barrage of information, images, and ideas we encounter daily, that percentage is going down. Many of the pieces we do have are out of date or lead to dead ends.

The focus of this book is to foster an understanding of addictive love—what it is and is not, how to identify it, and even more important, how to get out of it. It is intended to be a hopeful book that helps you identify the characteristics of healthy love and frees you to live life more abundantly. As you will learn, real love is not addiction, nor is addiction to romance and sex love. Yet, because of the human condition, these two experiences can come together and result in tremendous pain and suffering. Sex, love, and romance are delightful aspects of our humanness. We must be wise in the ways we express them. May you find some wisdom here that impacts your love life in a meaningful way. This book is not intended to cure specific problems. However, with increased awareness, we can begin to solve relationship problems with more compassion and with lasting effect.

My hope is that this book gives you a few more pieces to the love/relationship puzzle.

I

The Reality of Addictive Love

1

The Power of Love

Healthy Love

Of all the mysteries that enchant us, love may be the one most sought after. In *The Art of Loving*, Erich Fromm, the German-born American psychoanalyst, says most efforts to love fail unless a person has actively tried to develop his individual potential and personality. Fromm defines love as "the expression of productiveness [which] implies care, respect, responsibility, and knowledge; a striving towards growth and happiness of the loved person, rooted in one's own capacity to love."[1] Concepts we often associate with healthy human loving include affection, caring, valuing, trust, acceptance, giving, joy, and vulnerability.

Love is a state of being that emanates from within us and extends outward. It is energy, it is unconditional, it is expansive, and it needs no specific object. Love is free and available to all. It does not care what you look like, what you believe, what you do for a living, what your gender orientation is, and whether you are married, single, or in a relationship at all. It couldn't care less if you are a prince or pauper, sinner or saint. Though religion speaks to it, it is not cloaked in any dogma. We are *all* intended to be in the service of love. If you consider it, much human suffering results from denial of or resistance to this responsibility.

We must not confuse the power of love with sentimentality or physical love. It is far greater. Like food, it nourishes us and others. *In fact, love is the most cost-effective medical insurance policy and the cheapest medicine there is. And there is no end to its supply.* Love has been proven to strengthen the immune system, increase life expectancy, reduce depression, produce zestful children, and induce feelings of calm, safety, and trust. *And,* as you will learn, there is growing scientific evidence that some things we pass off as love are bad for our health.

Some have described love as the ultimate religious experience. It revels in the perpetual goodness that being in a relationship offers. Love is doing everything with a joyful heart and without trying to escape our pain. In deep love there is awe, mystery, gratitude, sorrow, rapture, ecstasy, grace, luminosity, and sacredness. The flood of emotions can run deep beyond measure. The love-inspired person often displays a nobility of character, and her virtues flourish. Witness a mother's love for her newborn, lovers in love, a person grieving the death of a beloved friend, a child reveling in the birth of kittens. When people bond in a loving way, everything seems to fall in place, even in times of chaos and doubt. When intimacy is profound, something inside of us says, "This is it." When love is present, no words are necessary.[2]

Hints of the idea of deep-partnership love were first recorded as appearing at the beginning of the twelfth century, when courtly or passionate love for another, rather than being considered sinful, was viewed as love emanating from the soul. Passion meant suffering. *Eros,* our longing for physical union, united with *agape,* the universal spiritual love of our neighbor, and became *amour,* a profound personal love relationship. This profound experience precedes any physical union. With amour, touch and sexuality are sacred.[3] This experience is in complete contrast to the lover of euphoria or the lover of a sexual high. There, pleasure is the primary goal. In healthy love, the senses are honored and respected as a meaningful part of the love relationship. There is yet another essential love we bring to relationships—*compassion.* A compassionate person sees and feels with the heart and wishes good things for others and self. Compassion requires us to make decisions in our relationships from love and not fear. It heals wounds and creates a feeling of safety that moves us through the difficult times.

Love can actually be experienced as emanating from the heart. We know who has an open heart, a warm heart, a callous heart, or who shows no heart at all. When two people are together, their hearts are always talking. Our hearts broadcast an energy field, and what is in that field—love or fear—deeply impacts those around us. Many spiritual schools emphasize how the heart is the bridge between our human experience and our spiritual experience. As Charlotte Kasl said: "We don't find love by chasing after it; we simply open our hearts and find it within us."[4]

But as we will see, most hearts have been injured, and it is an unhealed heart that is vulnerable to the unhealthy attachments to people, euphoria, romance, or sex that we will refer to as "addictive love." Think of the heart as having two sets of emotions. The lower emotions are connected to the hurts and injuries that lead to placing conditions on the love we offer to others. But our conditions are rarely fulfilled, and the result is that we end up feeling lonely, isolated, anxious, jealous, heartbroken, abandoned, betrayed, rageful, insecure, hateful, distant, or numb—once again. As we get to the source of these feelings and heal them, we begin to feel the higher emotions of the heart, those that lead to the deep unconditional love of self of which we are capable. When that happens, we are no longer dependent on our relationships to feel good. We want to reach out, share, embrace, give, nurture—all in the name of love. And a natural greening of Eros occurs.

Do not assume, however, that because you are in a relationship you are automatically in love. Love and relationship are not one and the same. Relationships are neutral places where we get to experience profound love as well as withhold it. Some relationships are toxic and mean. Almost every relationship problem is a love disorder problem. Love itself is not the problem, but it can be misunderstood, denied, distorted, mishandled, perverted, or betrayed—all of which can lead to addictive love.

The first love relationship we experienced was with our parents. Ideally, a parent's love unconditionally affirms a child's worth and life. The mother and father readily and easily fulfill the child's needs and give the child the feeling "It's good to be alive! It's good to be me! It's good to be with others! Love is terrific!"

Addiction

Stanton Peele and Archie Brodsky, authors of *Love and Addiction*, define addiction as "an unstable state of being, marked by a compulsion to deny all that you are or have been in favor of some new and ecstatic experience."[5] Any activity that can influence or shift our subjective experience holds addictive potential. As professionals continue their research into the biology of addictive love, they rely on common behavioral descriptions for clinical diagnosis.

Clinicians have found that an addiction is composed of three elements: obsession or preoccupation, a feeling of being out of control, and continuation of a behavior despite adverse physical or psychological consequences. Two other elements that may or may not be present are tolerance (progressively needing more of the object of addiction in order to get the same effect) and withdrawal symptoms. What these characteristics suggest is that what constitutes an addiction has more to do with how the object of addiction impacts a person's life than it does with the quantity of that object consumed or experienced. Using current standards emphasizing the above behaviors, we can see how sex, love, and romance qualify as objects of addictive behavior.[6]

Several researchers have shown that the euphoria produced by process addictions (e.g., sex, gambling, and spending) is the same as that produced by drug or substance (e.g., alcohol and other drug) addictions. According to Harvey Milkman and Stanley Sunderwirth, "We can become physically dependent on the experience of arousal, satiation or fantasy, independent of whether the capsule for transport is a substance or an activity."[7] Any activity, including love, that evokes any of these three sensations—arousal, satiation, and fantasy—brings about alterations to the brain chemistry. We are neurochemically vulnerable.

Our brains provide us naturally with these three sensations of pleasure as a way to experience life more fully. These three planes are controlled by hundreds of brain chemicals that we are only at the beginning stages of understanding. Without these chemicals, we would not have the ability to appreciate our own human nature. Phenylethylamine (PEA), for example, is a neurochemical that produces arousal states; it helps keep us alert and motivates us to action. Discomfort states, also produced by the activity of neurochemicals, help us identify our basic human needs so that we seek satisfaction and relief of the discomfort. Chemically controlled feelings of satiation then tell us we have had enough and allow our bodies to go into homeostasis, or balance. Still other chemicals are necessary for a rich fantasy life. This self-induced trance state helps us to luxuriate in a future of pleasant options, revel in a piece of art, experience a sunset, and feel great passion as we write a song. Contentment, creative passion, sexual excitation—each has neurochemical analogues.

Addictions tap into one or more of these same pleasure planes or "feel-good" chemicals. Some people crave arousal and exhilaration and get caught up in anything that is dangerous, risky, and stimulating: compulsive gambling, gaming, having illicit affairs, driving at high speeds, getting involved in dramatic relationships. Others opt for a rich fantasy life and soon get lost in it. Mystical preoccupation, romantic euphoria, objects of romance, and romance dramas are all means of tapping into or enhancing our neurochemical "highs." Still others "feel too much" and want a sedative to numb the pain, stress, and fear. Endorphins—the opiates of the mind—are the neurochemicals that kill pain and reduce anxiety. People seeking sedation may stimulate endorphins by compulsive overeating or by pursuing trancelike altered states of consciousness found in some new romantic love relationships. A love-addicted relationship can also provide a sense of satiation. One very effective way to combine the benefits of more than one neurochemical—a way to avoid pain, live out fantasies, and feel fully alive—is to participate in a love relationship.[8] The problem is, these benefits of our own brain chemistry can be addictive.

For our purposes, we will characterize addiction from three perspectives: (1) as a dysfunctional habit that has become unconscious; (2) as a compulsive ritual that is no longer a choice; and (3) as a psychological or physical attachment to the object, often character-ized by withdrawal or intensity of symptoms when the object is re-moved. Focus on the object of addiction can cause an interference with the normal social, occupational, recreational, emotional, spiri-tual, and physical aspects of a person's life. There is a minimizing or blatant denial of the abuse or pain resulting from this focus, and there remains a continued involvement with the object in spite of negative consequences. Addiction is a malignant outgrowth of our normal human inclination for arousal, fantasy, and satiation.

Our physical and emotional needs are legitimate. Sometimes, however, when getting our needs met takes time and attention away from other important life concerns, our needs become addictions. Words we often associate with addiction include *obsessive, excessive, destructive, compulsive, habitual, attached,* and *dependent.* And when you think about it, some of those words can also be used to talk about love relationships or our use of sex. Does this mean love is always a habit we have to kick? No, not at all. Our need to experience love is real—our purpose is to identify and then keep unhealthy addictive elements out of our love lives and bring healthy love in. Love relationships are not black and white, either/or, but have all of these elements. Most love relationships seem to have the characteris-tics of both addictive love and healthy belonging. There are healthy and unhealthy dependencies.

Most of our habits and practices can show characteristics similar to addictive behaviors, yet they are not necessarily unhealthy. Many things we believe we need, we really do need for biological survival or emotional security, and they deserve our attention. We need food, shelter, physical touch and other forms of physical stimulation, recognition, and a sense of belonging. Many of the other things we think we need are merely wants—we can survive without them. Though we need a house, for example, we do not need one with a three-car garage.

When we consider love, the question of need becomes much more complex. Recently, I heard someone say that we don't *need* love in order to survive. And it is true that even a dependent infant doesn't need love to physically survive; what the infant needs is attention and care that activate the body's nervous system and stimulate growth. A baby given adequate physical care that includes being touched but that is emotionally neutral will survive as well as one given very tender care. But a baby who is seldom touched or not touched at all may get sick, become depressed, or, in severe cases, become mentally handicapped or die.

Thus, in the most primitive sense, we don't need love to biologically survive. But without the experience of being loved as a child, the recipe for a whole, healthy human being is sadly incomplete. Without love, one may live, but may have difficulty developing self-esteem, love for others, or even love for life—all basic ingredients of healthy, nonaddictive love relationships.

Yes, people can live without love, but those I encounter who have difficulty loving themselves or others are usually people who were deprived of bonding, nourishing parental care, or unconditional love as children. Unconditional love is a love that says to a child, "I love who you are no matter what, even though I may not always like what you say, think, or do." Though there are conditions on behavior that serve as protective fences keeping the child from harm, unconditional acceptance of the child's uniqueness is always present in unconditional love.

Love relationships can be good or bad, depending on how they serve us. The questions we consider here are these: Does addictive love really exist? What is addictive love? How does love become addictive? How can something so wonderful become something that feels so bad? Is it love? Or is it addiction? What is a healthy relationship?

Addictive Love

My clinical experience of addictive love is that it is a reliance on someone or something external to the self in an attempt to get unmet needs fulfilled, avoid fear or emotional pain, re-enact trauma, solve problems, and maintain balance. *The paradox is that addictive love is an attempt to gain control of our lives, and in so doing, we go out of control by giving personal power to someone or something other than ourselves.* This attempt, then, results in an unhealthy dependency on others, romantic illusions, or sex. It is very often associated with feelings of "never having enough" or "not being enough." For many of us, this is because we did not get all of our needs met in an orderly way when we were children. Addictive love is an *unconscious* attempt to satisfy our developmental hunger for security, sensation, power, identity, belonging, and meaning. Addictive love may or may not include a romantic or sexual component. What we witness daily in the news confirms that the more extreme cases of sex, love, and romance addictions can be dangerous, even lethal. Homicide, suicide, stalking, rape, incest, HIV/AIDS, and domestic violence capture the headlines. Addictive love can range from an unhealthy dependency on a person, a romantic state, or sex sanctioned by society to violence and abuse abhorred by, but nevertheless promulgated by, that same society. It is important to know that these are but degrees of the same problem. We will address the less extreme consequences that touch the lives of most of us almost daily as well as some of the more extreme abuses of addictive love.

Three Types of Addictive Love

The psychological seeds of addictive love relationships, romance addiction, and sex addiction are usually sown in early life, when some of us experience overt and covert abuse from those we love. What starts out as healthy dependency becomes unhealthy. The roots of love, romance, and sexual addiction are similar and often overlap, but the addiction processes of each are unique.

When a person's object of love is also the object of his romantic and sexual desires, he will experience intense feelings resulting in irrational behaviors when the person/object withdraws or threatens to withdraw. If one considers the millions of people who get hooked on the daily drama of the jealous ex-lover who stalks her prey across the country, or the politician who is caught in a sordid sexual escapade, one can begin to imagine what it is like to be in such a drama itself. The neurochemistry of love can become a drug as difficult to give up as alcohol or cocaine. The number and variety of out-of-control behaviors that result when love is withdrawn are legion. The difficulty with addictive love, however, is that we often allow our dysfunctional behaviors in the past to stop us from loving or relating in the present and future. Therefore, we must be clear about what is love and what is addiction, and when it is that we cross the often-fuzzy line from one to the other.

Love Addiction

Love addiction refers to an unhealthy dependency on the object of love. It is a form of passivity in that we do not directly resolve our own problems or ask for what we need, but attempt to collude with others so they will take care of us and thus take care of our problems. *We take care of others at our own emotional expense, or we attempt to control others to meet our needs at their expense.* No matter how it plays out, we look to others to "fix" our fear, pain, and discomfort, and we tolerate or inflict abusive behaviors in the process. These "others" can include any important person in our lives with whom we unconsciously hook up: a child, a parent, a friend, a boss, a spouse, a lover. A key element of an addictive relationship is how we feel when that person disapproves of us, disagrees with us, moves away from us, or threatens us. An escalation in dysfunctional behavior will occur when the love object leaves or threatens to leave us.

Romance Addiction

Romance addiction refers to those times when the object of love addiction is also a romantic object. This object/person can be a romantic partner or live only in the love addict's fantasies. The "fix" may be an elaborate fantasy life not unlike the story line of a romance novel, or the euphoria of a new romance. In either case, the rush of intoxicating feelings experienced during the attraction stage of a romance—a state called *limerence* by Dorothy Tennov, Ph.D.—is like a drug that can become a substitute for real intimacy.[9] The pursuit of this high can become an addiction in itself. Often, it becomes a dramatic obsession that results in the stalking of the romantic love object by the obsessed person. The love addict seeks total immersion in the romantic relationship, real or imagined. Since the romance-driven high is dependent on the newness of the relationship or the presence of a person, romance addiction is often filled with victim/persecutor melodrama.

Sex Addiction

The power of sexual love is unequaled in human experience. According to author and sex addiction specialist Mark Laaser, when normal sexual love is distorted, repressed, or forbidden by religious or familial structures, it may result in sex addiction. He writes that "sexual addiction is a sickness involving any type of uncontrollable sexual activity which results in negative consequences."[10] When obsessive-compulsive sexual behavior is left unattended, it causes distress and despair for the individual and his partner and family.

Patrick Carnes, a pioneer in the field of sex addiction, stresses that sex is not about "good" or "bad," in any moral, social, or psychological context. Rather, it is the behaviors that accompany sex that determine whether or not it is an addiction. According to Carnes, sexual behaviors that involve the exploitation of others—behaviors that are nonmutual, objectify people, are dissatisfying, involve shame, or are based on fear—indicate the presence of sexual addiction.[11]

❧ Addictive Love: Anna's Story ❧

As a psychotherapist, I am acutely aware of how often my clients' adult love relationships exist in the shadow of early love experiences—especially childhood ties to parents.

The story of Anna graphically demonstrates how childhood traumas hover over many adult relationships like powerful, unseen ghosts. Anna's story vividly demonstrates an important truth: there is often more to love than sexual attraction, romance, and relationship compatibility.

Anna, thirty-two, was an attractive, intelligent woman and the mother of four children. She sought therapy for chronic anxiety and depression. Among the reasons for her melancholy were her troubled, tumultuous feelings for her supervisor, Andrew, who was fifty. Although Anna was fond of Andrew, she was upset because he had begun to make odd emotional and sexual demands on her. She had come to believe she was in his power and that she could not refuse him—although she did not know why. She only knew she felt a strong obligation to cooperate with him, to try to keep him from becoming depressed. Anna professed love for Andrew, but she did not like his sexual demands, which often occurred at work, where his job held power over hers. She knew involvement with him threatened both their marriages, and that the relationship was unhealthy, but she did not understand nor could she control her emotional helplessness when it came to Andrew.

One evening, a distraught Anna called me. She had made a vow a few days before to have no contact with Andrew except on a purely professional basis. But now, he had called her with a plea that she should come to him. In the throes of distress and longing, Anna found her conviction not to see him wavering.

"I feel compelled to see him," she said to me. "My body hurts, I'm shaking uncontrollably, I feel like I'm falling apart—that I've got to see him or I'll get sick or go crazy. Please help me—I feel so helpless!"

I asked her, "Anna, what do you think will happen if you don't see him?"

"I don't know, but it feels like something really terrible will happen, and I'm scared," she said. "And it all seems so absurd!"

I reassured Anna that nothing awful would happen to her. She calmed down a bit, and for the moment, the crisis passed. In a therapy session shortly thereafter, Anna renewed her commitment not to see Andrew. Yet as she said, "I will not see him," her body shook and she wept.

"Why are you so afraid?" I asked.

She struggled to explain. "It seems so crazy. I'm afraid that if I don't see Andrew, if I abandon him, something bad will happen to him. Maybe he'll be so upset that he'll hurt himself. I feel as though he needs me!"

"You're feeling afraid for Andrew," I said. "But Anna, what is your fear for you? You're the one who's upset and fearful. What is it you get out of this relationship? Why are you so attached to this man?"

The answer to that question did not come easily, but in subsequent therapy sessions, as Anna began to relate her childhood, her story offered many clues to her current predicament. The fear Anna felt about Andrew was a familiar one—it was the same fear she once had felt for her father, a man much like Andrew. Anna's father, whom she had seen as a refuge from her mentally ill, violent mother, caused conflicting feelings in Anna. Although he could be a kind, sensitive man, he had made many demands on young Anna—including sexual demands. While Anna's mother neglected her and inflicted violence, her father offered attention and protection—but at a terrible price.

Anna had grown up with an overpowering sense that her father needed her, that he could not do without her, and that she should provide his happiness. Much of her adult depression sprang from her wretched childhood. Anna's pain and guilt as an incest victim also led her to present herself as an asexual adult, but when her sexual feelings were aroused, she could not control the desire and emotions she so vigorously suppressed most of the time. She did not realize that merely because one has sexual feelings, one need not always act on them.

"Why did you believe you had to take care of your father's emotional feelings and sexual needs?" I asked her during one session.

"My dad was the only person I could count on to protect me from my mother," Anna said, relating episodes of emotional and physical abuse inflicted by her mother. She said, "My dad was my protector; he loved me."

Making her father feel good—even though he used her sexually—had given Anna the sense that she was lovable. I urged her to talk about the feelings she had when she acted as her father's servant. In the months that followed, the tragedy of Anna's first experience with love—the experience so mishandled by her father and mother—slowly emerged. It became clear Anna had never separated her love for her father from her agony and guilt over incest. The result was emotional turmoil over her father—and over the concept of love.

During one session, Anna said, "I needed to keep my father around, and to do that I believed I needed to make him happy, or he would either reject or leave me. Since I was a child, that meant I would die! What choice did I have but to cooperate with him and try to make him happy?"

There it was—her profound underlying belief that the presence and approval of another person—even one who sexually abused her—meant life itself. And, to some degree, there was an element of truth: Anna the child did need protection! That belief also pervaded her current adult obsession with Andrew; it explained much of her panic and helplessness in the face of his demands.

Consciously, Anna knew she could survive without Andrew. Unconsciously, Anna believed that without Andrew's acceptance, she would not be lovable and her life wouldn't have purpose and meaning. As a child, she was convinced she needed an intense relationship, or she would lose her mental balance—and eventually her life. Our focus in therapy was to prevent an awful history from repeating itself.

In therapy, Anna began to explore her archaic inner self—the dependent, frightened child—that governed so many of her adult emotions, including her penchant for men like Andrew. One by one, she discovered and wrestled with the powerful unconscious beliefs and traumatic moments that caused her terror.

"Well, you are no longer four or five, you are grown up. Is that true?" I asked.

"Yes, that's true, but that's not how I always feel. When I'm with this person, I often feel like I'm only four or five years old."

"But how old are you?"

"I'm thirty-two."

"And what do you know? Do you actually need this person to protect you?" I challenged.

She thought about it and said, "No."

"Do you need this person to believe you are lovable?"

She hesitated and said, "I'm not sure, since I really don't feel very lovable."

"Do you know anyone else who loves you?"

"Yes, I know some other people who love me."

"Does this person give you the only meaning in life?"

She hesitated and said, "No."

"Do you need this person to keep you alive?"

She shook her head, no.

The questions helped clarify her fears and the thoughts that supported those fears for the moment. Slowly, and through deeper trauma work, she not only learned the fear and behavior that had made sense to her in childhood no longer needed to have power over her, but also she reclaimed her sense of self. She was then able to confront Andrew and tell him she would no longer allow him to fondle or harass her. She ended her relationship with him and was able to turn her energies back to her work and family, including coping with marriage problems. Andrew received treatment for his sexual misuse of female co-workers like Anna.

Anna, whose insecurities ran very deep because of a childhood more troubled than most, must always be aware of her tendency to become obsessed with needy, demanding, abusive men who prey on her sexually. But she succeeded in handling one such situation and in laying bare the motivations for her behavior. This was no small accomplishment.

~

Love and the Unconscious Mind

Anna's case may seem rather extreme, but she is not unique. In fact, in family systems such as Anna's, the incest may never be physically consummated, and yet the psychological implications for the child may be nearly as severe in later life. Such cases are sometimes referred to as examples of emotional incest. Over and over again, a child is invited to take care of the parents' feelings. Sometimes the invitation is overt, sometimes it is covert. The child often misconstrues this silent seduction as parental love.[12] When the invitation comes from the parent of the opposite sex, it is covert incest. The parent asks the child to become a surrogate partner. Such partnerships set the child up for a role reversal that later translates into dependent love relationships and confusion about the nature of real intimacy.

Behind each obsessive, often destructive, relationship—which we shall call addictive love—lurks a belief that such dependence serves an important purpose. *To the unconscious mind, addictive love makes perfect sense;* it feels necessary to survival itself. And to an addictive lover, even a pathological relationship may seem normal and necessary. As we understand our fears and the ways we use addictive love, they often lose their holding power.

Addictive love is egocentric and self-serving. Anna, the child, loved her father not selflessly, but to meet her own needs. She believed she needed her father's attention and approval to sustain her self-esteem—and her life. Although that belief made sense during her childhood, Anna, the adult, no longer needed someone like her father to make her feel lovable and alive. She had her own sustaining qualities, including the potential to love freely, openly, and as an equal. Egocentricity also was evident in Anna's obsession with Andrew; she believed that without his approval, she would lose the small amount of self-esteem she had and would slide deeper into despair and perhaps even die.

The intensity of addictive love is often in direct proportion to the intensity of one's sense of unmet needs during childhood. Intense addictive love often accompanies low self-esteem. As discussed earlier, such obsession presents us with a huge paradox: we fall into it as an attempt to gain control of our lives, and in so doing we actually grant control to forces outside ourselves. Such willingness to give control away springs from fear: fear of pain; fear of deprivation; fear of disappointing someone; fear of failure; fear of guilt, anger, or rejection; fear of being alone; fear of getting sick or going crazy; and fear of death.

Addictive lovers usually labor under the illusion that the dependent relationship will "fix" their fears. We will explore the many complex reasons why addictive love exercises a powerful hold over people and why it is not easily given up. Like Anna, many people are drawn into it over and over again. But how do people get drawn into addictive love? The seeds of addictive love lie deep in our biology, our social education, our use of technology, our spiritual quests, and our psychological beliefs. We shall explore each of these in turn.

What you will learn is that each person in an addictive relationship followed an individual road map leading into it. Finding out how addictive love makes sense to its victims is necessary in creating a road map out of addiction and into mature love and belonging. We return to the puzzle: how does something that feels so good become something that feels so bad?

In the story of Anna and Andrew, Anna was addicted to the romantic high the relationship produced. Andrew, on the other hand, was addicted to the sensations sex and power produced for him. But underneath the romantic and sexual highs, both Anna and Andrew were attached to the need to be needed called love addiction.

You will be able to identify all three kinds of addiction—romantic, sex, and love—in the stories that follow. My years as a therapist have led me to one important conclusion: underneath a sex or romance addiction is a dependent love addiction problem that must be addressed for successful recovery. It is love-addicted relationships to which the human condition seems to direct most of us most often. It is so common that we frequently fail to recognize it until it wreaks havoc on our love lives.

The Roots of Addictive Love

The Role of Biology

The need to be close to other people—the yearning to be special to someone—is so deeply ingrained in people that it may be called biological.

The Biology of Bonding

Anthropologist Helen Fisher explains how emotional bonding evolved early in human history to guarantee regular sex and ensure protection of offspring. Such bonding became crucial in the evolutionary process when women lost their period of heat; ovulation was hidden, and therefore, women were more frequently responsive to sex. Women began to bear children more often and needed more emotional support and physical help from men. Males and females began exchanging favors, dividing labor, and tightening the relational "knot." Mating soon went beyond creating offspring. Females began looking for males who were good hunters, who were strong, and who could provide protection that would assure them that their children would grow into adulthood. Males sought the female who was most frequently available for sex in order to guarantee the continuance of their genetic legacy.

Eventually, emotional bonding grew beyond mere functional ties to sexual partners and dependent offspring. Both the female and the male began rewarding what pleasured and protected them. Babies began bonding with the man who slept with the mother. Personal relationships, the foundation of the family, were established. Along the way, complex rules governing such ties to others developed. With those rules came the fundamental human emotions that lead us to form and preserve our relationships. And it is true that most of the rules and emotions are healthy, delightful aspects of our humanity. To desire, to share, to protect, to nurture, to feel affection, and to live in organic harmony are intrinsic aspects of healthy love. With partnerships and sexual bonding came other emotions as well. Wanting to protect his genetic heritage, the male became jealous and possessive. Fearing that she and her offspring might not survive without the protection of her mate, the female experienced the first fear of abandonment.

Like other primitive fears and habits, many strongly emotional behaviors governing relationships have stayed with us. We still flirt; we still feel infatuation at the beginning of a love relationship, allegiance during it, and sorrow when it fades. We feel guilty if we are promiscuous and jealous or vengeful if we are betrayed. Men still worry about their wives being unfaithful; women still worry about being deserted. We no longer need to bond to guarantee sex or to keep our young alive, yet we continue to do so. Why? To be human, it seems, is to desire attachments to others. Like other behavior patterns from the past— fears of falling, of heights, of closed places, of the dark—the fear of being alone causes panic and despair. The urge to form emotional alliances with others appears to be an innate drive—one that makes us human, and one that will no doubt continue.[1]

Our desire for attachment, then, can be viewed as instinctual. Psychiatrist John Bowlby, borrowing from animal behaviorists Konrad Lorenz and Harry Harlow and their work with infant birds and monkeys, sets parental love in an evolutionary setting in his attachment theory. Most animal infants form a passionate attachment to their primary caregiver, usually their mother. When separated from the caregiver, the infants become anxious and then depressed. Biologically, this makes perfect sense; in the wild, an infant animal is vulnerable and could easily become food for a predator or die of hunger. Then, Bowlby points out: "The standard response to loss of loved persons is always urges first to recover them and then to scold them. If, however, the urges to recover and scold are automatic responses built into the organism, it follows that they will come into action in response to *any* and *every* loss without discriminating between those that are really retrievable and those . . . that are not."[2]

Daniel Amen, M.D., a clinical neuroscientist, explains that when we bond with someone, she actually begins to live in the neurons and synapses of our emotional brain. When that person is no longer there, the brain gets disoriented and desperately begins searching for the missing someone. The overactivity in the brain creates low levels of our feel-good chemicals, resulting in depression, loss of appetite, obsessing, and even physical pain. We become a neurological mess.[3]

The Biology of Attraction

Breaking love down into chemical components may seem to take some of the mystery and magic out of love, but doing so can help us distinguish between healthy belonging and addictive love. Neuro-chemical research is showing that anything that generates significant mood change can become an obsession.[4] We know of more than three hundred chemicals that affect brain function, yet we have a working knowledge of less than one hundred. Some of these pertain to our love lives, and we can become addicted to the chemical highs that love relationships produce in our brains. It has now been con-firmed that the rush of intoxication is associated with the neurologi-cal release of endorphins and many other mood elevators. Michael Liebowitz, in *The Chemistry of Love*, states that a specific neuro-chemical, PEA, is critical to courtship and produces a high arousal state similar to that caused by amphetamines. Its intense impact seems to taper off with time and when the object of affection is not present. But not to worry. We have other ways to turn on our chemi-cals, including, but not limited to, some of the darker sides of love. Fear, for example, can biologically escalate desire, and large quantities of PEA have also been found in people involved in divorce-court trials.[5] And there is considerable evidence linking the high-risk emo-tions of anticipating danger, fear, excitement, and rage—emotions often present in love relationships—with chemical highs.

With alcohol and other drug addictions, the chemicals we take into our bodies interact with the chemicals in the brain to produce the high. In addictive love, we unconsciously use the objects of love, sex, or romance to stimulate the chemicals in our neuropathways to provide the high. Since it is impossible for us to sustain the fix (other people won't always conform their behavior to our neurochemical cravings, after all), we eventually crash and are flooded with feelings of disappointment, depression, anxiety, hopelessness, or powerlessness. To get back on keel, we attempt to use again. Or, when the love object does not sustain the fix, we can develop an obsessive fantasy in which that person is fixing us, or we arouse ourselves with the excitement, fear, rage, or melodrama that exemplify addictive love.

The Brain in Love

When it comes to forming love relationships, one theory has it that three distinct and yet related brain circuits go to work. The three brain systems have correlative feelings and behaviors that are referred to by Dr. Helen Fisher as lust, attraction, and attachment. For our purposes, I will refer to them as *sexual arousal, romantic attraction,* and *emotional bonding.* Each has a unique place in the larger brain and unique chemicals that support the accompanying emotions.[6] Our brain is a factory producing the chemical concoction needed at a specific time in our love relationships.

According to this model, to complete the mating game, we must first experience lust, the craving for sexual union. *Sexual arousal,* or libido, turns us on to what is sexually desirable. It is controlled primarily by the gonads—which produce testosterone and estrogen, plus nitric oxide, pheromones, and other arousal chemicals. Given that there are many to whom we are turned on sexually, the second brain system, *romantic attraction,* kicks in to help us narrow the playing field. At this point, we begin to crave a passionate connection with one potential mate. Unrequited love is driven by a cocktail of chemicals consisting of the reward and motivation chemical dopamine, the adrenaline rush chemicals epinephrine and norepinephrine, the love chemical PEA, and nature's antidepressant serotonin.[7] This chemical experience is tenacious and difficult to control.

While we may want to linger in the euphoric state, we must move on to the third phase of a love relationship, *emotional bonding*. Our third brain system facilitates a deeper, longer-lasting love that encourages commitment. If our partner is the right one, at some point the romantic high biochemically shifts to a calmer, more secure sensation that provides the safety to continue growing in love. We are less driven and can postpone gratification and emotions. The excitatory chemicals diminish, and the bonding chemicals, oxytocin and vasopressin, step in and urge us to cuddle, touch, express affection, and commit.

Unlike other hormones, oxytocin can be stimulated by both physical and emotional cues. A certain look, a smile, a gesture, a richly woven fantasy, or a memory may be enough to hormonally stimulate the smooth muscles and sensitize the nerves to project a relaxed body that invites closeness. A chemical symbiosis occurs between two people and generates the experience of "it's safe to be close." A cross-cultural research study found that 91 percent of women and 86 percent of men would not commit to a marriage if they were not in love. The research showed that most prefer monogamy or serial monogamy that has all three brain systems working together.[8]

How does this theoretical model relate to addictive love? While these brain circuits and emotions work with each other in a safe and fulfilling love relationship, they can and do function *independently* of one other. As the stories in this book tell us, you can be bonded to one person, infatuated with another, and have sex with yet a third person. Yes, we can compartmentalize our love lives. *The three-brain system theory explains why and how sex, romance, and love addiction can be experienced separately or together.* Some become addicted to the chemical high sex produces, and it becomes their "drug" of choice. Others discover that when the euphoria of infatuation dwindles, they become depressed or restless and jump from one romantic high to another. There are still others who, for the many reasons we will discuss, cannot make the full leap into an intimate bonding and opt for love addiction, which simulates real love but is not. And, we can have more than one of these addictions in one or more relationships.

Men's Brains and Women's Brains

Research is affirming that men and women *do* have major brain differences. Getting the Y chromosome from Dad sets off dramatic differences in the development of the male brain and body. A male gets his first burst of testosterone in the womb and another burst in early adolescence. By early adulthood, he has twenty times more testosterone than a woman, which gives him an advantage when it comes to developing the part of the brain that is interested in sex. While essential to his maleness, testosterone also has a close connection with aggression, surges of anger, the need to control, and interest in risk taking.

Getting the X chromosome from Dad, a female's development is much different. From the onset, female brains foster relationships. Female infants tend to smile more, communicate, and be interested in security and people. The emotional memory part of a brain ends up being larger in women than in men. That is why it is easier for her to remember the time of the first kiss, the song that was playing, and what he promised last week. And studies show that estrogen, the hormone that makes her uniquely female, helps a woman live a more balanced life and provides connections within and between the two hemispheres of the brain. The left brain is analytical, logical, detail-oriented, and good at conceiving and executing plans. The right brain is creative, is intuitive, sees the bigger picture, knows when a problem exists, and knows when a problem needs to be taken seriously. While men tend to be more left-brained, women can and do use both sides of their brains and are generally better at multitasking and communicating.

A woman is often the first to notice a problem in a relationship, and the man tends to be the one who wants a quick and logical way to fix it. If something doesn't seem practical, a man often does not want to waste the neuronal time on it. Frequently, when a couple comes in for therapy, the woman wants to be heard and understood, and the man wants to know how to get from A to Z, how long it will take, and how much it will cost him.

Brain scans show that, in general, a woman's brain is very active, especially in the emotional and bonding regions; a man's brain is quieter and is more active in the lower, more primitive areas of the brain. According to a study by Ruben Gur, an expert on gender differences in the human brain, when a man rests, 70 percent of his brain shuts down. When a woman rests, 90 percent of her brain is active. When she wants to talk, he wants to rest or seek things that are stimulating to him. Women, who tend to be the more skilled communicators, crave relational conversations, while men want something new and exciting. Women may be content with family involvement and turn down outside excitement. Men, on the other hand, may become lonely or bored and seek outside stimulation.[9] To foster healthy relationships, we need to understand these biological differences, work with them rather than against them, and let men love as men and women love as women.

The Biology of Needs

Physically, we strive for inner balance. Infants identify their survival needs through physical sensations and cravings: hunger, thirst, warmth, cold, satisfaction, and irritation. Babies feel discomfort and cry out until there is a soothing response from another person. When their needs are met, they feel comfort and balance again until the next need presents itself. Life feels good; they feel safe and cared for. They experience trust in themselves, others, and life. Emotional security develops. This diagram illustrates an ideal situation.

NEED→	SENSATION→	ACTION→	RESPONSE→	BALANCE
	pain indicates a need (hunger)	reaches out to others (baby cries)	receives satisfaction (baby is fed)	trusts self, others, and life; basis for mature love (feels content)

Sometimes, for any number of reasons, parental care is inadequate—needs are not met and discomfort escalates. Our parents could not always be there as our needs arose. Sometimes we were separated from our parents, and we were cared for by people who seemed strange to us. Infants seem to know instinctively that if certain needs are not met, they will die. In such situations, panic sets in. Now, the situation looks like this:

NEED→	SENSATION→	ACTION→	NO RESPONSE→	NO RELIEF
	pain indicates a need (hunger)	reaches out to others (baby cries)	discomfort escalates; panic felt; sensation suppressed	distrusts self, others, and life (basis for predisposition toward addictive love)

The recollections of such fearful times are recorded in our nervous systems; we don't ever want to experience such helpless panic again. Adults, too, may be unconsciously convinced that they will suffer or even die if certain compelling needs are not met. Thus arises the intense, often irrational fear and panic when someone rejects or leaves us. Despairing adults seem to forget that they can now take care of themselves, that they can solve most of their problems alone. We have the capacity to think and can therefore postpone needs, problem-solve to get our needs met, or meet our own needs. Often, what we perceive as a need is merely a want and something we can survive without.

Now let's look at a model for adult problem solving.

NEED →	SENSATION→	REASONING→	TAKE AN→	RELIEF
OR	OR	OR	ACTION/	OR
WANT	FEELING	PROBLEM-SOLVE	COMMUNICATE	GRIEF
	Pain	What am I	Do or let go	Need
	indicates	feeling and why?		met or
	a need.	Is it a want or a need?		not met
		Is it realistic and		
		possible?		
		Can it wait?		
		How can I get it?		
		How can I ask for it		
		in ways that consider		
		self and others?		
		What kind of action?		
		What do I do		
		if I don't get it?		

The diagram above—which represents a normal, healthy, adult reaction to a problem—is useful in therapy, where the goal is to help people understand their needs and desires so they may take appropriate action to gain emotional relief or balance. Unfortunately, many of us have learned to deny pain or to limit our problem-solving options; thus, we fail to take reasonable action, and we continue to feel physically and emotionally uncomfortable. Instead of reacting logically, we are moved by the infant within us to panic and to cling to another, craving the other to "make us whole" and provide us with a sense of balance. Sometimes, we are not aware of what we need because we have learned to shut off the sensations and feelings of discomfort that identify our needs. Sometimes we feel discomfort, but fail to figure out what we need. Sometimes we feel and identify the reasons for those feelings, but wait in a state of discomfort and fail to take action. And sometimes there is no way to have our desires fulfilled, and we grieve over our losses as a way to regain our balance. At times, our grief is so intense we feel as though we are going to die of a broken heart. The paradox of love is that we must be willing to embrace both joy and sorrow.

The Role of Culture

We don't become love addicts in a vacuum. To comprehend how and where we have learned the erroneous ideas about love, romance, and sex that lead to addiction, we must examine what our culture teaches us. The messages are both subtle and blatant, and they are ubiquitous and unrelenting. These messages often become deeply internalized and unconsciously accepted as fact from an early age.

We live in a world of image and ownership. We are measured by how good we look, how much we have, and whether we have someone by our side who supports a good image. We have, sadly, been groomed to look outside ourselves for happiness and love. Our society's obsession with sex, romance, and love pervades every aspect of our culture—the Internet, movies and television, advertising, song lyrics, and even great works of fiction, poetry, drama, and art. You find it on Madison Avenue, in Hollywood, and all the way to Disneyworld. Each day, in a variety of ways, our society encourages us to seek addictive relationships. Our culture idealizes, dramatizes, and models a dependency that says we cannot live without another person or without sex. When we love, we naturally feel lustful, feel romantic, and desire to bond with a special someone, but these should be balanced by a healthy appreciation of our independence and self-worth.

We also live in a culture that promotes sex incessantly. Sexually charged images or situations abound on television, in magazines, and in film. How often is sex being connected to a deep emotional and spiritual intimacy where body, heart, and soul are relating? Very rarely. There is a staggering amount of denial in our culture regarding out-of-control sexual behavior; it is often glorified, despite the mounting negative social consequences of sexual compulsion. People are dying of AIDS; the incidence of sexual violence continues to rise; professionals are publicly shamed and even prosecuted for sexual improprieties and illegalities; and unwanted pregnancies, lost jobs, incarcerations, and broken homes are the results. Sexual exploitation by people in positions of power seems epidemic. The cost of this addiction to our society is more than financial. The fabric of our spiritual, emotional, and relational lives is affected as well.

Our society trains us to be effective at getting what we want, and when we cannot control others to give us what we want, when we want it, we feel anxious or take it. For proof, all we need to do is turn on the news. In one newscast, you can hear many dramatic stories: "Young woman ends abusive love relationship and is brutally murdered"; "CEO charged with sexual harassment"; "Coach arrested for sexually abusing students"; "Domestic abuse charges filed by wife of a professional sports star"; "Governor caught in sex trafficking."

We are all guilty of attempts to control our love lives at times. We must learn how to accept our relationships' limitations and not attempt to control them, for the need to control others is one of the greatest offenses of addictive love. Men and women have the same need to belong, to be intimate, and to experience fulfillment in love. Both have a need to experience physical, emotional, and spiritual bonding. Both men and women suffer in love relationships. The following story illustrates how cultural distortions contributed to one man's suffering.

✐ Rick's Story ✐

Rick, a young and successful businessman, came into therapy with reluctance. He was painfully trying to extricate himself from an emotionally abusive relationship. Separation anxiety attacks brought him to therapy. Though he was bright enough to know the relationship was toxic and that he did not know what real love was, he felt compelled to reach out to his former and abusive partner whenever he experienced anxiety. Their sexual relationship was intense, and that pull made it difficult for him to end it. His partner fit society's description of the "beautiful, sensuous woman," but Rick experienced her as hollow and callous. She lied, manipulated, and sexually betrayed him. The following is an excerpt from his journal:

"I admit that I have measured the level of love on how pleasing a woman is to me physically. I have mistaken a strong desire by a woman for sex with me as love for me. When men talk together, they reinforce that tradition. Men comment on whether my new date is 'hot' and attractive. They rarely ask what her goals in life are and what she does for a living. They are still much more interested in her looks and sex appeal than her interests. All of this is amply promoted by the media and advertisers: dishonest men and glamorous women. I actually buy women's magazines to see what is being promoted to women. It's worse than what guys are being sold. Affairs, multiple partners, lying, cheating, and divorce are all portrayed as glamorous. With all of this garbage being sold to men and women, how can we ever hope to find a normal, honest, healthy relationship? Maybe I take all the media stuff too seriously. I do think that it all feeds into our brain and gets stored somewhere. If we ignore it (which takes a lot of energy), it still sits in there and helps form our attitudes in general."

Family Role Models

Our families can direct us into addictive relationships as well. Though their influences are primarily subtle and nonverbal, they are powerful and pervasive. From the time we are very young, we observe how adults act in relationships. We learn to respond to certain gestures, smells, idiosyncrasies, styles of dress, and manners. We become accustomed to styles of living—to order or chaos. And in our families, we first learn the definitions of love, power, and what it means to be a man or woman, definitions that can become locked in our psyches and interpreted in adulthood as universal truths that are not to be questioned. From these definitions, we develop the roles we live out and the base of power from which we operate in those roles.

These early experiences create a "love map" that helps determine whom and how we love. It doesn't take long before we discover that the map can lead us repeatedly to dead ends. Often, our models lack knowledge about healthy love relationships, healthy sexuality, problem solving, and the importance of individuality and autonomy. And many grow up in a closed family—that is, a family in which the children are expected to believe and behave as their parents did. As one man told me, "The message in my family was to follow the tried and true, and that meant becoming an addict and looking for cold women. I played by the rules and still do not know how to do a relationship."

The Role of Technology

Modern technology can be credited for amazing feats. Today, we have cell phones with us twenty-four hours a day; we communicate via e-mail or instant messaging; we research virtually anything on the Internet, including sex; we communicate with romantic interests in chat rooms; and we look for a lifelong partner online. And, much of it can be done in our own private world. It's yet to be determined how the lightning-fast information exchange will influence the evolution of brain chemistry and the future of sex, love, and romance.

For many, the Internet can too easily become an insane world that negatively impacts attitudes about sex, love, and romance. For the shy and depressed or just plain bored, cyber connections are easy to maintain or hide behind. The fantasy world substitutes for the real world. Cyber love relationships become highly charged and addictive. The ability to communicate for hours on the Internet, easy involvement and abrupt endings, and the euphoria of romantic fantasy create a use-and-crash cycle that can be devastating and lead to depression and suicidal ideation. Cyber relationships often carry as much emotional weight and pain as face-to-face ones, and their impact should never be underestimated. And then there is sex.

The Internet is a place where the gap between fantasy and reality may become wider. Recent studies have shown that so-called cyber-sex addicts spend between fifteen and twenty-five hours per week pursuing sexual material online. The same study indicates that the nature of the Internet provides a lure that may lead individuals who would not have otherwise developed problematic sexual behavior to develop compulsive online sexual behavior.[10]

Pornography is everywhere on the Internet. If you are not out looking for it, it will find you. Take normal curiosity, pressure from peers, and the sheer amount of time people spend on the Internet, then throw in unsolicited instant messages with pop-ups of sexual images, add a dose of immature impulse control, low self-esteem, shyness, or anything else going on in the mind, and you have a recipe for compulsive use of sexual imagery.

More than 60 percent of all site visits and commerce on the Internet involve sexual purposes.[11] Patrick Carnes's seminal book *Out of the Shadows,* published in 2001, estimated there were 100,000 pornographic sites at that time, with two hundred new ones being added daily.[12] The Internet itself is not the problem; nor is pornography. Rather, the problem is how cybersex is used and how long it is used. Sexual images hit a part of the brain that triggers cravings for more and more arousal images, and I have known a person to become addicted to pornography on the Internet in as short a period as six weeks, when used consistently. Another major survey showed that cybersex is a major contributing factor in divorce. Of the couples surveyed, 68 percent had lost interest in relational sex.[13]

Cybersex is delivered in three forms: the online exchange of pornography in snapshot and video formats, live communication such as chat rooms and interactive home pages, and the downloading of pornographic software and files. Regardless of the form, the cyber world of sex can result in isolation, fantasy, objectifying people, and relationship problems. For some, it progressively escalates and becomes addictive.

Cybersex is referred to as the Triple-A Engine—it is anonymous, affordable, and easily accessible. The anonymity encourages users to communicate in a more open and frank manner than would be their norm.[14] An introverted woman can turn into an uninhibited woman of the night in cyberspace. A repressed, unassuming man can become a Don Juan. The behaviors of each produce a "high" that is both immediately rewarding and ultimately addicting.

And what about the sites for married people looking for other married people to develop sexual or romantic love relationships? The initial attraction may be to fulfill a fantasy need or to experience some excitement, but the addictive quality of the medium often pulls the person into other online or offline sexual escapades. I have worked with many women and men who risked losing their children and partner to cash in on a long-term Internet relationship by meeting to have sex. One client, Jennifer, said to me: "I know it is crazy, but I fell in love online, and I feel compelled to meet this guy in person and have sex with him. I also know it is more about feeling special and desired than about the sex. I am afraid that I am so into this relationship that I will let my urge to meet him take me over. I'm afraid for myself, as it has happened many times before."

Despite all its benefits, technology can create problems in our love lives—the compulsive use of sex and romance, the need for high-arousal relationships that can end in sexual or physical abuse, and the development of unrealistic expectations of our partners. Another great concern is that it can lessen the direct human contact we are in need of.

Yet there is a positive side to sex, love, and the Internet. It is also easy to find legitimate sites that talk about everything from birth control to abstinence, sexually transmitted disease, sex myths, love advice, sex advice, and personal health, as well as special interest chat groups that allow a person to legitimately meet a potential partner online. I personally have seen this lead to many successful relationships.

The Role of Spiritual Quests

Many would say that experiencing our spiritual nature is as profound an experience as we humans can feel. We do not need to be involved in a specific religion, though that can play a role. Spiritual pursuits may be defined as those that transport a person beyond material needs and worldly pleasures on a very personal, profound quest for meaning that aligns him with a higher purpose for living. Our spirit seeks to continue growing. Like the blade of grass that pushes through hard dirt to reach toward the sun, we, too, continue to quest for the experience of awe, wonder, mystery—union with God. In spirit, we can experience love everywhere and in everything. When we become intimately involved with something or someone, we experience a growing love for that thing or person.

Spiritual questing is meant to guide us to stop looking outside of ourselves for happiness. Instead of regarding love relationships as our source of happiness, we can see them as places to express and share our happiness as well as other higher emotions: compassion, sorrow, gratitude, and joy. When we participate in shared love, we experience a sense of "oneness" or spiritual ecstasy. We experience ourselves in the other and the other in ourselves.

Spiritually as well as biologically, we do want to belong. Once we know that we are capable of such a "divine experience," we seek it. Some even become addicted to the spiritual high of ecstasy, bliss, awe, and transcendence and choose to live more in that reality than in practical daily life. Though it is natural for us as spiritual beings to yearn for transcendent experiences through which we merge with something greater, this must come through a gradual and balanced process. Some people feel urgency about these experiences, and their experiments result in highs not unlike those resulting from experimentation with chemicals. When the spiritual turn-on is the goal, a person can become addicted. Spirituality is not an escape from the world, but a way to live in it. When we try to use spiritual searching as yet another form of escape from the painful realities of life, the result can be less than holy.

Because few people have learned how to develop their spirituality, addictive love may be embraced in the misguided belief that one dependent merging with another is the highest spiritual experience. And it is easy to understand how this might happen, for at the beginning of a love relationship or in a moment of sexual union, one often feels euphoria and ecstasy of almost mystical proportions, and rational thought is subordinated.

Self-Actualization

Psychologist Abraham Maslow, who believed that theories of personality and motivation must emphasize healthy, normal development, proposed a needs hierarchy to describe development from physical, instinctive motives to more rational, transcendent ones. Maslow's theory of "self-actualization," useful in understanding the importance of spiritual questing, states simply that humans tend to move toward being all they can be. Maslow's pyramid of human strivings is illustrated here.

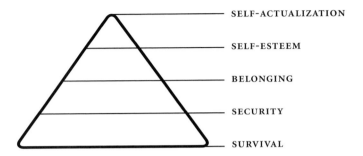

SELF-ACTUALIZATION

SELF-ESTEEM

BELONGING

SECURITY

SURVIVAL

Listed here are the characteristics of people who are near self-actualization.

1. They accept reality.
2. They accept themselves, other people, and the world for what they are.
3. They are spontaneous.
4. They are problem-centered rather than self-centered.
5. They have an air of detachment and a need for privacy.
6. They are autonomous and independent.
7. Their appreciation of people and things is fresh rather than stereotyped.
8. Most have had profound mystical or spiritual experiences, although those experiences are not necessarily religious in character.
9. They identify with humankind.
10. Their intimate relationships with a few specially loved people tend to be profound and deeply emotional rather than superficial.
11. Their values and attitudes are democratic.
12. They do not confuse means with ends.
13. Their sense of humor is philosophical rather than hostile.
14. They resist conformity to the culture.
15. They transcend the environment rather than just cope with it.[15]

Maslow distinguished between two types of self-actualizers: *non-transcenders* and *transcenders*. Nontranscenders were "practical, realistic, mundane, capable, and secular." They were healthy reformers of life, but had no experience of transcendent "highs." Transcenders, on the other hand, "had illuminations or insights" that motivated them to transform their lives and the lives of others. They felt a sense of destiny, sought truth, did not judge, and viewed pain, even in their love lives, as an opportunity to grow. Maslow considered peak experiences, mystical visions, and self-creation as natural parts of our higher circuitry.[16]

While our human nature focuses on survival and security, our spiritual nature seeks personal growth and fusion with others. Maslow believed that nature recognizes our need to belong, our need to be part of the human group.

Obsessive erotic love often is a misplaced attempt to achieve that fusion we so deeply desire. We want to end the feelings of isolation caused by our learned restraints against true intimacy. In a sexually aroused state, one often is willing to suspend those restraints in order to merge with another. If the merger is dependent and immature, the result is a barrier to self-actualization. Life energy is directed toward the pursuit of gratification rather than toward growth. As Erich Fromm said, "This desire for interpersonal fusion is the most powerful striving in man. It is the most fundamental passion, it is the force which keeps the human race together . . . Erotic love . . . is the craving for complete fusion. It is by its very nature exclusive and not universal."[17] To be sure, erotic love beautifully complements spiritual love in mature people. But sadly, for many, sexual desire often is nothing more than an attempt to relieve the fear of aloneness, to try to fill a void. In that sense, such love is addictive. Without agape, universal love of others, erotic love remains narcissistic.

The Role of Psychology

We would like to believe we know everything we need to know about ourselves. We do not. What we consciously know about ourselves is but the tip of the iceberg. Our life experiences are recorded in the body's nervous system. From early experiences, good and bad, we combine our perceptions into beliefs on which we make our adult decisions. Those include, of course, decisions—conscious or unconscious—about love. In our lifetimes, we will use but a small portion of our physical, emotional, intellectual, and spiritual potentials, all of which play a role in true love. Why do we limit ourselves so? And how does this limitation relate to love? The answers to these questions can help us understand the psychological roots of addictive love. That is the focus of the next chapter.

The Psychology of Addictive Love

There is a psychological reason for unhealthy dependency on people, romance, or sex. Discovering the psychological basis for such behavior is necessary in overcoming it. Psychological addiction appears to result from unfulfilled dependency needs and a quest to get those needs met, heal from trauma, and make our psychological beliefs come true. On an unconscious level, addictive tendencies function as misguided sources of protection, as warped, ineffective aids to emotional stability and survival. The goal of all good therapy and self-help books is to provide tools to help people live less frustrating, more fulfilling lives, and independent of a therapist. Transactional analysis, developed in the 1950s and 1960s by psychiatrist Eric Berne, is a model of personality development that has proved especially effective in understanding addictive relationships. It can be helpful in rooting out the underlying life drama that sustains addictive behavior. Here are some principles of this system.[1]

A Psychological Understanding of Dependencies

Transactional analysis divides our personalities into three distinct parts: the Parent, Adult, and Child ego states. If healthy,

The **PARENT EGO STATE** nurtures and protects.
The **ADULT EGO STATE** thinks and solves problems.
The **CHILD EGO STATE** feels and identifies needs.

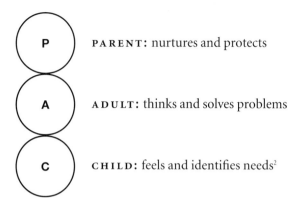

PARENT: nurtures and protects

ADULT: thinks and solves problems

CHILD: feels and identifies needs[2]

Child Ego State

The Child ego state is the first part of our personalities to form. It is the source of our strongest sensations and feelings. In our Child ego state, we experience life primarily through our senses—through strong feelings and desires. It is the Child ego state that identifies what we need and want and that reaches out to the world, trusting to get the needs met. Long before "inner child" became a buzz phrase, transactional analysts knew of its importance. The Child ego state is where the myths that support addictive love begin when needs are not met. "It's not safe to get close," "I'm not lovable," "Love hurts," "Men can't be trusted," and "Women are manipulators" are some examples.

Adult Ego State

The second part of the personality to unfold, the Adult ego state, acts much like a computer, collecting information, processing it, and giving answers. Rational problem solving, not emotion, is its hallmark. If the Adult ego state receives accurate information, it will provide workable solutions. Unfortunately, the information is often inaccurate; merely operating in one's Adult ego state is no guarantee that solutions for problems will work. If a role model demonstrates that the way to deal with pain is to have another drink, that how-to is recorded in our brains.

Parent Ego State

The third and last part of the personality to form is the Parent ego state, the function of which resembles that of a parent. It is a master plan consisting of guidelines, rules, and permissions for living. It is meant to love unconditionally. It provides protection from harm. It tells us what to do in order to live productive lives. Setting boundaries is a Parent ego state function, as it demonstrates tough love: "Stop hurting me," "Stay safe." But sometimes it controls, criticizes, is overly permissive, enables, rescues, and stunts the childlike part of us. "Don't bother me" or "You're bad" are examples of this.

Three Types of Dependency

There are three kinds of relationship dependencies we may experience, but not all are addictive. Grown-ups have access to all three ego states, but children do not. Infants can't think or protect themselves; they form a healthy, necessary dependency on their parents and, with them, function as one person. They borrow their parents' Adult and Parent ego states until they have their own. In a normal, healthy, child-parent relationship, the parent provides love, protection, and nourishment. This is called a *primary dependency*. It is necessary if the child is to thrive and develop the ability to be intimate, spontaneous, independent, and, finally, interdependent. *Autonomous dependency*, or interdependency, assumes two adults have all three ego states available to give and receive in healthy ways.

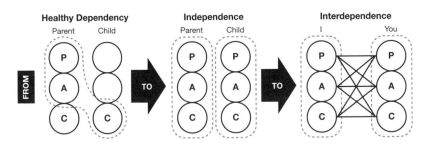

But for the child to move from absolute dependency to autonomy, her specific needs must be met at every stage of development by the parent figures and with minimal trauma. Since few, if any, of us get everything we need from our primary dependency in infancy and childhood, a secondary system develops as we strive for survival and growth. This dependency, which I refer to as *addictive dependency*, is the basis for adult addictive relationships. Think back to Anna in chapter 1, whose abusive childhood made it difficult for her to learn self-esteem and self-sufficiency. Such a system dominated her adult behavior as she took care of others with the belief that in so doing, she would gain security, self-esteem, and self-sufficiency.

The Child Within: Addictive Dependency

The Child ego state is worth further scrutiny in our examination of addictive love. Within that state, Berne says, there are three components: the Natural Child, the Little Professor, and the Parent in the Child.[3]

At birth, only the Natural Child is present—the source of sensations and feelings that tell us what we need to survive. The Natural Child spontaneously reaches out to the world in hopes of getting what it needs. And it will continue to do so unless it is stopped, ignored, or scared.

At about six months, the Little Professor appears. It is our intuitive thinker, the master of childish calculation. The Natural Child knows it needs certain things—food, elimination, warmth, protection, stimulation, touching—to stay alive; in short, the Natural Child knows that *it must keep those big people around in order to survive*. It is the Little Professor's job to answer the question this knowledge raises: *How to keep them around?*

Parent in the Child

Little Professor

Natural Child

At the age of three, the third part of the Child ego state—the Parent in the Child—develops. This stage, which lasts until age six or seven, is the kingdom of myths and magic, of Santa Claus, bogeymen, and monsters. Thus, when your mother said, "You make me so mad!" or "You make me feel so good!" you took her literally; you believed you had the power to control her feelings and she controlled yours. You thought in black and white—no gray—because that was the only way your mind could work then. The Parent in the Child is the holder of myths, which it believes to be truths, which sustain addictive love.

These parts of our personalities have the same function today as they did in childhood. The Natural Child knows it needs something; the Little Professor figures out how to get that something; and the Parent in the Child carries out the plan to keep that something—those essential people—around. In a child, such dynamics are perfectly normal. In an adult, they can be troublesome when they sustain beliefs that turn love—that most precious of human experiences—into unhealthy dependency.

The Myths behind Addictive Love

Behind each addictive love relationship lurks a childhood story dominated by magical thinking and strongly held myths that become a self-fulfilling prophecy. One such story is Brent's.

❧ Brent's Story ❧

Brent was a financially successful professional, well respected in the community, who came into therapy with high self-esteem. His problem was his inability to establish relationships that met his needs for support and closeness. He had a number of love affairs with women whose needs were so great or who were so independent they would not respond to his needs. Intellectually, he was aware of his patterns and selections; still, he was unable to understand them. In exploring his background, much of which he had consciously forgotten or dismissed as not important, the following story emerged.

One ordinary day, four-year-old Brent hugged his mother and ran outside to play; life felt good. Time passed, and as children do, Brent went home for his periodic check-in with Mom to assure himself that his world was in order. When he walked into the house, he found his mother crying, holding his baby brother, who was also crying. (Although Brent had no way of knowing it at the time, his mother and father had just argued over the phone.) Brent's world suddenly seemed threatened, and he felt terror. *What have I done or not done?* he asked himself. Looking for comfort and reassurance, Brent asked, "What's wrong, Mommy? Is everything okay?" Brent's mom said, "Oh, honey, I'm so glad you're here. Tell Mommy everything will be okay." Brent felt momentary confusion and then quickly acted on his mom's suggestion. He patted her arm, smiled into her eyes, and proudly and magically said: "It's okay, Mommy, everything will be all right. I just know it!" Mother smiled and said, "You are my wonderful little man. I don't know what I'd do without you."

Brent's world was in order once again. But something significant had happened. The four-year-old boy could not perceive that the incident was a natural and isolated occurrence and that the comfort he offered his mother was not the result of some magical power he possessed. A myth was born and grandiosity established: Brent began to believe he had the power to make his mother (and perhaps everyone) feel good; moreover, he had to do so in order for his own needs to be met. The child-belief that prevailed was "I'm in charge of making people feel good or bad; what I say, think, feel, or do will keep them around or drive them away."

Brent's story may sound rather poignant and sweet: a child caring for his melancholy mother. But Brent was a child who needed his mother to be a big person who would care for him. Like other children of this age, who are not yet able to separate pretend from reality, he feared that if something happened to his parents, his world would not last. He also believed he might be the cause of his mother's pain; parents often unwittingly say things—like "You make me feel bad"—that a child takes quite literally. As an adult, Brent would have responded to the situation by reasoning, *Mom is upset. I'll offer her sympathy, though I can't make everything better.*

As a child, Brent needed information and reassurance he didn't receive. He needed Mom to say, "Thank you for caring about me, and I'm fine." Instead of receiving maternal comfort for his *frightened* Child ego state, Brent was invited to take care of his mother's sad Child ego state, *suppressing his own fears and needs in the process.* Brent had cared for his mother at his own emotional expense; he continued to do so in his adult relationships. From a child's point of view, Brent's decision was creatively adaptive: *I'll stop feeling scared and needy and take care of her.* And it did seem to work! Mom did stick around. And she even smiled![4]

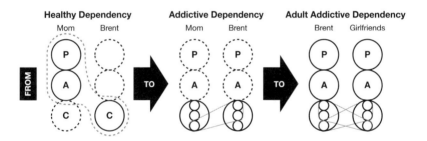

Because Brent continued his unconscious pattern of suppressing his feelings and needs, he unconsciously chose needy women who supported his belief system. Thus, he actually got what he wanted in his troublesome addictive relationships: his partners were psychologically self-serving and prevented him from having his own needs fulfilled. In a variety of subtle ways, his partners supported his earlier conclusions: *My needs are not important, and I have the power to make a woman (Mom) feel good.* The tragedy is that Brent needed and had a right to his own feelings, desires, and support; he needed to be cared for without always having to care for others first.

In addictive love, the ties of dependency run from one partner's inner child to the other's. Addictive lovers believe that they need to be attached to someone in order to survive and that the other has the magical ability to make them whole. This is why a love relationship often goes wrong. Addictive lovers don't believe they can be whole alone. The pervasive feeling that something is missing directs them in adult relationships to unconsciously seek out others to meet their unmet needs. The difficulty is that a person out of touch with his real needs tends to seek out people similar to the original person (i.e., a parent) who did not have the capacity or information to meet those needs in the first place.[5]

Only when Brent, like Anna and so many others, was able to examine the unconscious fears and beliefs connected to his unmet needs from a new adult perspective was he psychologically free to establish healthy interdependency with women.

Immature, childish love believes "If I take care of you and love you the way I want you to love me, then you'll love me that way, too." We may think of a child's love as generous and innocent; but often it is not. Children are not yet capable of spiritual love; their love is egocentric. They love in order to survive, in order to avoid pain, fear, and want. And that pattern, as we're seeing, haunts adult addictive lovers.

Addictive Love as a Response to Trauma

No sooner do we begin to know other people than we discover their broken heart.

JACOB NEEDLEMAN, A Little Book on Love

Each story in this book illustrates that there is usually a direct correlation between addictive love and trauma. At a specific emotionally traumatic moment, we began establishing psychological beliefs that counter our ability to establish or maintain true intimacy. It was in such a moment that Brent concluded, *My needs are not important.*

Traumas of All Kinds

Childhood trauma, if unresolved, will continually produce symptoms that impair our ability to form healthy, secure relationships or will direct us to romance or sex addiction. When we hear the word *trauma,* most of us think of a single, horrific experience that forever terrorizes us. But trauma, particularly childhood trauma, does not have to be extreme to leave an impact. There are four types of developmental trauma I look for in my work. I do not know anyone who has not experienced at least one of them. They are

- trauma of omission
- trauma of commission
- shock trauma
- post-traumatic stress disorder (PTSD)

Trauma of omission is subtle and often overlooked. In our psychological maturing, we need to accomplish specific developmental tasks in an orderly way to ensure a healthy sense of wholeness. We need to hear certain affirmations and permissions that affirm our right to be who we are. None of us got everything we needed in just the way we needed it during childhood. These unmet needs are called *omissions.* As adults, we walk around unaware that we have holes in our psyche and that we are trying to fill them any way we can. Children who have a chronically depressed parent or whose emotional needs are not met because of ignorance or ineffective parenting, for example, fall into this category.

Trauma of commission refers to things that are said and done to children that never should have been said or done—physical beatings, name calling, put-downs, shaming, deliberate neglect, harsh punishments, and emotional incest. In an emotional state, we may draw conclusions about ourselves, others, and life that get locked in our psyche: "I am bad," "No one will love me as I am," and "It's not safe to be close."

Even more shocking events may occur that we have little or no control over and have to adjust to anyway. *Shock trauma* can occur when a child experiences a difficult birth, a hospitalization, an auto accident, a serious illness, or the loss of a parent, friend, or sibling. It includes peer shaming, bullying, being publicly humiliated, witnessing parents abuse each other, or watching a sibling getting a beating.

Some children are exposed to more catastrophic life events: sexual abuse, rape, kidnapping, brutal beatings, witnessing a shooting, witnessing one parent kill another, being in a war zone, or experiencing a natural disaster such as a fire, flood, earthquake, or tornado. Such life-threatening or chaotic events overwhelm the psyche, flood a child emotionally, and leave the child in a trancelike state, numbly watching the world go by. This is known as *post-traumatic stress disorder.*

Healing from Trauma

It is not our fault that we were traumatized, and we could not help but be impacted. When a child's needs are not realized, when cruel words are said, or when a child finds herself alone in a traumatic moment, the child feels betrayed or abandoned. Not having the words or perceived power to stand up for herself, a child often stops trusting. Trauma = betrayal = broken heart = loss of trust = fear = addictive love.

Healing trauma is probably the single most important factor for successful long-term recovery from sex, romance, and love addiction. And though we have innate capacities to heal from trauma and its incapacitating symptoms, we must understand that the symptoms are physiological as well as psychological. Trauma does not heal on its own, nor is it forgotten by the body and psyche. Our brains are set up to remember painful experiences on a deep level, even when we push them out of our current memory. Dr. Paul MacLean's triune brain theory explains how the three parts of our brains—the reptilian (instinctive) brain, the mammalian (emotional) brain, and the neocortex (rational)—work to make this happen (see page 53).[6]

The reptilian brain is responsible for keeping us alive. Involuntary and unconscious, the primal brain cannot *not* respond to life events. When a tiger comes into the room, we experience perceived danger, and our primal brain puts us into fight, flight, or freeze mode. When we see a chocolate cake, we salivate. When a sexual image is

The Triune Brain

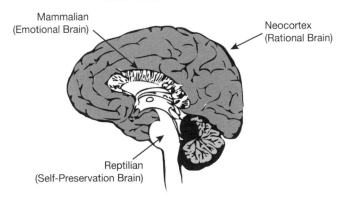

Mammalian
(Emotional Brain)

Neocortex
(Rational Brain)

Reptilian
(Self-Preservation Brain)

put before us, we feel sexually excited. If a child, such as Anna, is sexually abused, her brain is wired to the trauma. If she sees a reminder in the future, her body automatically experiences the same sensations whether she wants to feel them or not.

The mammalian, or "limbic," brain is our emotional brain. Structures within this section of the brain relate to impulsiveness and anger, and they also encode emotional memories and conclusions made in an emotionally traumatic experience. For example, in a state of fear Anna concluded that she must care for her father at all costs in order to be protected. This became a learned fear waiting to sabotage her adult love life.

The neocortex is our rational brain. This "captain" of the cortex lies in the front of the brain and is called the prefrontal cortex. It is our conscience, the part of us that works to control urges and make sense out of our behaviors and relationships. Its job is to plan ahead, consider consequences, and manage emotions. What got Anna to therapy was her rational belief that neither she nor Andrew would die if she was not sexually involved with him.

Fight, Flight, Freeze

Unresolved trauma trapped in the body and mind generates trauma in our love relationships. When we have a traumatic recall, known as "getting triggered," the lower two brains—instinctive and emotional—take over rational thinking and immediately bring past memories into the present, to the extent that the past trauma feels as if it is happening again. According to trauma expert Dr. Peter Levine, "Traumatic symptoms are not caused by the 'triggering' event itself. They stem from the frozen residue of energy that has not been resolved and discharged."[7]

According to Dr. Levine, a threatened human is not unlike his reptilian and mammalian relatives. When we feel threatened, even in our love relationships, the biological part of us instinctively reacts with a primary fight, flight, or freeze response that is not under our conscious control. Most people are more familiar with the fight-or-flight mechanism than with the freeze response because of how we interpret it as a culture.

The freeze response, or *immobility response,* is often seen as pure cowardice or is resisted because of its deathlike quality. Nature has two good reasons for a freeze response: playing possum may guarantee survival, and entering this "frozen" state eliminates the experience of pain should our predator get us. When animals are traumatized, they are not left with residual effects, because when the trauma is over, they allow their bodies to fully release by shaking. They do not have imperatives that tell them they are weak if they shake off the fear in their bodies. Our rational human brains, on the other hand, become confused and override our instinctive healing mechanisms. What results is that our bodies—including our hearts—become frozen in fear. We hang on to this possumlike state by shutting down emotions or keeping others at bay in anticipation of being hurt.

The body trembling that occurred in Anna's story was old fear still trapped in her body and being triggered by the relationship with Andrew.

✂ *Lindsay and Kevin's Story* ✂

Childhood traumas, including traumas we are not aware of, get re-enacted in our adult relationships. Lindsay and Kevin's story speaks to four types of trauma and tells how each individual's trauma fed off each other.

Lindsay: I unknowingly married a man who was a sex addict. Demoralized and furious when this came out, I blamed many of our relationship problems on him. Since he was the one who broke the trust, my self-righteous anger was justified. He had to change so I could get rid of these thoughts going off in my head. But then I got suspicious, as I kept hearing myself interpret his actions as a statement about me. I was the one who felt unimportant, unattractive, and stupid. And while these feeling-related thoughts could be explained given Kevin's addiction, I couldn't stop them even when our relationship started to heal. They were deep. I finally got help. My therapist insisted that I look at what was going on inside of me that kept getting "triggered" in the relationship.

As I got into my story, I realized my past experience was the filter through which I was viewing myself and Kevin. I really thought I had a good childhood. Then I started to remember. I remembered being ignored and feeling lonely. I remembered being verbally abused by an older brother. When I asked my parents for help, they blew it off. I decided that all of the negative things my brother said were probably true because my parents seemed to side with him.

The feelings I had back then were exactly what I felt when I learned about Kevin's sexual addiction. Every time we had a big argument, in my mind I heard him saying, "Lindsay, you are stupid," or "Your opinion is not important to me." I would take it one step further and hear, "And I am going to leave you for someone who is more attractive than you." I had been working hard to change Kevin so he could become the partner I needed him to be—someone to affirm what my family had failed to affirm. I realized *I* had to heal my trauma, and *I* had to believe in my importance, beauty, and intelligence.

Kevin: I am recovering from sex addiction. I didn't even know I had a problem until I realized that although I married the woman I loved, I could not stop my compulsive use of pornography and Internet affairs. I got caught by Lindsay, and going into recovery was a condition of her staying in the marriage. At first I took on the brunt of the relationship problems because I had disturbed the trust in the relationship. But after being in recovery for a year, I realized we both brought stuff to the table from our pasts. I hate to admit to the cliché, but Lindsay reminded me of my mother. Even though she was not saying it out loud, what I heard her saying was "You are really bad." When I first told her how I felt, and she became defensive, I told myself that my feelings were not acceptable. We would get into some heated power struggles.

I went headlong into my trauma history. I had a very hard time feeling anything, but I thought this was a guy thing. I had been suppressed for years. As I started to remember experiences, amazing emotions surfaced—terror, rage, grief. I shook and cried when I recalled a time I had to watch my brother being beaten by my father and wasn't able to stop it. That my mother was cold and failed to protect me and my brother was not as bad as her tying me to the bed for hours at age five. I remember being terrified at first, and then I began going somewhere else in my mind and shutting down my feelings.

Such experiences led me to believe that I was bad and that my feelings did not matter. Waiting for Lindsay to magically rescue me from my beliefs was futile. Instead, her trauma collided with mine. There has always been legitimate love in our relationship, but there has also been a hidden need to fix our wounds. Of course we did not know this. Now we talk about our triggers when we recognize them, and we are learning to appreciate the little boy and little girl in each of us that has a story to tell.

Because traumatic events from the past are rarely remembered, and because the psychological motives that promote addictive love are usually not conscious, we must look at behaviors and patterns in the here and now to assess whether we are in love or addiction. Let's move on, then, to examine the warning signs of love addiction.

II

How Do I Love Thee?

Love Addiction

Controlling and caretaking create unmanageability.

MELODY BEATTIE, Codependents' Guide to the Twelve Steps

Most, if not all, love relationships harbor some elements of love addiction. Narrowing our focus to one mate is a natural setup for both healthy and unhealthy dependence. Let's face it—blissfully harmonious, mature interdependency is just an ideal we are striving for. If we are to achieve mature love, we need to have experienced as children the steady, strong parental love that helps us to love ourselves. Parental love gives us a strong sense of well-being and allows us to experience giving for the sheer joy of it. This allows us, as adults, to experience and express our full spectrum of emotions and desires. We can think clearly and separate illusion from reality, and we can confidently give voice to our thoughts and determine how best to meet our needs. If we are to be capable of mature love as adults, we need to develop an internal system of self-parenting that offers unconditional self-love, wise self-guidance, and strong self-support.

In addition to strong parental love, we need to have grown up in a society that worked to free its children from the illusion that others hold the key to a life full of constantly fulfilled promises: absolute safety, unearned trust, instant gratification, power, and perpetual comfort. That culture would be honest and admit to us that human beings don't inherently possess all of the tools needed to form conscious, intimate relationships with others—that we are in need of constructing a whole new curriculum. Contrary to what love songs would lead us to believe, this curriculum would say love is not all you need, and living love is not easy. The curriculum would say, "Go easy on yourself; a conscious, intimate, loving relationship is a rarity."

Few people are lucky enough to have all it takes to be a completely mature individual and lover. But there is much that adults can learn about love and freedom, and that is our goal here.

Infantile love operates on the principle "I love because I am loved." Mature love embraces the idea "I am loved because I am love." Immature love says, "I love you because I need you." Mature love imparts, "I like loving you"; immature love says, "You must like me before I will love you." Mature love allows for individuality and for free expression of ideas and feelings; it consents to discussion of values—and even, at times, to confrontation. Immature love does not. Mature love nourishes; immature love can be lethal. Immature love leads us to love addiction.

Identifying Love Addiction

Love addiction is a psychological and behavioral disorder in which a person looks to another person to satisfy a hunger for security, sensation, power, identity, belonging, and meaning. It is an unconscious attempt to fix or avoid pain, present or past. Rather than a bonding, it becomes a psychological bondage. In the process, a love addict becomes emotionally and biologically dependent on the love object. The gradual enmeshment with the love object occurs over time and can have a soothing, satiating effect on the brain, not unlike alcohol. Like an addiction to alcohol and other drugs, a dependency on love begins to feel like an unstable state in which a person begins to lose herself to the experience. Love addicts deny parts of themselves to keep people, even toxic people, around and ensure predictability. In their attempt to control a relationship, they slowly go out of control. Physical and emotional problems increase as the disorder continues.

Based on fear, love addiction begins to anticipate hurt, rejection, disappointment, and betrayal. And then, as with a self-fulfilling prophecy, love addicts create that which they fear. Underneath, there is a fantasy hope that the drug of choice—a person—will complete them. A love addict will employ indirect means to get a need met and is willing to use others or allow self to be used in the process.

For many of us, looking outside of ourselves for affirmation and worth, wanting approval and acceptance, taking care of others' feelings at our emotional expense, and struggling for power have become well-established patterns by the time we reach early adulthood. Even though we have the illusion of freedom, we are unaware of how our psyche has already been programmed, how our love maps have been set, and what trauma seeks resolution. Love addiction demonstrates what Freud called the repetition compulsion, or the impulse to re-enact earlier emotional experiences and to seek out players that fit our script. The repetition ultimately results in more pain than pleasure. Though the love addict usually hopes to create a positive ending, the repetition compulsion is so ingrained and the roles so intact, that it typically takes a major life event to recognize love addiction and change it.

Love Addiction and Health

People often ask me why a person should get out of love addiction. My answer is "because it is deadly to stay there." In love addiction, there are actual physical ramifications. As Anna's and Brent's stories illustrate, love addiction starts out as a role reversal in childhood, when a child attempts to fix the parent's feelings. This situational role reversal also results in physical aches and pains that can actually disable. Let me explain. There are two mutually beneficial positions in healthy dependency: provider and receiver. There are two energy-depleting roles assumed in love addiction—the *grandiose* role and the *victim.*

In the story in chapter 3, the child Brent, whose rightful position was receiver, assumed the grandiose role instead. In order to become "Mom's little man," he had to push himself to grow up, and in so doing did injury to his body as well as his psyche. His body, meant to be relaxed and open to receiving, became tense. He carried the grandiose role, body tension included, into his adult relationships. Love addicts who primarily assume the grandiose position in relationships often end up with illnesses such as hypertension, rheumatoid arthritis, migraines, and neurodermatitis.

It is not difficult to identify someone in the grandiose role. They feel energized, powerful, obligated, agitated, and driven. They want to fix things and people to keep their world in order, but they have trouble stopping and feeling for themselves. Displaying "parent feelings" of pride, self-righteousness, impatience, outrage, and guilt, they come across as superior, suspicious, and independent. They are good at projecting their problems onto their partners as a coping mechanism and to maintain their position.

Others, such as Brent's mother, are groomed to be in the victim position. Her rightful position was to be the provider. But her passively postured body, turned-down mouth, furrowed brow, and beseeching eyes invited Brent to care for her. Love addicts who assume this position often realize physical ailments such as bronchial asthma, peptic ulcers, diabetes mellitus, and colitis. Their muscles are slack, their complexions sallow, and their breathing shallow.

You can recognize someone in the victim role quite easily as well. They are often lethargic, flabby, confused, lonely, and depressed. They feel inferior, helpless, regretful, and shameful, and they are quite adept at manipulating people to take care of them. They make excuses, are self-pitying, and on occasion assume a hysterically depressive position. Denial is their major coping mechanism.

In love addiction, there is a strong investment in the grandiose and victim positions. But since these roles are energy depleting and impossible to sustain, an explosion or crash is inevitable. The roles will reverse, or the two people become competitive. Eventually, love addicts will demand fulfillment of their magical expectations.[1] If one person refuses to play his or her role or removes himself or herself, there will be intense withdrawal symptoms of an emotional, physical, and behavioral nature. And it does not matter who is stepping out and who is hanging on. Both will feel the impact.

Since elements of unhealthy dependency creep into even the best of mature love relationships, the challenge is to identify and acknowledge love-addictive behaviors, uncover the myths that support them, do what we can to change them, and build on the best aspects of a relationship.

How do we know if our love is an addiction? For the answer, let's take a look at twenty prominent signs of love addiction.

Twenty Signs of Love Addiction

If you recognize several of the following characteristics in yourself, there's a good chance you are in the midst of a love addiction:

1. overadapting to what others want
2. boundary problems
3. sadomasochism
4. fear of letting go
5. fear of the unknown
6. stunted individual growth
7. difficulty experiencing intimacy
8. psychological games
9. giving to get
10. attempting to change others
11. needing others to feel complete
12. wanting, wishing, and waiting
13. demanding and expecting unconditional love
14. refusing or abusing commitment
15. looking to others for affirmation and worth
16. fearing abandonment
17. repetitive bad feelings
18. wanting and fearing closeness
19. attempting to "fix" others
20. projection, personalizing, power plays

Now, let's look at each of these signs in more detail.

Overadapting to What Others Want

To adapt means to adjust or conform to a situation or person. You accommodate others. You live cooperatively. For example, I agree to meet you at 8:00 a.m., and I do. We stop at red lights and we get to

work on time. Such adaptations are healthy and keep our relationships and communities working well. But in love addiction, we overadapt. We accommodate others out of fear and minimize or give up
our thoughts, feelings, creativity, spontaneity, authenticity, and capacity for intimacy to keep others around, get their approval, or not
make waves. Remember Brent's story in chapter 3. As a child, he used
intuition to determine what put smiles and frowns on the big people
and adjusted his behavior to them. He learned to suppress his feelings and needs and take care of others' feelings instead. And that pattern caused pain in his adult relationships. Examples of overadapting
include the following:

- smiling when you are angry or hurt
- withholding the truth so as not to hurt someone's feelings
- behaving against your own values
- not standing up for yourself
- letting someone talk you out of your decisions
- not telling people what you really feel
- putting others' needs first
- adapting your life to others' schedules
- postponing your life
- sabotaging your success when someone is threatened by it
- lying to keep the peace

It should be noted that rebellion is the flip side of overadapting.
Some people overadapt thinking they will be appreciated for their
sacrifice, and when they are not acknowledged, they justify rebellion
in any of its forms, including sexual acting out.

Boundary Problems

This means other people so totally dominate our egos that it becomes difficult to know who is thinking what, which feelings belong
to whom, and who is responsible for which actions. Or, on the other
hand, it means we are so closed off that others cannot get close. Our
ego boundaries should be open enough to allow for the free flow of

thoughts and emotions, but not so open that our energy is sapped and our identities become blurred with the identities of others.

✺ *Mario and Jill's Story* ✺

I noticed with one couple, Mario and Jill, that whenever I asked Mario what he *felt,* Jill quickly answered for him. When I asked Jill what she *thought,* Mario replied. At first, they were unaware they were responding for each other, but they soon realized Jill was primarily responsible for the feelings in the relationship, and Mario for the thoughts. It then became clear why Mario and Jill feared separation: they functioned together as a whole and unconsciously allowed themselves to act as mere halves.

They learned that the romantic notion that urges two "to become one" sounds ideal—but this concept is neither romantic nor an ideal worth pursuing. We don't have to lose ourselves to be close to another person. Every relationship has three entities: an "I," a "you," and a "we."

Boundary, by definition, refers to a landmark that distinguishes one piece of territory from another. In relationships, it suggests marking our psychological territory. A fence is an easy dividing line to recognize; psychological dividing lines are more complex. We use words to describe these ephemeral boundaries: "I feel invaded." "I don't know where I stop or another begins."

A healthy boundary is permeable, so that it allows a free exchange of thoughts, actions, words, and feelings while serving to protect us from psychological invasiveness. But boundaries can be too weak or too rigid.[2] Examples of weak boundaries include the following:

- having intimate conversations with people with whom you have not established trust
- falling in love with anyone who reaches out
- being sexual solely to meet someone else's needs or desires

- acting on a first sexual impulse
- disregarding personal values to please someone
- accepting things you do not want—food, sex, touch
- failing to recognize when your boundaries have been violated
- failing to stop others from violating your boundaries
- saying yes when you mean no
- letting abusive people remain in your life
- trusting anyone
- telling all
- adulating others

Examples of rigid boundaries include the following:

- trusting no one
- using black-and-white thinking
- compartmentalizing life—keeping people and activities in one's life isolated; failing to integrate various aspects of life
- holding out—refusing to yield or compromise
- putting up a wall—not sharing thoughts, feelings, energy with others; becoming physically rigid, withdrawing
- lacking in empathy
- being intimate only when sexual
- being unwilling to be vulnerable
- feigning emotions
- avoiding love—not accepting caring from others
- living a secret life
- observing life versus fully living it
- exhibiting a hardened attitude—being set in one's ways, being constrained, lacking the ability to empathize or show feelings

Sadomasochism

A sadistic person is one who is mean, vicious, heartless, and even cruel. A masochistic person is one who allows himself to be dominated and treated cruelly. *Sadomasochism* implies two people agreeing to take each role. Though it is often used to denote perverse sex, sadomasochism in love addiction can be subtle, as when one person is the brunt of jokes or is constantly presented as "the problem" in the relationship. In a restaurant, I heard a husband say to his wife, "I am really hungry," and her response was, "All we have done on this trip is eat." He tried again by saying, "They have your favorite cheesecake." Predictably, her response was, "The last thing I need is cheesecake." Yes, love addiction can sting.

In many unhealthy relationships, one partner generally gives more while the other takes more. One partner may unconsciously enjoy hurting or disappointing the other, while the other unwittingly enjoys being hurt or disappointed. In severe cases, one partner physically abuses the other. Usually, this is related to past trauma, and it is familiar—even desirable. We become comfortably miserable; it is what we know. It is as though we are addicted to the drama, the chaos, and the pain. Edie is a classic example.

✎ *Edie's Story* ✎

Edie came in surprised to find herself in a state of anxiety. She and her husband were "getting along well," she said. He was actually honoring the contract he made to stop his rageful outbursts. They'd even had a heated argument, and he did not become aggressive. But instead of feeling better, Edie had a panic attack. Both her body and psyche were poised for the usual attack and remained in anticipatory mode, wondering when the "boom" would fall. She said to me: "I liked when he would attack, because then I knew it was over with and I could then relax—for a while. I do not trust him. I am waiting for the hit. My father was a raging alcoholic. Even though I hated his outbursts, they were predictable. Once out—I could relax."

It is no surprise she chose a man who so easily fit her first experience with love. And it was no surprise that she set herself up by having an affair and that her jealous and rageful husband would find out about it.

Fear of Letting Go

Because love addiction is so intense, there is a fear of letting go. As a result, some pathological relationships may endure for years.

ᘓ *Marty and Larry's Story* ᘓ

Marty and Larry's relationship had been emotionally dead for years. Although they often talked about ending their relationship, they avoided taking steps toward it. Exploring their dread of letting go in the face of the irredeemable loss of their love, they found that their fear of being alone and lack of confidence in their abilities to cope with separation and change were keeping them together and unhappy. As children, both had been abandoned physically or emotionally by their parents, and neither wanted to relive the pain of loss or rejection. What they had seemed preferable to what they feared. Marty and Larry failed to trust their individual abilities to be independent, to cope with separation, and to experience fulfilling relationships in the future.

ᘓ

We all have experienced loss in our lives, and it hurts. We have been rejected, and it is painful. Some people empower their pain by believing they cannot stand it and by doing everything to avoid it. Rather than facing the pain and trusting it will end, they hang on to unhealthy relationships to avoid grief. But loss and rejection are part of life; to think we can avoid them is magical, mythical thinking. Grief is a natural, healing response to loss. Contrary to what we might believe, we do have the ability to handle pain. Addictions are a misguided attempt to increase our comfort level.

Fear of the Unknown

Another element of love addiction is its illusion of safety and predictability, which prevents a person from exploring the unknown.

No matter how badly a person may treat us, that person is the drug that we have become dependent on. When my son was young, I asked him, "Why do you think winners might have more losses than losers?" He thought about it a bit and said, "Because they take more chances and try more things." And that's true. Winners don't stop when they make a mistake; they don't kick themselves when they lose. They ask, "What can I learn from this? How can I do it differently next time?" But love addicts hang on and on and on, because it is what they know. They may think or say, "How do I know it will be better next time?" "What if I never find anyone?"

✺ *Candi's Story* ✺

Candi sought therapy, she said, "to learn to grow up." She was dating Mike, who accused her of being immature and a hanger-on. Mike had told her that if she didn't "grow up," he would leave her for another woman he had been seeing. Candi's motive for trying to change was to please Mike; she didn't want to lose him. But Mike did not really want Candi to change. He hoped to justify his relationship with the other woman by blaming it on Candi's inability to grow up. When Candi realized Mike really favored her dependency, she dropped out of therapy, still fearing she would lose him.

A year later, she was back in therapy, saying this time it was for herself. She knew she deserved to feel grown-up and happy; if Mike wanted to join her, fine. If not, she felt ready to risk the unknown and move ahead with her life.

Stunted Individual Growth

In love addiction, the lovers stagnate; they often are satisfied with a monotonous lifestyle as dreams and passions are put aside in service of connection. They put more energy into concern about their relationship than into personal growth—self-actualization. As Abraham Maslow discovered, humans have a natural urge to grow. When that urge is neglected because of an addictive relationship or a compulsive habit, we are, in a sense, dying—if not physically, then mentally, emotionally, and spiritually.

To deny oneself growth is personal abuse and often results in emotional or physical illness. The reason for this is that we each have a certain amount of energy to be expressed in feelings, thoughts, and actions. Energy has to go somewhere. When it is suppressed or blocked, it will eventually either be directed inward, leading to physical or mental illness, or it will explode outward, and we will strike out at others.

✌ *Barbara and Gary's Story* ✌

Barbara was bright and creative. Encouraged by her husband, Gary, she returned to college after their children entered school. In time, Barbara earned a graduate degree and began to expand her interests and activities. In many ways, it seemed she was surpassing her husband's education and success.

Then Gary's insecurities surfaced. He complained that Barbara's job was more important to her than their marriage. Barbara, anxious to please him, began to limit her friendships and activities, and in time, she became ill.

At that point, Barbara and Gary went to see a counselor. Their therapy focused on teaching Gary to explore his fears and insecurities, freeing him to appreciate and encourage Barbara's creativity and success. It also helped Barbara explore her tendency to deny her needs, and to find a balance between the demands of her career and her marriage.

Difficulty Experiencing Intimacy

The word *intimacy* has different connotations to different people. For some, it suggests a profound emotional closeness. For others, it is interchangeable with the word *love*. For still others, it's a euphemism for "sexual closeness," often suggesting illicit overtones.

If we accept Eric Berne's definition of *intimacy* as a "profound exchange of thoughts, feelings, and actions in the here and now," intimacy potentially includes all life experiences.[3] Because intimacy, by Berne's definition, is happening now, it suggests an emotional openness, vulnerability, risk taking, and unpredictability. It does not hide in the past or future. It can feel good or bad. Soldiers in combat feel heightened intimacy. Watching a loved one die is intimacy. Expressing anger to stop hurtful behavior is intimacy. Resolving conflict is intimacy. Even domestic abuse can be considered intimacy. It is happening now! In moments of intimacy, a person is vulnerable and thus absorbs the experience into her psyche. Considering that, even early childhood trauma occurred in a moment of emotional intimacy! In some cases, the pain of intimacy was so great that we may have promised ourselves never to be that intimate again. Such self-promises close us off to more ecstatic states of intimate love.

In intimacy, then, we are naked and free to reveal the truth of who we are, including our emotional wounds, our fears, our walls. In intimacy, relationships are processes, not perfect products. Intimacy—the exchange of thoughts, feelings, and actions in an atmosphere of openness and trust—is a profound expression of our identities and, when positive, leaves us in a euphoric state. Love addiction gives the illusion of intimacy without our having to be fully vulnerable. That illusion—that we can have human closeness without risk—is a large part of the attractiveness of love addiction. But as with all addictions, the premise is a false one that will always betray us sooner or later.

Recall the Natural Child component of the Child ego state: true intimacy involves contact between the Natural Child in two people. But addictive lovers suppress that state in their attempts to care for others. And, often, they mistake unhealthy dependency for intimacy.

✑ *Audrey's Story* ✑

Most complaints in therapy are related to emotional intimacy. As Audrey said: "I have been married over twenty years, I have four children with this man, and I do not know him." In her response to his question "How much do you love me?" she answered: "I can only love you as much as you will allow me to know you. All I ask is if you would expand yourself more so I will know you and in time can truly love who I know." She said she was not going to make the first move. She wanted him to open up before she risked being honest and expressed love to him. It was just too scary to be the first one rejected. "I want certainty," she said. And then she laughed at what she'd just said.

Psychological Games

Psychological games replace intimacy in addictive relationships, providing interaction and drama, and are a roundabout way of seeking fulfillment of our desires and needs. Although asking for something in an indirect fashion—through game playing—is less risky, we're also less likely to get what we want this way. We did not start life as game players. As young children, we identified a legitimate need, communicated directly to a parent figure, and asked for what was needed. We either got a positive response, no response, an inadequate response, or a negative response. It was in our reaching out without success that we stopped being direct and played our first game.

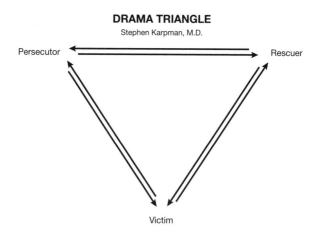

DRAMA TRIANGLE
Stephen Karpman, M.D.

Persecutor   Rescuer

Victim

A game player adopts one of three roles: *victim, rescuer,* or *persecutor*.[4] And there is always a switch of roles somewhere in the drama. Here are common themes of each position:

- victim: enjoying misery, inviting put-downs, copping out, proving I am less okay, inviting in rescuers and persecutors
- rescuer: saving others, enabling victims, proving I am more okay than you, inviting in victims and persecutors
- persecutor: blaming others, finding fault, getting even, proving I am okay and you are not, inviting in victims and rescuers

Games look absurd to outsiders, who often recognize them for what they are, but the games seem perfectly normal to the players. In our more ordinary, less melodramatic lives, the games we play are very subtle and thus not always easily recognized. We may not be consciously aware of game-playing dynamics at all—that is, until we feel the pain they cause. Even then we do not always fully comprehend what happened. Instead, we feel confused.

❧ *Gina and Randy's Story* ❧

Gina and Randy were inveterate game players. Gina was a depressed, sexually unresponsive young woman whose favorite game was "Ain't He Awful?" She was referring to her husband, Randy, who was very aggressive sexually with Gina—and with other women. Randy's favorite game was "Poor Me," and his self-pitying litany was "How can you expect me to be faithful with a wife who won't let me touch her?" Gina cited her depression and anger to justify her inability to respond; Randy cited his frustration and anger to justify his unfaithfulness.

In reality, both were content with the story line they had concocted. Both feared commitment and intimacy, and their games allowed for warped contact, interaction, and melodrama. Meanwhile, they didn't have to cope with their problems or make tough decisions about change.

Giving to Get

In love addiction, what appears to be altruistic giving often is not. Love addiction is conditional; the underlying hope is "If I do the right things, I'll get what I want." Asking directly for what one wants or giving spontaneously often is seen as giving up, giving in, or losing part of oneself. This occurs because, on an unconscious level, the one who asks does not believe it is okay or safe, and the giver has promised not to grant control to another. Yet being straightforward does not guarantee a person will get what she wants, as Joan's story illustrates.

ℐ Joan's Story ℐ

With the help of therapy, Joan, a very hesitant, quiet woman of thirty-five, had accomplished many new things. She could talk honestly about her feelings and directly ask her partner, Clark, for what she wanted instead of giving and expecting to get. One day, she came to me in anger. "I did everything I was supposed to," she said. "I wanted Clark to do something for me, and I asked him in a clear, gentle way. Do you know what he said? He said no! He refused me."

Joan had done the right things, but she had made a common mistake: she thought if she asked in the right way, she'd get what she wanted. Although this is often the case, it is important to ask the right person at the right time, and even then accept that the person might say no.

People often get into trouble when they expect to get what they need or want. Needing or wanting things is natural, but expecting or demanding to receive them only sets us up for disappointment. Healthy love is willing to let go, not of a partner, but of expectations. The reward is that in asking, no matter what the outcome, we have been self-honoring.

Attempting to Change Others

Because we may experience ourselves as incomplete and therefore seek other people in search of wholeness, love addiction involves attempts to change others and scrutiny of others for faults.

My clients say, "If only Gina wasn't unresponsive, I wouldn't act out sexually"; "If only Candi would grow up, I'd be content"; "If only women would really love me, I'd be fulfilled at last." Over and over again, people try to change others in an effort to camouflage their own fears and inadequacies.

Candi's partner, Mike, expressed self-confidence, yet his need for dependent, insecure women in his life revealed his uncertainty. After he admitted his uncertainty, he and Candi were able to love each other with more calm and honesty.

Remember, your love addiction fits you like a glove. Stop putting the problem on the other. Why do you need an unresponsive woman? Why do you need an angry man? Why do you work for a tyrannical boss? How does your relationship fit you?

Needing Others to Feel Complete

Love addiction is a parasitic arrangement. In it, people feed off each other. The love addicts need each other to feel whole, balanced, and secure. Anxiety occurs whenever this unhealthy symbiosis is threatened. Often, that anxiety explodes into emotional or physical violence, as Hank and Joann's story reveals.

❧ *Hank and Joann's Story* ❧

Hank was a cold, prejudiced perfectionist. He grew up in a family that placed great emphasis on looking good on the surface, yet emotional and physical abuse occurred in the privacy of their home. Hank's wife, Joann, was warm, insecure, shy, and passionate. Hank bluntly expressed his lack of emotion for Joann: "She is there, but I don't feel anything for her." Whenever Joann questioned the relationship or discussed leaving Hank, he became furious and abused

Joann verbally, sexually, and physically. Although Hank did not love nor want Joann, he pathologically needed her. The thought of her leaving caused him intense anxiety. Primal feelings of ownership, a well of unmet needs from childhood, and role models who nonverbally said, "Men get what they want by bullying and staying distant," "Men have to control," and "Women keep men happy," surfaced each time Joann said she had had enough. But Joann had no intention of leaving. In fact, Hank's behaviors were, in a skewed way, welcomed by Joann. They suggested to her that she might really be needed and therefore was lovable. She developed an odd sense of security in Hank's perverse behaviors. This is often the paradox of violent marriage: two people feel strongly that they need each other, but they slowly destroy each other in spite of—or, rather, because of—that perceived need.

Wanting, Wishing, and Waiting

Closely related to the above is the habit of looking outside ourselves for change to happen. Many of us still think magically, like children who believe in Santa Claus, and are passively wanting, wishing, and waiting. Ask yourself how many times you have heard, thought of, or said the following statements:

- "If only I had someone . . ."
- "I wish she would change, then . . ."
- "When he has more time, then . . ."
- "After the kids are grown, then . . ."
- "Next year, things will be better."
- "If only I had done more, she wouldn't have left."

Instead of direct, assertive requests or realistic appraisal and action, we cling to our childish beliefs in magic. We must accept that we are responsible for ourselves and for our actions. Failure to rely on oneself leads to frustration, unhappiness, and illness.

My client Meghan is living evidence that wanting, wishing, and waiting for others to provide us our happiness—and empowering them to do so—does not work.

❧ *Meghan's Story* ❧

"Five years ago, when I was thirty-five, I finally went into treatment for longtime alcoholism. Sobriety is a miracle in my life. Before I became sober, I tried to cope with and avoid all my problems with alcohol and other drugs.

"I grew up with an alcoholic father and dealt with my unhappiness by being secretive and passive. I was a people pleaser and acted as mediator between my mother and father. During this time, I was sexually molested by my father. My mother knew what was happening, but did not stop it and chose to blame me, a ten-year-old child. During the years that followed, I clung to the belief that when I finally left home, my life would change. I wanted to get married and be rescued by someone stronger and healthier than myself.

"But 'rescue' was not forthcoming. As a young adult, I coped with my pain by being an 'achiever,' and by excelling in music, playing in local music groups. Before performing, I took tranquilizers for my anxiety. I also began to drink heavily. As the result of my very low self-esteem, my music suffered. Most of my social life and contacts involved drinking. I met my husband in this atmosphere.

"When I drank, I felt powerful, in control. I felt high and happy. *So this is how people manage,* I thought. But after a while, alcohol no longer helped with my depression. I found myself weeping more and more. I felt helpless and alone. Mark, my future husband, 'rescued' me. He gave me alcohol, took over my finances, made decisions for me, and wanted to marry me—even after I told him about my wretched childhood and history of promiscuous sex.

"Yet as our wedding approached, he began to throw my past at me, resulting in terrible quarrels in which I always ended up crying and begging for his forgiveness. I was sure no one else would have me, and I wanted desperately to belong to someone; I still believed marriage would mean the end of my troubles. I had forgotten my childhood beliefs: 'Men are abusive and scary'; 'No one can ever love me.' However, it wasn't long before these beliefs became a living nightmare.

"Only a month after we were married, Mark began to beat me. I once left him for several days, then returned because I believed no one else could love me. I cringe now when I think of how little love I had for myself. I tried to please Mark, believing if only I behaved properly, all would be well. The only positive result of this behavior was that my drinking declined during these years because Mark objected to it.

"One way I could feel good about myself was by being a hard worker. After my children were born, I continued to work, partly because my job helped me feel good about myself and partly because I did not trust Mark to provide for us. I passively handed over my pay to him; if I needed anything, I had to beg him for it. It never occurred to me that my income was my own, and I could handle finances.

"Meanwhile, I continued my role of rescuer, protecting my mother from my father's alcoholic rages. I felt important when I got her away from the house or argued with my father on her behalf. I had no real friends; my time was spent with Mark or my mother. I used my mother to provide me with tranquilizers and antidepressants; Mark would not pay for them, but she would. Mark also would not pay for clothing for me or the children; he said there were bills to be paid. My mother paid for these things, too. Nevertheless, I still felt Mark was taking care of me, and although there was no affection between us, I stayed with him. My mother and I would commiserate together about our marriages.

"I finally realized that my marriage and lifestyle were unhealthy, and I asked Mark to see a marriage counselor with me. He refused, and I left him. A few days later, Mark agreed to enter counseling, and we reconciled. We spent the next six months in a counseling group. After our sessions, we would go out and drink together. Mark no longer objected to my drinking; in fact, he encouraged it. Suddenly, we were both using alcohol to numb our unhappiness. As a result, the counseling was unsuccessful; we refused to face our problems.

"Then my mother died. This was a turning point in my use of

alcohol. Even though I knew it was wrong, I drank heavily to avoid pain and grief. I was pregnant with my fourth child, and I consider it a miracle that my daughter Daniella was not born with fetal alcohol syndrome. The day before she was born, I was so drunk I could hardly walk.

"One night shortly after Daniella was born, Mark and I got drunk, then got into a vicious argument. He beat me up, saying that during the months of marriage counseling he had been waiting for an opportunity to show me who was in charge. For some reason, I had never seen the brutality of his behaviors before; I was shocked. I knew I could not trust him, and I began to fear for my life.

"I decided I had to leave, but I didn't know how. I trusted no one; I fell into silence, barely speaking to Mark for months. I continued to drink heavily; Mark was drinking heavily, too. Then he got into deep financial trouble because of gambling debts, and he swore off alcohol. In a terrible incident witnessed by our children, he beat me up again. The next day, I took the children and fled. I got an attorney and eventually a divorce. Now, I thought, all my problems would finally end.

"But they didn't. I kept drinking and chose to be with men just as abusive as Mark. After about three years, I realized I *had* to quit drinking. It was out of control, and my job was in jeopardy. I finally sought professional help for my drinking.

"While in treatment, I learned a lot about myself. I learned how I had blamed others for how I was. I learned I had been unwilling to take any action toward change.

"I was sober for about six months before I began to allow myself to really feel again. Suddenly, my sorrow, built up over all those years, poured out, and I shed many tears. It was not an easy time, but it was necessary. I slowly began to put my life back together as I stopped wishing and waiting for someone to save me."

Demanding and Expecting Unconditional Love

The only time we really needed *only* unconditional love was when we were infants. After that, we began to receive conditional positive strokes for cooperating and conditional negative strokes for doing something wrong. Unable to love, nurture, or protect ourselves, we needed care and guidance from others to keep us alive and growing. If this guidance was underwritten with unconditional love, we would soon learn that we are not our behavior and that love does not get removed when we do something wrong. We also know we do not need to earn love. Unfortunately, many of us did not have this experience as children, and we continue to look outward for unconditional love.

It is perfectly legitimate for adults to want and to receive unconditional love, but to demand it is an unhealthy, unrealistic expectation. In love addiction, we may refuse to love ourselves unconditionally and rage or weep when others fail to love us in that way. And if we do not love ourselves unconditionally, we are more apt to believe we must earn love or become needy and cling to others.

✋ *Dorothy's Story* ✋

Dorothy, who sought therapy for chronic depression, appeared to be a demanding, whiny, angry young woman. Her need for love and approval from me, her counselor, seemed insatiable. She was angry that she had to pay for therapy; she was angry that the sessions weren't longer. "After all, isn't it my right to be loved?" she would ask. Her unspoken message to me was, "My parents didn't love me like I deserved to be loved, so you'd better!" I told Dorothy I was sorry she hadn't received the positive, unconditional love she had a right to as an infant, but I could not and would not make up for that loss. When she made demands for unconditional love, I felt compelled to pull back from her rather than come close. And if I, her therapist, felt this way, how might others in her life feel?

Dorothy acknowledged that her love relationships had been disastrous. Her neediness alternating with rageful demands to be the central figure in her partner's life resulted in two failed marriages marked by verbal and physical abuse. Her current marriage was also on dangerously thin ice. Her husband, a passive man filled with insecurities himself, would attempt to please Dorothy any way he could. Rarely satisfied, Dorothy would often verbally demean him, which suggested to him that he was not enough. He was very close to leaping out of the relationship to keep from striking back. Both Dorothy and her husband needed to learn to love themselves unconditionally and to place healthy conditions on their behaviors if the abuse was to stop. Paradoxically, this would also allow the deeper goodness of each person to be expressed and unconditionally affirmed by the other.

Refusing or Abusing Commitment

Love addiction often appears to be antidependent, to exhibit a clear refusal of commitment. In reality, this antidependency is the flip side of dependency. Our need to belong is real. People who say, "I'll do my thing and you do yours, and if we meet, so be it," promote a false independence. Most people who exalt their independence harbor many unfulfilled dependency needs. They've learned to avoid pain and fear by becoming overly self-sufficient. As they've assumed the "grandiose" role in a relationship, control is important to them; when they were children, they often felt one or both parents were attempting to overpower them or each other. Paradoxically, those control-obsessed parents failed to meet basic developmental needs in the child, and often the child's response was, "No, I won't, and you can't make me!" or "I'm okay; you're not!" These were important ways the child maintained a sense of personal power and dignity in an uneasy, unhealthy situation.

Having weak, ineffective parents can lead to similar results. The children are forced to take care of themselves rather than entrust dependency to others. However, this self-promise to be completely independent makes it difficult to commit to a mature love relationship.

It is not uncommon for an antidependent stance to turn into an abuse of commitment. A "you owe me" or "I own you" attitude has led to many unthinkable domestic abuse stories. Antidependence is pseudoindependence. Healthy independence assumes that one has had a healthy primary dependency relationship with parents as a child.

✐ Richard's Story ✐

Trauma can generate fear of commitment—and even terror. I have known people who panic when they think of a commitment to a love relationship. Their hearts are under lock and key. In a euphoric state of sexual excitement or romantic high, they may open up temporarily to feed the senses and then go back and lock them. As my client Richard so aptly put it: "I have seven gates around my heart. The closest I have let anyone get is to gate three. Only I have the keys. The more they push to get in, the more I resist." At forty-five years of age and after two failed marriages and numerous romantic liaisons, he has not known sustained, committed love and views others' pushing as the problem. In truth, he has old unhealed wounds and fear behind the gates. He may look at himself as strong, but until he has the courage to expose his heart, he remains in a self-imposed prison. This man may know sexual and romantic love, but until he unlocks the gates, he will not know sustained heart-to-heart bonding.

Looking to Others for Affirmation and Worth

Very few people love themselves without reservation, yet everyone wants to be loved that way. Like young children, we search the world for people who will love us totally, and when a love affair ends, our self-esteem wanes.

✌ *Judith's Story* ✌

Judith, who had very low self-esteem, wrote the following letter from her addictive self to her healthy self to describe the unconscious motivation for her many bad habits.

"Judith, the reason you are eating, smoking, and drinking so much is obvious. What else can you do? Behind your defenses is an empty shell, absolutely nothing. There is not a Judith. Your house, your job, your family, your car, your furniture, your plants, your clothes are all things that can be removed. You needed to think all these things were you, but you know better now. There is no you. I don't think you exist. *The only times you felt like you existed were when you had someone to love you or you belonged to someone.* And you don't have someone now. So you smoke, eat, and drink—at least they're something to help you feel alive."

People like Judith need to realize that it is their choice to enhance their lives. Most of us can be far happier and feel more fulfilled than we currently do. Our stumbling block is our belief that someone else will do it for us. We overlook our ability to choose to develop ourselves. We not only can make our own choices, we can create our own chances.

Fearing Abandonment

Pathological aloneness is characterized by chronic panic, anger, despair, and emptiness; it differs from mature aloneness, which is a healthy wistfulness for an absent lover. Love addicts are unable to sustain comfortable memories of the beloved, and fear of abandonment often accompanies even the most routine separation. The love addict has trouble trusting the other person will return. This phenomenon seems to be the result of having missed an important developmental lesson in childhood. It is essential that infants bond with and trust in the permanence of their parents. As they do, they begin to comfort themselves with the memory of parental love during the parents' absence, trusting they can have it again. When children learn to distrust that inevitable return, they are unable to call on pleasant memories to sustain them during parental absences. As adults, they may have trouble trusting their partners unless the partners are always in their sight.

✍ Jean's Story ✍

As a child, Jean was emotionally neglected by her parents. They seldom responded to her needs, and they often were physically abusive toward her. In therapy, Jean, an unusually hesitant and dependent young woman, took in positive messages about self-esteem and autonomy, but she was unable to trust and use those messages outside of therapy. Outside of my presence, Jean panicked and feared I would leave her and that her fragile new self-affirmation would vanish. Jean needed to learn to trust her memory and to use the lessons from her therapy in her daily life. At first, she had to work hard at this, restating and revisualizing our discussions to recapture the good feeling she had about them. She learned we have the capacity to recall both pleasant and unpleasant feelings and memories, and that we can control that process. I could not put anything new into Jean, only affirm what was already there and encourage her to develop self-worth.

Repetitive Bad Feelings

Another prominent feature of love addiction is the recurrence of bad feelings like emptiness, depression, guilt, rejection, anxiety, self-righteous anger, and low self-esteem. These recurring feelings generally result from psychological games played out by love addicts. People generally have their own favorite set of feelings supported by unconscious myths about themselves, others, and life. Such feelings interfere with meeting psychological needs and make intimacy difficult.

❧ *Carla and Ken's Story* ❧

Carla's favorite bad feeling was sadness. Ken's favorite bad feelings were rejection and self-righteous anger. Each knew how to get their bad feelings to pay off. Carla and Ken worked together and frequently met after work for drinks with other co-workers. Carla was flirtatious, and Ken responded. One night he invited her to his home for dinner. Carla only intended to be Ken's friend, and Ken believed her behavior indicated she was willing to have sex with him. When Ken made unwanted advances to Carla and she told him she wasn't interested, he felt rejected and ashamed, and he self-righteously lashed out at her. Carla felt misunderstood and burst into tears.

Similar to Kevin and Lindsay in chapter 3, these two would trigger each other and perpetuate their drama.

Wanting and Fearing Closeness

A great paradox of addictive love is that we really do want to love and be loved, but our addictive selves fear closeness. At the basis of most relationship problems, addictive or otherwise, is a betrayal of trust. When trust is violated, we lose our innocence and step into fear. Once again, love addiction is grounded in fear: fear of rejection, fear of pain, fear of losing control, fear of loss of self or loss of life. Love addiction's intent is to connect *and* avoid what we fear.

❧ *Nancy's Story* ❧

As a child who observed her parents' miserable, quarrelsome marriage, Nancy vowed to be cautious in love—in fact, to avoid it altogether. Yet Nancy fell in love while still a young woman. She deeply committed herself to a man who, without warning, broke off their engagement shortly before they were to be married. Nancy's pain ran doubly deep because she had broken her vow to herself. Her experience of being jilted confirmed her unconscious conviction that love inevitably led to pain. Unknowingly, she renewed and amplified that vow.

Several years later, she fell in love again. In spite of her deep affection for her new lover, she was unable to fully let go of herself in an emotionally committed or sexual way. Whenever she found herself opening up to intimacy, she felt fearful, guilty, and angry with herself. Careful exploration of her feelings helped her discover her unconscious vow, and she was able to see the futility of such thinking. Nancy eventually became willing to take risks in love—even though pain might be involved.

☙

Attempting to "Fix" Others

Perhaps the most pronounced characteristic of love addiction is this unwritten rule: "You take care of my feelings, and I'll take care of yours. You make me feel whole and good, and I'll do the same for you."

Taking care of another adult's feelings is very different from caring about someone. The first assumes a person can read another's mind, know another's needs, and "fix" the other's ill feelings. Such an assumption makes one lover responsible for the other's well-being. But true caring about someone means, "I care about what you feel; I'm here to lend support although I do not have the power to make your pain go away or to help you feel complete in yourself." The first belief system is based on fear and guilt, the second on compassion and realism.

How often we expect others to read our minds and know what we want! "You should know; you've lived with me long enough," we say. How often we assume the other knows what we want, even though we've never asked for it. Maybe the other does know sometimes, or can guess correctly, but we will get more from our relationships by learning to read our emotions, understand our wants and needs, and then communicate in ways that our partners are most likely to hear. We must ask clearly and with consideration for the other's position.

Emotional dishonesty is one of the major problems in addictive love. It creates a breakdown in communication and results in a lack of emotional bonding.

ℐ✥ *Stan's Story* ℐ✥

When Stan's marriage began to fail, he entered therapy with his wife, Pat. He had a hard time understanding why things weren't working out; after all, he was doing all the "right" things to make her feel good. He was a loyal husband; he liked to please his wife. He worked hard, he was strong and didn't demand much, and he provided a lovely home for his family. Pat, however, was unhappy because of poor communication, a feeling of being smothered by Stan, and Stan's frequent, seemingly unprovoked, angry outbursts. The more depressed she became, the harder he tried to fix her. In fact, he said to me: "The real reason I am here is to learn some ways to fix Pat's unhappiness. There must be something I can do. Just tell me and I will do it."

Stan did not realize that while he could care about Pat, he could not fix her unhappiness. An even more complex problem was that Stan didn't know how to identify and express his own feelings, or ask for what he needed and wanted, because he was so focused on Pat. He had to relearn what he had known as a child—that his feelings offered clues to what he needed, and it was his responsibility to let others know what that was. Pat needed to do the same.

As Stan became more familiar with his emotions and put them out for Pat to see, Pat felt closer to him. She was happier now that Stan wasn't trying to fix her. The bonus was that he did not have out-bursts as he expressed himself more frequently.

Projection, Personalizing, Power Plays

Love addiction is heaped with denial. Denial is fertile ground for the "three Ps" of dysfunctional relationships: projection, personalizing, and power plays. The Funk & Wagnalls dictionary definition of *projection* is "to throw or forward into space or upon a surface as an image or shadow." Metaphorically, this definition accurately describes psychological projection. Projection means shifting blame onto another, or perceiving a quality or characteristic in someone else that one denies or does not wish to claim in oneself. *Personalizing* refers to those instances when we internalize the projections others make onto us, accepting them as truths about ourselves. It also refers to the times we "take personally" what others say and do even when they are not projecting onto us. *Power plays,* which will be discussed at some length in chapter 5, are attempts to give back the projections and maintain control.

The first step in the dance of projection, personalizing, and power plays occurred in childhood. When others were too fragile, too unaware, or too afraid to vent their pent-up feelings, they took the dark side of their own personalities and placed them on us. They saw in us, or attributed to us, what they denied in themselves. We were not perfect enough, caring enough, and successful enough. We were sick, unappreciative, wrong, crazy, stupid, too sensitive, too angry, or too seductive.

The second step of the dance occurred when we personalized the words and actions directed toward us. Not having the ability to stand up for ourselves, or in a misguided attempt at being loyal to those we loved, we absorbed the projections of others. We became the "problem" or the victim of their inadequacies. This inequality began for us an ongoing struggle for personal power and integrity.

Power plays were the third step of the dance. Manipulative behaviors designed to maintain inequality in a relationship, they ensure that a person is either one-up or one-down with another person. Power plays are habits of relating that can become a way of life. Subtle or not so subtle, consciously devised or completely unconscious, power plays are sometimes hostile in nature and are always covert. In essence, they are schemes to get another to behave in ways we think will bring us inner satisfaction.

Christine's story illustrates several of these dynamics. As a child, she knew what she needed and asked for it in direct ways. When others failed to respond, she personalized the lack of response by telling herself that she was unimportant. As an adult, she believed she had to fight for power. Though she was criticized for acting powerless, her friends and family actually supported this behavior.

Christine's Story

"I repeatedly experienced a dream that ends in exasperation and terror. As a young child, my bedroom was located in an area behind my parents' tavern. In my dream, people were coming in and out of my room without knocking. They were loud, drunk, and scary. I got very irritated and went out into the bar and attempted to kick people out. While I was doing this, my sister was in my room rummaging through my clothes deciding which ones she would wear the next day. My father and his friends played music as loud as it would play. No one paid any attention to my pleas, or they told me I was too sensitive.

"What I learned from the dream was that, as a child, I felt powerless. I had been unable to take a stand in any situation where there might be a chance that someone would tell me no. I accepted put-downs; I looked to others for permission to do what I wanted to do. These others were my father early in life, my husband later, and my best friend, even now. My goal is to stop seeking others' approval, stop taking on their projections, have approval stem from my accomplishments, and believe that I have personal power."

Let's now look at power plays in more detail.

Power Plays

When love is without power, we take care of others at our own expense. When power is without love, we hurt, injure, and abuse others—ultimately at our own expense.

BRENDA SCHAEFFER, Loving Me, Loving You

Power

One of the most pronounced features of love-addicted relationships is the use of power plays to gain a misguided sense of control over a partner. As mentioned in chapter 4, power plays are manipulative behaviors that keep two people relating on an unequal basis. Learning to recognize such behavior is a step toward purging it from our relationships or avoiding relationships based on power plays.

The word *power* is used in many ways. In regard to the search for love and interdependence, the power we strive for springs from self-esteem (personal potency), not from control over others.

The myth underlying power plays is this: there is not enough power for two; one person must maintain control. The myth is based on the belief that people with power have control, and they can get what they want and need. Without such control, life seems tenuous and uncertain. And, of course, we all want to feel certain. Competition for the mysterious thing called "control" is often fierce, as is evident in wars. Often, we don't even know what we want to control. Moreover, power players—aptly called "controllers"—mistakenly believe that other people provide or take away their personal potency. Where do such beliefs come from?

The Beginnings of Power Plays

As children, we started to fight for power at about age two, when we were told by our parents it was time to stop being the center of the universe, and cooperation with "the big people" was now necessary. We could remember, we could talk, and we could act in socially cooperative ways. If we didn't cooperate, we were often punished or rejected. In this situation, children have three options: they may rebel, overadapt, or cooperate.

Rebels say, "No, I won't go along, and you can't make me," and fight to have their own way. We've all seen children attempt to overpower and often win over a parent by saying no, holding out, and throwing temper tantrums.

Overadapters are often overpowered by a parent. They may feel they are being swallowed up, that their freedom is being stripped away. They may feel grief and fear because their behavior and freedom of choice are being suppressed, not directed. And so they adapt and withhold anger.

Those children who are guided to cooperate and to recognize that others have needs slowly learn cooperation, and growing up can be a joy. Power sharing and yielding, base components of healthy love, become normal parts of life.

There was no need to overpower our parents, nor did they need to overpower us with directives, bribes, threats, demands, and physical punishment. Parents and children alike can be powerful in their own ways, and in sharing power, they construct bridges of communication, support, and love. That is normal development.

Every two- or three-year-old child moves through the rebellious stage. Some emerge with few emotional scars, though everyone I have met has some problems with trying to control others. The roots of adult power players' behavior often can be traced back into childhood. There are many ways in which children can be helped through this difficult time, even taught that power need not be something one person has at another's expense.

When my daughter, Heidi, was three, she toddled into the kitchen where I was washing dishes and thinking about the chores I had to complete that evening. "Mommy, read me a story," Heidi said, tugging on my skirt. I looked down, grimacing at the toys scattered across the floor of the kitchen and living room. I thought, *Well, I've got time to either read her a story or pick up those toys.*

I started to say, "Go pick up your toys and then we'll talk about a story," but I suddenly stopped, realizing I would be issuing an irritated order. Instead, I said: "Heidi, I only have time to do one thing; read to you or pick up all those toys. Why don't you decide which I should do?"

I had given the child a choice, and Heidi was startled. She had no cause for disappointment or a temper tantrum, because it was her choice. And she chose: she ran to pick up the toys herself, then returned for the one thing I had time for—reading the story. Getting her to think and choose affirmed her personal power.

The transition from childish omnipotence to power sharing seems to be something we all struggle with in childhood and adolescence, even in adult life. Confusion over the uses of power is evident in unhealthy, uneasy adult relationships. What are some of the power plays that sabotage adult love relationships?

Twenty-Three Power Plays

Following are examples of power plays often present in addictive love relationships:

1. giving advice but not accepting it
2. having difficulty in reaching out and in asking for support and love
3. giving orders; demanding and expecting much from others
4. trying to "get even" or to diminish the self-esteem or power of others
5. being judgmental; using put-downs that sabotage others' success; faultfinding; persecuting; punishing
6. holding out on others; not giving what others want or need

  7. making, then breaking, promises; causing others to trust us and then betraying the trust

  8. smothering, overnurturing others

  9. patronizing, condescending treatment of others that sets one partner up as superior, the other as inferior; intimidation

10. making decisions for others; discounting others' abilities to solve problems

11. putting others in no-win situations

12. attempting to change others (and unwillingness to change self)

13. attacking others when they are most vulnerable

14. showing an antidependent attitude: "I don't need you"

15. using bullying, bribing behavior; using threats

16. showing bitterness or self-righteous anger; holding grudges

17. abusing others verbally, emotionally, sexually, or physically

18. being aggressive and defining it as assertiveness

19. needing to win or be right

20. resisting stubbornly or being set in one's own way

21. having difficulty admitting mistakes or saying "I'm sorry"

22. giving indirect, evasive answers to questions

23. defending any of the above behaviors

To feel powerful, a power player attempts to overwhelm and control another. Such a person is unconsciously saying, "I fear I'm powerless and need others to control so that I may be powerful." This false belief suggests another person is in charge of our personal potency, and we need to control the other person to be secure and strong.

The power player struggles to keep others in the position of a victim so they can be rescued or persecuted. Such melodramatics are not the essence of true personal power, but of dependency. Ultimately, power plays are the cause of much unhappiness.

Power playing is not easily given up, for it masks unconscious and often suppressed fears. In each incidence where I have explored the roots of a client's need to control another person, I've found a traumatic experience or imagined threat that led him to interpret loss of control as a loss of self, which is a dangerous and terrifying idea. Or, perhaps, the client had been allowed to overpower her parents, and thus developed a belief that "I am more powerful than you, and I can get my own way."

"Besides," reasoned one power player, "being powerful feels much better, so why give up that behavior?" They fail to recognize that these positions are unstable and unhealthy, and are based on false beliefs. People attempting to control others can avoid dealing with their own private fears, insecurities, and doubts because they always have someone else who is "less okay" to focus on. Keep in mind that power players and their victims both play the game. The victim sees benefits, too. Cooperating keeps the other person around, helps the victim avoid looking at his own fear, keeps life predictable, and provides recognition, stimulation, and a sense of security. Perhaps most important is that it validates the inner beliefs that the victim has carried for years: "Power does not belong to me"; "I can get what I need by being still"; "Power is scary"; "I won't get hurt if I cooperate"; "If I am powerful, people will leave me"; "I'm not important enough, smart enough, strong enough to speak up."

Because we may have designed our power plays in childhood to protect us from harm, they are deeply embedded behaviors, and our resistance to giving them up will be very great.

Power players who strive to maintain the one-up position seldom reach out for help or indicate they want to change. This is largely due to their domination by delusion and denial, as well as their belief that they are better than others. Generally, they are forced into therapy or change when they experience a trauma—such as a partner's threat to leave. Even then, their goal may be to regain control over the rebellious partner. At this point, the partner usually is no longer willing to be a victim. Sometimes, the partner may be angry and may even be competing for the dominating position. Neither person will be ready to give up power playing until the insecurities that motivate them have been explored.

❧ *Pete's Story* ❧

Power players often interpret loss of control as a loss of self. Pete, who was seeking help for his depression and low self-esteem, wrote the following letter to himself from the side of him that needed to control.

"You've always had a strong ego and been so self-sufficient, and now you are thinking of turning all that over to another person who will cause you to lose control. You don't really want this, do you? I've tried to protect you in a thousand ways. Maybe you forgot how I stuck with you and wouldn't let others get close to you. I've kept you alone and in complete control. You are so intelligent and above others who try to help. You don't need them because you can figure it out for yourself. It's worked quite well all these years, right?

"Why you want to admit defeat or the need for help mystifies me. You can be in the driver's seat. The powerful ones are the ones in control; this is where you want to be and stay. Most of your problems stem from others trying to thwart you. Push them out of the way and things will really start happening for you."

Pete listed all the ways he would attempt to con me in therapy:

1. laugh or smile hurt feelings away
2. dominate the conversation
3. get me to feel sorry for him
4. become defensive when things get touchy
5. convince me others are to blame
6. keep the sessions nonserious
7. intellectualize
8. appear flexible
9. overcooperate
10. find my soft part and capitalize on it
11. find out what pain I have suffered and commiserate
12. try to become emotionally involved
13. try to induce self-doubt
14. question my motive for helping
15. talk around the subject at hand

Pete was using these cons to reinforce his need to control. With the help of therapy, he later learned that his personal power did not come at another's expense. Our personal power comes from within; there is no need to win control over another. With self-confidence, we let go of the need for power and control.[1]

～

Options

Once we identify the power plays sabotaging our relationships, we have three options.

First, we could cooperate and respond passively as a victim, agreeing to forfeit our own potency and to accept our one-down submissive position. It is easy and familiar, even though addictive. Needless to say, this is no way to live fully, although many people do it. These people usually end up with the feelings the other person is trying to avoid—shame, guilt, inadequacy, and fear. "She overpowered me," "He took my power away," and "I'm powerless when it comes to her seductions" are delusions that suggest that personal power is a commodity controlled by others rather than being our life energy.

Second, we could seek the one-up power position, but we may become snared in a competitive addictive relationship. In this case, two antidependent people vie for the power position, living in constant conflict as each tries to overwhelm the other with creative and destructive power-play tactics. "I'm giving you back your power" and "I'm taking my power back" are statements that reinforce the belief that power is an item controlled by another. Unfortunately, most relationships alternate between options one and two, seesawing through life.

However, there's a third, much healthier option—to respond from an affirmative position that acknowledges equal personal power. In this position, we are saying, "We are both okay and personally powerful. Sometimes, your behavior is not acceptable to me." We acknowledge that "I acted as though I gave her my power," "I acted as though he owned me," or "She acted as though she had power over me." Such ownership is empowering.

It is a matter of consciously reclaiming our power over our own lives. When our lives become unmanageable because of a toxic attachment, we can either work to change the relationship or remove ourselves from the attachment. The slogan "Let go and let God" does not suggest that we passively wait for intercession or deny our own personal power. On the contrary, it suggests power sharing, doing what we can do in a situation and then letting go.

When we choose this option, it is important to recognize how power plays have victimized both players and to work to nurture a new sense of personal power and dignity for both.

Listed here are things we must do if we are to withdraw from power plays.

1. Acknowledge that power plays are real.
2. Take an inventory of the power plays we most often use.
3. Learn to identify our personal cues: feeling confused, trapped, guilty, uncomfortable, threatened, and competitive; doubting ourselves; making sarcastic rebuffs; being defensive; projecting blame; avoiding our partners; giving evasive responses.
4. Examine our personal negative beliefs that are supporting power plays and change them.
5. Detach ourselves; believe we are equals.

We win by learning an internal process: how to live with ourselves. If we have a sense of confidence, we no longer need to "win" at another's expense.

The Goal: Mutual Respect

You may find that when an argument stems from the power-seeking behavior of a partner, the less you say in response to verbal challenges, the better. The urge to defend or to agree can lead you directly back into addictive behavior. Short, one-word responses are most effective in staying detached from power competition. Or, you may choose to state your position: "When you _(Action)_ , I feel _(Feeling)_ , and hear in my mind _(Thought)_ . What I prefer/need is _(New Action)_ ." You are responding from a position of equal personal power; you are educating the other. Make the statement at a time you are most likely to be heard, not when you are angry or in the midst of an argument. The following is an example of a couple moving toward a healthier relationship based on each partner's equal personal power.

✨ Jennifer and Brad's Story ✨

Jennifer and Brad had a potentially good relationship. But Brad was obsessed with his role as rescuer and adviser to many people—holding power over others. Brad had many "victims" demanding his time and energy, people Jennifer called "hangers-on" and not true friends. Though Brad often complained that these people ate up his time, he could not say no to them.

Jennifer often felt neglected, but for several years she said little, always hoping the situation would change. Her style, learned in childhood, was to say nothing and feel bad. Because she had not experienced power sharing in her family, her fear of confronting Brad, possibly causing him to grow angry and reject her, was very real.

When she finally gathered the courage to confront him, she did so with great feeling and honesty. She told Brad she was no longer willing to postpone her own needs for those of his acquaintances. She said, "When you cancel our weekend plans because a friend wants you to help him move, I feel hurt and very angry. I think I am unimportant. What I want is for you to consider my needs in your decision making." She had begun to recognize that her behavior was a pattern carried over from childhood. She no longer wanted to do this.

At first, Brad listened sympathetically; later, he verbally attacked Jennifer, accusing her of manipulating him with tears and trying to control their relationship. To regain his equilibrium, Brad began to criticize her, to withhold affection, and to lecture her on how their marriage should and would be from then on.

Jennifer knew she could comply, stand and affirm her personal dignity, or leave the marriage. Fortunately, she was strong enough to recognize that although Brad's behavior hurt her, it stemmed from his fear of losing control and being hurt himself. Determined not to remain a victim, Jennifer maintained detachment and did not take his criticism personally.

When an opportune time arose, she told Brad how his behavior affected her, although she knew she could not realistically expect to change him and that changing lifelong patterns would not be easy. She also made it clear she wanted a healthy marriage in which both of them could contribute their own thoughts, feelings, and ways of doing things as equals without fear of reprisal. Jennifer hoped such an ideal could be achieved; if it couldn't, she said, she would have no choice but to consider how or if she would remain in this relationship.

Fortunately, both Jennifer and Brad now are working to achieve a stronger, freer relationship. It hasn't been easy for them, but mutual respect has allowed them to move from a controlling, addictive relationship to one that supports—yet frees—them both. There are fewer power plays, and they are better for that—individually and as a couple.

I continue to be amazed at how frequently people begin getting what they want and need in relationships when they are willing to give up the need to control. Perhaps they can do this because one partner senses that the other's power lies confidently within and, in awe and respect, is moved to reach out and give. Or, perhaps, they discover that control over others is an illusion and the answer is in letting go. In a storm, it is the tree that bends with the wind that survives to grow tall.

Because we have the brain circuitry to experience bonding, romance, and sex separately, we will look at how romance and sex become addictions and how to recognize when they do in the chapters ahead.

6

Romance Addiction

This beast that rends me in the sight of all,
This love, this longing, this oblivious thing,
That has me under as the last leaves fall,
Will glut, will sicken, will be gone by spring.
The wound will heal, the fever will abate,
The knotted hurt will slacken in the breast;
I shall forget before the flickers mate
Your look that is today my east and west.
Unscathed, however, from a claw so deep
Though I should love again I shall not go:
Along my body, waking while I sleep,
Sharp to the kiss, cold to the hand as snow,
The scar of this encounter like a sword
Will lie between me and my troubled lord.

EDNA ST. VINCENT MILLAY, Fatal Interview

Romantic Love

The euphoria of romance is one of the most intoxicating of life experiences. At a very young age, we hear stories of its magic and its power. It arouses a princess from a coma, changes a depressed prince into an enchanting hero. In most stories, love arrives out of the blue, it abducts the lovers, and the rest of the story line seems out of their control. Fatal attraction is as old as time itself and is filled with pathos, longing, and calamity. In romantic love, lovers step into the attraction stage of a love relationship where they are bathed in self-induced ecstasy chemicals. When the love potion wears off, which it will, the blinders come off long enough to see that this person I am in love with was not right for me, and I leave for the right reason. Or, if true love is there, bonding will eventually occur.

Romance is a double-edged sword. So aroused, we are willing to be vulnerable and show our best qualities. We forget those who have hurt us, open our heart, and let another see us for who we are. On the other hand, we become a bit crazed as total immersion into the romantic experience or fantasy begins to consume us. When we attempt to hang on to the relationship, out come our vices—neediness, anger, control.

But the *rapture* of romantic love—limerence—is far different from the longing of sexual release or romantic infatuation, both of which can be short-lived. It is the experience of being *lost* in love. According to Dorothy Tennov, Ph.D., "Limerence is a particular state—known only to those to whom it has happened and mystifying to those to whom it has not."[1] It is a specific state of *is* or *is not*. And when it *is* there, without help, it cannot just be turned off. It is involuntary. Even when it drops to a low ebb after you get the love object out of your mind, it can be spiked up again if you run into this person in the future. You can be "almost over her," until she calls to say hello. It is a special kind of bonding that seems to go beyond chemistry and captivates a person psychologically.

Being "lost in love" can be experienced at any time of life, by anyone, and can be long-lived. It does not require face-to-face contact, as the many virtual romantic affairs prove. It is often hidden from others or minimized out of shame. It can be mutual, as in the story of Romeo and Juliet, or one-sided, as Scarlett O'Hara demonstrates in *Gone with the Wind*. Psychologists refer to the two as *reciprocated* romantic love—filled with elation, ecstasy, and fulfillment—and *unrequited* love—filled with agony, longing, and sadness.[2] According to Dr. Tennov, in addition to the euphoria, ecstasy, and obsession observed in romantic love, there is also an involuntariness of thought, exclusivity, and sensitivity to the love object's actions. "Everything is measured by the [love object's] anticipated approval or disapproval.

Limerence is a pull of tremendous force toward another person. It seems to end only with reciprocation or starvation, and even then it may endure."[3]

Romance Is Addicting

Romantic love *is* addicting. Dozens of chemicals are involved in telling us what effect a person has on us. It is an emotional speedball, a wild ecstasy, a bewitchment, a preoccupied madness. When we are newly in love, our brains contain high levels of the reward chemical dopamine, which accounts for the euphoric state, and norepinephrine, which accounts for the sweaty palms, racing heart, increased blood pressure, and excitement we feel. Romantic love simulates the experience of psychedelic and euphoric drugs, mystical preoccupation, and immersion into romance novels. Research on the chemistry of romance has shown that the initial rush of intoxication is a necessary step in the mating process. Yet it is also important to understand the depth of joy and pain this state produces. Brain scans show that the love-stricken brain is similar to a brain high on cocaine and opiates.[4]

If the symptoms of the romantic process—narrowing our focus to one person, giving the object of our love special meaning, aggrandizing the person, experiencing intrusive thoughts, having mood swings, and reveling in the ecstasy, passion, and yearning—are normal, what makes romantic love an addiction? The elements that characterize it as addiction are (1) obsession or preoccupation, (2) loss of control resulting in negative consequences, and (3) continuation in spite of negative consequences. Two other elements may or may not be present: tolerance or needing more of the experience to get the same effect, and withdrawal symptoms when the love object is removed.

Though romance addiction is often mistakenly lumped in with sex addiction and has not yet gained widespread recognition as a separate disorder or been included in the *Diagnostic and Statistical Manual of Mental Disorders* (the diagnostic manual that clinicians use), romance can meet the criteria of an addiction. In fact, romance addiction, with its load of feel-good chemicals and intense focus on one person, in my experience, can be the more powerful of the two addictions. "I can't get you out of my head" is no joke. If you ask someone to have sex with you and they say no, you do not threaten to kill yourself. But read the news. People live for love, die for love, and kill for love.

Emotional Affairs

An emotional affair, more fantasy than reality, approaches the category of romance addiction when the emotional attachment begins to exclude others, including a partner or spouse. Emotional affairs usually go unattended until they become an obsession, or until it becomes hard to keep the relationship at a friendship level. Warning signs that indicate a relationship has crossed the line of friendship and is now taking on the characteristics of a romance addiction are obsessing or constantly daydreaming about the person, neglecting or postponing important areas of life, thinking this person understands you better than anyone else, monitoring the person's behaviors and attention to others, spending an inordinate amount of time anticipating seeing the person again or making plans to do so, minimizing the impact the relationship has on a person, insisting "We are just friends," needing to keep aspects of the relationship a secret, making this person the most important confidant, and going to this person first with issues. Contrast this with healthy, nonaddictive behaviors where a person stays in reality, has clear boundaries, keeps it a friendship, and feels comfortable sharing the friend with a partner or other friends.

Twenty Signs of Romance Addiction

It is important that an "in love" person recognize repetitive negative patterns as an alarm bell. In addition to the signs of love addiction in chapter 4, which may also apply to romantic love relationships, here are those specific to romance addiction:

1. obsession
2. intense jealousy
3. possessiveness
4. depression and melancholy

5. dependence on intoxicating feelings
6. heightened anxiety
7. romance interferes with life
8. living on the edge of perfected love
9. exaggerated fantasy life
10. choice of entertainment is romantic, dramatic, or euphoric
11. stalking the love object
12. chasing the illusion
13. lured by intermittent reinforcement
14. longing for reciprocation
15. withdrawal symptoms when the love object moves away
16. friends and family express concern
17. hanging on to the unavailable or abusive
18. outcomes are disappointing
19. distortion of reality
20. melodrama

Attraction Problem—Help Required

The problems in love relationships are universal. Here is an e-mail request for help from a South American man, Ricardo, which includes many signs of romance addiction. It also demonstrates how confused we can become regarding what is love and what is an addiction.

Dr. Schaeffer,

I would really appreciate help with an issue. I have been a friend for almost one year with a woman at work who is very striking and fun to be with. We have spent a lot of time together and I have developed this very strong romantic pull to her. We have never had a romantic relationship or commitment; we have never been sexual. Then we had a feud over the fact that I saw other women, and she decided to stop being my friend. She said it was cheating. It has been several months since we stopped being friends. My problem now is that even though I do not want a long-term relationship with her:

1. *I miss the good moments we spent together and realize that just being with her and fantasizing about her was giving me a romantic high. Losing that high is painful.*
2. *I have this extreme physical and emotional attraction toward her that doesn't seem to die. When I don't see her for a while, the pain dies out, but then I see her, and the trauma is back.*
3. *I can't stop thinking about her and getting her back. Maybe I just want her because I can't have her.*
4. *I get very jealous if I see her with other men. I then call or e-mail her, and she tells me I am stalking her.*
5. *I am becoming more depressed. I tell myself that if I had tried a little harder, she would still be my friend.*

How do I get over this strong physical and emotional attraction toward her? I feel I am a little obsessive, and it may be that I cannot face the rejection and want her back. Whatever it is, I am hurting and need some advice badly. Could it be love by any chance?

Gratefully,
Ricardo

I will let you, the reader, assess whether this is an addiction as you review the following signs of romance addiction and then decide how you might then answer the query. Here are some of the darker sides of romantic love.

Obsession

Obsession can be as mild as intrusive thinking—going over and over a mental thought—or as extreme as a feeling of being held captive, where the mind is gripped in a fixated or fanatical preoccupation. With romance addiction, a person goes into a private world and becomes lost in obsessive thought of the romantic object or relationship. He or she is your first thought in the morning, you wonder what she or he is doing or thinking during the day, and you close the day with thoughts of him or her. Everything is seen through the lens of the current love as though in a fog.

In a study featured in her book *Why We Love,* Helen Fisher found that 79 percent of men and 78 percent of women newly in love reported that when at work or in class, their minds kept going back to thoughts of their beloved.[5] Obsession can become a mental illness or create physical illness. The word *obsession* refers to any intrusive thought, emotion, or behavior that exerts such a powerful and persistent influence upon a person's life that it interferes with normal functioning. As Ricardo indicated, his mind felt possessed or captured with his former relationship as he scrutinized the "what ifs" and "maybes."

With love relationships, real or imagined, the preoccupation is with the love object itself, and such immersion becomes consuming and robs energy from other important areas of life. Oftentimes, in a new romance, both individuals are lost to this experience, and a certain amount of obsessive thinking is normal. At other times, the preoccupation takes a one-way direction and may even involve an elaborate fantasy life about an actor, actress, or political leader. Bizarre acting-out behaviors, such as stalking, are often a by-product of obsession.

Intense Jealousy

In the *Art of Courtly Love,* Andreas Capellanus wrote that jealousy was the "nurse of love" in that it kept the flame of love alive. And to some extent that is true. Jealousy is a universal phenomenon associated with romantic love. Cross-culturally, it is known that both sexes can and do get very jealous. Oftentimes, men, fearful of being cheated on, react strongly to threats of sexual betrayal, and women, fearful of being abandoned, often react strongly to perceptions of emotional betrayal by their partner with another woman. Both fears have historical roots and make sense in the development of family. Jealousy can strengthen a love affair or destroy it.[6]

Jealousy is rooted in fear: fear of pain, fear of abandonment, fear of being alone, fear of the future, fear of betrayal, fear of not being enough, and more. Because of the intense reliance on the love object to fix what one fears, one or both lovers will closely scrutinize the love object's actions and attention to others. If there appears to be a slight wavering of attention or a threat to the relationship, jealousy will occur. While a certain amount of jealousy may be expected, in romance addiction it can escalate to verbal and physical abuse as a punishment for such wavering. Often this behavior stems from broken trust in the past.

℘ David's Story ℘

"I had been in the relationship for four months and I knew in my head that she was safe and genuine. Then I asked her if she ever had a one-night stand. She said, 'Yes, and I did not enjoy it.' Since then, I have been obsessing about her past sexual escapades and telling myself that she is not the safe person I thought her to be. I get jealous very easily. I watch her carefully as though I want to catch her at something and leave before she does. It is ridiculous, as I have had many one-night stands myself."

David, having had his trust broken in early childhood and in a recent love affair, said to me with deep sincerity, "I want to get this relationship right."

Possessiveness

Closely related to obsession and jealousy is the desire to possess or control the love object. In romance addiction, the person is the stimulus for the good feelings. If the person moves away, the addict will likely react with manipulative control tactics to keep the love object around. Such tactics might include threats, bribes, and intermittent reinforcement. Romance addiction is, after all, unconsciously attempting to medicate something on a psychological level. This makes the pull to keep the relationship alive even more important, as Patrick's story demonstrates.

✣ *Patrick's Story* ✣

Patrick escaped an unhappy home life by getting into love relationships very early. He wanted the high that love produced, and he wanted certainty. At the same time, he did not want to lose himself entirely. In came Jan. Younger and inexperienced in the ways of love, she was easily controlled in the beginning of the relationship. But as the high of romance gave way to more of the reality, she decided to move on. Patrick became angry and attempted to manipulate Jan with varying tactics: inducing self-doubt in her, controlling the conversations, bribing her with promises of change, threatening, and showing softer emotions. When his tactics failed and Jan left, Patrick switched from anger to deep depression. In therapy, he learned that love is not a possession nor a drug to fix pain.

Depression and Melancholy

Some wistful feelings of melancholy seem to go along with love stories, but when using romance addictively, there is both a biological and a psychological crash that is experienced as depression. Often, tragic romantics fail to seek counseling or speak to family or friends about the depression. Some are even attached to the sweet melancholy, which reminds them they are in love. These depressive moods may initially be short and are relieved by using the romance object or fantasy to feel good again. But keeping consistent with the use-crash-use cycle going on in the brain when an addiction is present, the moodiness eventually lasts longer and gets deeper.

The use of romance is no longer enough to relieve the down mood, which in some cases has been there all along. Depression also contaminates the person's ability to think clearly about the relationship. When depression follows the end of a romantic affair, the person may experience trouble moving forward with life and cling to the person or dream of perfect love.

Here are signs that depression may be present. A person only needs a few of these symptoms more days than not for two weeks or more to have a depression.

- feeling blue, moody, or depressed
- sleeping too much or too little or having trouble staying asleep
- changes in eating habits or appetite that cause weight loss or gain
- difficulty focusing, distractibility, memory problems
- low energy or frequent fatigue
- trouble motivating self
- feeling hopeless, helpless, worthless, or guilty
- crying spells
- social withdrawal
- vague physical pain
- thoughts of death or suicide
- increased irritability

If these signs are present and persist, seek professional help. Medication and therapy can help a person think more clearly, make better choices, and move forward more quickly.

Dependence on Intoxicating Feelings

The chemistry of love is something we think we have control over. The romance high is invisible, and we can create an incredible fantasy life to keep the high going. Most love addicts start out attempting to meet some known or unknown emotional need and then become dependent on the intoxicating feelings.

The Internet has proven to be a convenient way for people to compulsively seek out romantic relationships to get their fix. When a person "meets" another in a chat room, she can idealize this anonymous person. This creates excitement, danger, and pleasure as adrenaline and dopamine are released. Yet such relationships create a false sense of emotional and chemical security.

❧ *Julie's Story* ❧

"When one of my friends told me about her 'other life' of having romantic affairs on the Internet, I thought she was crazy. She suggested I look into sites for married men and women, and I did so out of curiosity. I got hooked rather slowly. At first the talks were friendly and safe. I felt a kinship with the men I was meeting online and felt important. Then I began to narrow it down to one person, and we began to have private exchanges. I justified my actions because these conversations put me in a better mood for my family.

"Then I fell in love. I became consumed with thoughts and fantasies of being with Nick. We chatted intimately for hours. I longed—no, ached—to meet him. I fantasized about him for hours every day; I was ready to give up everything, marriage and children included, for the projected life I would have—being in a relationship with a man who tenderly loved me. How crazy is that?"

Heightened Anxiety

In addition to a depression cycle, romance addiction can generate a high level of anxiety that interferes with ordinary functioning. We may carefully monitor the behavior of the other and feel anxious when he moves away or signals disapproval. This is often related to a specific trauma in the past, a fear of separation, or the inability to develop a trust in the romantic partner. The anxiety can also be a fear of getting too close.

❧ *Nikki's Story* ❧

Nikki had come to therapy with these universal questions: "Why do we have certain attractions?" "Why do we both want and fear love?" She had come in feeling a distinct pain in her heart and a feeling in her body she identified as panic. She was exploring a new romantic relationship and recognized familiar sensations and feelings in her body. "It is terrifying" were words she used to describe the possibility that this person might not accept her. She monitored every nuance, every gesture he made, and every word he uttered. "What do I need to do to be wanted?" she asked. Struck by her question, I asked her where it came from.

She proceeded to tell me about her childhood and feelings of being unwanted. "My parents were forced to marry because of me. My mother told me she cried for days before and after my birth and became very depressed. She gave up a great career. My father was not even there when I was born; he was off doing his thing. He was not in love with my mother. They lived a miserable existence for sixteen years and finally ended it. My father told me he suffered each day of his marriage. I blamed myself for their unhappiness and lived in anxiety. I have never felt wanted. I'm afraid I am attracting men who do not want me. I also believe I am as terrified of being close as I am of being unwanted, and so I do things that upset my romantic relationships."

Romance Interferes with Life

Addiction zaps a person of energy. The quest for the high, the experience of the high, and the hangover after the high gradually take over a person's life. With any addiction, there are negative consequences, yet the person continues the relationship with the drug or behavior of choice. Romance addiction is no exception. In romance addiction, the intense focus on the love affair diverts a person from other important life pursuits, and the biological and psychological consequences mount. Consequences may include the following:

- lower work performance
- poor health
- loss of friends
- relationship conflict
- letting go of personal goals
- emotional problems
- neglect of children

✒ *Nadine's Story* ✒

As Nadine, a returning client, said to me, "I feel shame telling you that I have been romantically involved with a man who is in another relationship, and I stayed there on a hope and a promise. What is worse is that he came into my life right after I achieved my goal of getting my counseling license, and I have totally put my dream of starting my own practice aside. I have broken up with him several times, but I get so depressed that I go back. I think of the wonderful moments we have had and how unhappy he is in his current relationship. I have let go of him—again—and I really need you to help me be accountable this time. I am emotionally worn out, and if he were to call as if nothing had changed, I would be tempted to see him. We have a very strong pull to one another."

Nadine admitted to being lost in her romantic affair at the expense of her physical and emotional health, her career, her financial stability, her friendships, and her dream.

Living on the Edge of Perfected Love

Romantic love helps us taste the deep, heartfelt love we have been searching for. It is an idealized love that seems tenuous and sometimes illusive. *Amour,* a word that refers to a romantic affair, is experienced as a state of bliss, awe, and wonder—all refinements of the soul. *Amour,* to the twelfth-century troubadours, was more the love of the virtues seen in others and self. Empowering the love object with these virtues, we fear that we will lose the greatness stirring inside of us should the relationship end. Living on the edge—not fully stepping into this idealized, and sometimes forbidden love—allows us to cling to the illusion of perfected love and its virtues. Often we fail to understand that love relationships do not make us virtuous but rather are places we can chisel ourselves into better human beings. Without this understanding, we will spiral down into pathos, sadness, and longing should the relationship end.

✄ *Clint's Story* ✄

When a romantic relationship ends, it seems our virtues do, too. My client Clint was in grief, having ended what he claimed was the most complete love relationship of his life. He felt desperate to be in another romantic relationship "just like it" so he could be and feel that way again. I reminded him that his lover had not put anything in him that was not already there. The romantic relationship had invited him to be himself, and in that regard, it was a gift. I asked him what he liked about himself when he was in the relationship. He responded: "I was free, I was more fun, I laughed, I enjoyed life, and I was kinder." I then asked him how he was as a little boy. He recalled being sent to his room for being too exuberant. He rarely had fun, and open affection was frowned upon.

He got the message. He did not have to live on the edge of perfected love or wait for another person to open him up or be close. The experiences he had were potentially there all along and his to energize as he so chose.

Exaggerated Fantasy Life

Fantasy is intended to enrich our lives as we design images in our mind, write poetry, and anticipate being with the person we love. These are all good uses of the feel-good chemicals that make life bearable. There are times, though, that life seems unbearable, and a person wants to escape from the pain by getting lost in fantasy. A romantic love relationship can seem a perfect way to do this. For some, the escape through fantasy began in childhood and continued into adult love relationships. Such is Kari's story.

✄ *Kari's Story* ✄

"As young as three years of age, I remember escaping the pain of loneliness by leaving my body and traveling to far-off places. As I entered my teens, my craving for love and attention intensified. I fantasized being chosen by older, popular guys and about being the most popular girl with them. I worked hard to make my fantasy reality. Yet nothing seemed to fill the big, empty hole inside of me. It seemed a vicious circle. I went from painful feelings—to fantasizing about a new romantic relationship—to acting out the fantasy—to painful feelings—to another fantasy.

"My cravings persisted into adulthood. Looking for someone to fix the wounds of a childhood filled with loneliness, I sought romantic love. I continued in my rich fantasy world of magical deliverance in multiple romantic affairs. Then, I met Cliff. I really thought I'd found the one I had been looking for. We fantasized about our shared life together. We seemed not to be able to get enough of each other. I was in a magical whirlwind for months. Then a sexual addiction I had not known about surfaced that led him to another woman. I was devastated. I am now grieving the loss of the magical 'us.' I think I am getting the lesson. It is time to let love be love and not a fantasy fulfiller I became addicted to. It is time to heal the roots of my need to take flights into fantasy."

Choice of Entertainment Is Romantic, Dramatic, or Euphoric

A person using romance addictively looks beyond the romantic object to find other ways to enhance the trancelike state. The addict may gravitate to media that are romantic in nature, reinforce fantasy, or induce melancholy and longing—for example, romance novels, love songs, country music, soap operas, reality shows, romantic chat rooms, euphoric art forms, or euphoric recall.

❧ *Nancy's Story* ❧

Nancy, a recovering romance addict, described her past ritual for getting into a romantic mood. She would come home from work, put on romantic music, think about her lover, recall a highly romantic moment, take a sensuous bath, dress in sensuous clothes, put on sensuous perfume. "By the time he came over or I went to see him, I was already in a romantic high. And I could get to this feeling even when not in a romantic relationship and preparing to go out to scout for a new lover. And though I needed to be sexually attracted to someone, it definitely was not the sex I was after. It was the romantic thrill."

⌐∽

Stalking the Love Object

Webster's dictionary defines *stalk* as "to pursue obsessively and to the point of harassment." Another definition is "to approach sneakily for the purpose of killing, as in hunting." Sexual desire, territoriality, aggression, and jealousy can result in some very volatile behaviors. Today we are seeing some very unhealthy ways to deal with the fear of the end of a romantic love affair. When romantic love is an addiction and the love object moves away, or even threatens to move away, the romance addict often becomes a stalker. Once again, the first biological and psychological impulse when someone important leaves or threatens to leave is to cling to the person. The second inclination is to get angry. These are old survival instincts we do not need as we approach adulthood. But the stalker has another agenda—*control*. The stalker, on a primal hunt, wants to know what the other person is up to, where the person is going, and if he has anyone else in his life.

Though the stalker may be experiencing a tremendous psychological pain of rejection, he is also driven, in part, by soaring levels of dopamine and norepinephrine. In addition, when these chemicals rise, serotonin levels lower, and therefore it is more difficult to control violent impulses. Although humans have sophisticated mechanisms to control impulses, we also carry within us a "fatal reflex," as psychologist William James referred to it.[7] Most stalkers let the fatal reflex take over. Unable to control their impulses, they can be dangerous.

❧ *Lance's Story* ❧

"This is a true story," said Lance, a therapist himself. "My daughter was dating a man who, prior to dating her, had ended a chaotic romantic love relationship. His former girlfriend did not accept the ending and began to stalk him and my daughter. She would appear out of the blue in the driveway, follow them on the freeway, or show up at a restaurant they would be at. The most dramatic event was that his ex-girlfriend came to me for therapy and lied about who she was and concealed her real intent until my intuition detected something was not right. I put two and two together and found out her true identity. When I questioned her, she finally told the truth, and I referred her to another therapist. Some people will go to any lengths to hang on to their drug."

Chasing the Illusion

When I listed this sign of romance addiction, "chasing the illusion," many stories involving political leaders and their sexual acting out came to mind. In such cases, it seems that the younger women involved are chasing the illusion and, in their young idealism and position of lower power, are most vulnerable. After all, these women were raised on the same fairy tales we all were. Infatuated with the charm, power, and beauty of the prince, they believe they cannot resist the older man's charm. As though pierced by Cupid's arrow, all sanity goes out the window. There is no thought of consequences, no taking into account that these men might have difficulty controlling their own sexual urges. Oblivious to the fact that they are deeply entrenched with a wife and family, the women cooperate. Some part of these women believed in the illusion and fell deeply and painfully in love with these leaders.

But what about an older man chasing the illusion—a younger woman who is using him? Here is Don's dramatic story.

❧ Don's Story ❧

"I am a sex addict who fell in love with one of the prostitutes I was seeing. I started an elaborate fantasy life around being with her. She played me to the end. She would hold out sexually and then give me enough to stay in the game. The intermittent reward worked. I gave her money, gave her a credit card, took her on vacations, bought and paid for her cell phone and services. She used heroin, so I tried it. It would make the sex more exciting. I let her male friend with hepatitis C inject me only to find out he had injected me with his blood. I learned she had it, too. I kept going, as now the romantic illusion of saving her from a terrible life became my drug. I saw her as the victim, not me.

"I bought a condo to move into and to share with my fantasy partner. I told my wife I wanted a divorce. Looking back, I feel deep remorse for the pain I caused my wife as I continued to immerse myself in the fantasy relationship. No matter, I could not stop and see straight. As a last resort, my wife asked if we could give the marriage one last chance. That stirred something inside of me, and I agreed to see a counselor with her. Still, I was not certain if I wanted to give up my fantasy. The therapist was very direct in pointing out that *I* was allowing myself to be made a fool of; that *I* was living a fantasy that would kill me; that *I* was fortunate to have a wife that was willing to give me one last chance. Gradually, I recognized my own crazy thinking and knew I needed to save me. This woman was not capable of a relationship, nor was I. The work toward sobriety and a healthy relationship with my wife included looking at what in me made me so vulnerable to my sexual and romantic delusions, and I found a history of emotional incest, loneliness, and very low esteem."

Lured by Intermittent Reinforcement

Addictive love is not unlike addictive gambling. A notable highlight of a gambling addiction is what is called intermittent reinforcement. There are several ways to encourage the continuation of a certain behavior. We can positively reinforce a behavior by continuously acknowledging it. For example, when a child gets a good grade, he gets praise. We can also reinforce a negative behavior by consistently giving it attention. Or, we can limit a behavior by giving it a negative consequence. "Friends are off-limits on Friday nights if grades go down," is an example. If you change the way you stroke behaviors, the behaviors can be changed somewhat readily.

The most challenging reinforcement of a behavior is intermittent. You never know when you will be rewarded or punished. In gambling, for instance, you might play for an hour on a slot machine and not win anything. Then just as you play the last quarter, you're rewarded with ten more. Now you are likely to play again. This is also true of highly addictive romantic relationships. You may put in more than you receive and, just as you are about to end the relationship, you are given just enough to feel hopeful about the possibility. Thus you stay.

৵ *Trent's Story* ৵

Trent, a forty-year-old client, told me he had a serious love addiction problem. He had given up on a dull thirteen-year marriage to begin a search for love. He could not imagine his life without achieving it. He met Cassie and fell deeply in love both romantically and sexually. The problem seemed that Cassie wanted to be both in and out of the relationship and continued to give Trent "come close, go away" messages. He moved in with her and then was asked to move out. He would be ready to face the pain of a breakup, and she would call him and want to see him. He could not refuse. One day, he would know she was not able to meet his needs, and the next day he was the center of her world. As this intermittent reward pattern continued, Trent began to feel desperate for Cassie's approval and felt more hooked into the possibility that eventually she would want him all of the time. The good times seemed to negate the bad. It was as though he had only one leg to his table—Cassie—and if it was not there, he would collapse. I encouraged him to build a four-legged table, with all of the legs being his.

Longing for Reciprocation

In romantic love, there is a delicate balance between hope and uncertainty—just enough to hold the tension. The chemical outpouring helps explain the physical yearning to touch and be touched. A person not only craves being with the romantic interest, but hopes the other craves her as well. When the romance object is not there, feelings of longing and sweet melancholy appear as a person simply fantasizes reciprocation. Longing and melancholy have a trancelike quality and feel less like pain than a reminder that we are in love. The hope of reciprocation will not be abandoned easily given the romance addict's extreme emotional dependency. These feelings and experiences become a problem when a person is blinded to reality or allows them to interfere with more important aspects of life.

❧ Back to Trent ❧

Trent's story illustrates how internal wounds can prevent a couple from being able to move into a sustaining intimacy or bonding yet hang on to the hope of reciprocation. For three years the longing, desperation, and cravings kept Trent on the edge of love. His body felt tense and on alert. But in looking at his history, this had always been the case. His mother had become pregnant with him to force his father to marry her. She used Trent, and his dad rejected him. He desired to be loved from day one and lived in the tension of not getting it. The tension he experienced now was familiar. He was looking for love to finally complete the gestalt—to get from Cassie what he did not get from his father and mother *and* to confirm his right to be alive. Psychologically he had a lot at stake. The problem was that he was now attached to the familiar hope of love returned. Being with Cassie was like being home.

Withdrawal Symptoms When the Love Object Moves Away

I received a call from a young man in another state asking for help recovering from his breakup with a girlfriend.

❧ *Darren's Story* ❧

Darren had been through drug rehab and, as a result, was familiar with the experience of withdrawal from drugs. He said he was having the same kind of uncomfortable symptoms coming off his romantic relationship, and he was having a hard time finding anyone who would take him seriously. "Just get over it" did not work. He *did* want to get over it. He, in fact, had ended the relationship and for good reasons. And he was concerned that the intensity of symptoms would cause him to relapse into his cocaine addiction. Given the similarities between how romance addiction and drug addiction affect the brain, his concern was legitimate.

When I told him I understood exactly what he was going through, he felt some immediate relief. "Thanks for not telling me I am crazy. These feelings are every bit as painful as the ones I wrestled when coming off drugs." I explained the biochemistry of love and how the brain itself develops cravings. I also shed light on how normal grief also has neurochemical responses and how it differed from what Darren was struggling with.

The more intense a romantic relationship is when it ends, or the more attachment trauma a person had earlier in life, the more pronounced the withdrawal symptoms will be. Some of the more serious withdrawal symptoms from a romantic relationship ending are the following:

- panic attacks
- irregular heartbeat
- chest pains
- tightness in chest

- stomach pains
- profuse sweating
- diarrhea and vomiting
- difficulty sleeping or eating
- trouble breathing
- urges to use or actual relapse into other addictions
- depression
- extreme craving to make contact with the person
- trouble focusing

A person experiencing such withdrawal symptoms may respond by jumping into another relationship or by numbing out the pain with risky behavior. When many of the symptoms are present and persist, it is important to get help.

Friends and Family Express Concern

One of the telltale signs that a person is hooked on the drama of romantic love is the honest feedback from friends and family who know him or her well. Sometimes others can see what a person needs to see and cannot when in the midst of new love. Sometimes this includes blatant abuse. What is disturbing is that many people interpret this abuse as proof that the abuser really loves them.

✌ *Beth's Story* ✌

Beth's mother was the first to identify her daughter's bruises. Beth lied and told her mother it happened at work. What was actually happening was a very abusive romantic relationship. Beth was "madly" in love with Kirk, who was a few years older, very good-looking, sexy, and emotionally going through some hard times.

Kirk's jealous streak and more bruising created concern on the part of Beth's friends and mother. They encouraged her to end the relationship, but instead of heeding their advice, Beth moved into Kirk's apartment. The dramatic relationship continued. On one occasion, Kirk, high on drugs, became angry and began to verbally lash out. Beth, fearing for her life, began to pack her bag. Kirk grabbed her and slammed her against the door. Terrified of his anger, yet still in love with him, she yielded and stayed.

One night, when Kirk was high on drugs and Beth was not, the abuse started once again. Displaying focus and courage, Beth called the police and friends. With the unconcealed bruises and lucid story, she was able to get a restraining order, move to a safe setting, and get help to heal from the trauma. As difficult as the trauma was, it was even more difficult to put Kirk out of her mind. Beth's low self-esteem and the loss of her father at an early age made it easy for her to interpret Kirk's behavior as a sign of being desired and loved.

Hanging On to the Unavailable or Abusive

There can be considerable abuse in love relationships, as many of the preceding stories demonstrate. One study of adults going through divorce court battles indicated that the same chemicals released in sexual or romantic arousal can be released during the heat of going through a divorce. This suggests that going after someone who is unavailable or staying in an abusive relationship can also provide a high. It can be the result of relationship training in childhood. Karen's story points this out.

ℱ *Karen's Story* ℱ

As an adult, Karen fell in love with Bill, who seemed like an all-American dream guy. Their first year together revealed a few warning signs that he was abusive, but the excitement and thrill of being newly in love helped her to minimize them. Gradually, things began to change. In front of others, Bill treated her well. In private, he was verbally and mentally abusive. There were good days and bad days, and this yo-yo pattern continued for another year. Karen wanted to leave the relationship, but she kept remembering the great times, the dreams of having his children, his good qualities. And, she was in love.

Eventually, Karen began behaving erratically as well. One day she would live in fear and adapt quietly; the next day she would explode and demand that he change. He would walk out or abusively tell her to get out of his life. They would come back together, make love, and live peacefully for a while. This pattern continued until she became physically ill from the emotional roller-coaster ride and reached out for help.

What she learned in therapy is that she had once bonded with an unavailable person—her abusive and distant alcoholic father—and had unconsciously looked for the same in a romantic relationship. In a private session, Karen's father, who had gone through treatment, made a heartfelt amend to Karen for his past rough behavior. And, without reservation, he told his daughter that she deserved to feel safe and loved in all future relationships. Karen seized Dad's words and let go of Bill.

Outcomes Are Disappointing

A person addicted to romance fixates on *making* a fantasy come true. *Finally, someone has arrived who will fulfill my emptiness, relieve my pain, and prove I am lovable,* the person imagines. Filled with expectation and unaware that the partner cannot (and even should not) fulfill the fantasy of making him whole, the person feels abandoned, and the dream of a storybook ending begins to fade. Followed by frustration, anger, and disappointment, the relationship withers and dies. Then, the search begins once again. Joanie was a person who went from one disappointing romantic relationship to the next.

✐ *Joanie's Story* ✐

"I had no standard for who I fell in love with. Anyone who would have me long enough to get my claws deep into would do. Without a romantic love in my life, I would feel really desperate. When a person pulled back or did not return an e-mail or phone call within sixty minutes, I panicked. I experienced horrible withdrawal symptoms—dizziness, the shakes, nausea, and heart palpitations. When the person was there, the symptoms subsided. So you can imagine I did everything to keep a person there. I made myself indispensable. I dressed seductively. I had sex when I did not want to. I fantasized and planned an elaborate future together. I convinced myself that the person loved me as much as I loved him.

"Of course, having unrealistic expectations, I always ended up disappointed. The center of my world would eventually leave me, and I would fall into a horrendous slump. It did not take me long to be in love again, and it did not take long to feel disappointed. I do not think I ever gave myself time to mend a broken heart or understand what I was doing until the last love relationship broke me. I ended up making an attempt on my life that got me into the hospital and then into therapy. When I finally accepted that I was powerless over making my expectations come true, I began to heal."

Distortion of Reality

The phrase "love is blind" is more truth than fiction when it comes to romance addiction. When a person falls in love with someone, that person is put on a pedestal, at least in the beginning. Everything the love object says or does becomes attractive. The romantic fog influences perceptions and interpretations with a positive slant and often keeps a person in a love relationship far too long. Romance addicts have a remarkable ability to see what is not there and, through vivid fantasizing, interpret the slightest positive or even neutral action by the object of their love as reciprocation. Such distortions provide temporary relief from unrequited love and the fear of rejection. Romance addicts also have an uncanny ability to avoid and minimize the not-so-nice qualities of their partner that are obvious to others. They will even take responsibility for the times they are mistreated. Such cognitive distortions keep hope alive and allow the sensations of elation to continue.

ℐ✺ *Maren's Story* ℐ✺

Maren was astounded that she was so blind. She had fallen in love with an "amazing" man, who she later learned was amazing to other women as well, including her co-workers. "I put him on a pedestal from the start," she told me. "I took every crumb he threw my way and interpreted it as a sign that he deeply loved me. He was charming and wonderful; he would say nice things, and then he would stop calling. He would be crabby and irritable, then when he suspected I knew he was seeing others, he would turn on the charm, take me on romantic dinners, and be very attentive. When he turned on 'nice,' I told myself that I was wrong, others were wrong, he really did love me above others, and we would get back to where we started. I had this internal double-talk. One part of me said he was not a good person, and the in-love part of me would rationalize how wonderful he was.

"My thinking became so distorted that I even blamed myself for weeks of mistreatment. I cannot believe what he got me to do for him. I cleaned his entire house after he moved out and put so much into it that I injured my back. And he did not even show up to help. I would pick up his dry cleaning and buy his groceries because, in my contaminated thinking, I interpreted his asking me to do things for him meant I was important and he loved me. What was I thinking?"

Melodrama

In the game of romance, the desire for reciprocation cannot be requested directly; it's too risky. Thus there is a delicate interplay, a courting, if you will. There is a progression to ecstatic mutuality that involves minor deceptions, shyness, and pronounced sensitivity or hypervigilance. A person becomes dependent on the love object's responses and behaviors. The subtle imbalance of hope and doubt keeps the passion alive. Fear of not getting the prize leads to caution. Open declarations of true feelings may interfere with the process and so are hidden or carefully put out. In romance addiction, the paradox is that a person wants and does not want the prize, for once it is realized, one has to take the relationship to the next stage—mutual commitment. A fear of taking the next step may surface, and so it seems better to hold the tension, the desire, the longing. Another option is that you hang in limbo, so you never have to take the risk of being rejected or abandoned. Or, if you get the prize and there is a letdown, you may leave.

❧ *Back to Ricardo* ❧

Go back and look at Ricardo's e-mail at the beginning of the chapter. How many signs of romance addiction are in his drama? Are obsession, jealousy, possessiveness, mood swings, or depression present? Is he getting a high when he is in the relationship or feeling anxiety when his love object is absent? Is the romance interfering with parts of his life as he holds back and lives on the edge of perfected love? Is he escaping through a rich fantasy life and craving the feelings of ecstasy? Is he stalking his friend or chasing the illusion? Is he hooked on the intermittent encouragement his friend puts out and feeling withdrawal when he is not with her? Is he hanging on to fantasy and an unavailable partner to reduce his pain? Is Ricardo's fantasy outcome disappointing to him? Does he distort reality to keep love alive? Are melancholy, longing, expectation, and melodrama recognizable as he pursues the soothing thought of being in love?

You are getting the picture. How would you answer his e-mail? If you are in a romantic relationship, how would you rate yourself?

As we will see in the next chapter, the drive to merge sexually with a lover is meant to be a good thing. Yet since there are so many confusing messages being tossed at us, sex can be misused and mishandled. Let's move on and look at twenty signs of sex addiction.

Sex Addiction

We all get unusual or sneaky thoughts; that is normal.
When they get out of control, it may be a sign
that the brain needs help.

DANIEL AMEN, Sex on the Brain

Dark Eros

The power of sexual love cannot be underestimated. The first stirrings of erotic love feel both good and disturbing. To be caught up by Eros is a passage into a new world. The messages we receive about sex in early life lead us either to joyful expression of our sexuality or to confusion. We soon learn that sex is not love and love is not sex. Yet these two experiences come together, and when they do, we get to experience our sexuality on multiple dimensions. Sexual love helps us feel excited and aroused; it sets the stage for and fortifies emotional bonding; it deepens our passion and longing for union; and it satisfies our search for oneness and ecstasy. Sex is not addiction, and addiction is not sex. But these two experiences can come together as well and result in pain and suffering. Sometimes it seems we have no control over which sexual path we take—the path of love or the path to addiction. As you have been learning, there are many reasons for that. Sex is about biology. Sexuality is about biology, emotions, passionate living, and love. Dark Eros does exist.

Having listened to hundreds of life stories, I can tell you that early experiences with sex rarely have loving heart in them. In fact, somewhere in their therapy, many men and women who have used sex compulsively come in with the embarrassing question, "What *is* healthy sexuality?" The fact that 97 percent of those who use sex compulsively suffered emotional neglect, 81 percent experienced sexual abuse, and 72 percent experienced physical abuse as children and teens says something.[1] It says that we have a lot of cross-wiring about sex and love to untangle in our brains before we can know what healthy sexual love is. It also says trauma wounds leave scars that must be healed before we can fully appreciate our sexual energy. It says we must discover safe ways to enjoy our sexuality and share it with loved ones. And when sexual trust has been broken in a relationship, it says we must rebuild that trust to feel safe enough to bond once again in a love relationship. No easy task.

When sex addicts are in a love relationship, they become increasingly dissatisfied with sex in that committed relationship. No amount of love, attractiveness, or sex will satisfy active sex addicts. Their demands for amounts of sex and types of sex invite low self-esteem, confusion, or guilt in their partners. As hard as they may try, partners are left with feelings of not being enough or not doing enough. This tension brings out anger and turmoil that begins a process of shutting down sexually or becoming hypersexual in an effort to please and control the sex addict.

Sex as an Addiction

The concept of sex as an addiction is quite topical and is not without its critics and doubters. It has been dismissed or overlooked by society, individuals, and many professionals in the mental health field. Disparaging terms have been used over the years to label those with out-of-control sexual problems—*nymphomaniac, sexual deviant, Don Juan, satyr, lothario, womanizer, dirty old man, whore, slut, fallen woman,* and *harlot*—suggesting that compulsive use of sex was mere choice and easy to stop. The idea of sex as an addiction came forward in the mid-1970s, when a recovering alcoholic identified his out-of-control sexual behavior as parallel to his alcoholic behaviors and referred to it as sexual addiction. Looking at compulsive use of sex from the addiction model gave such behaviors an explanation and a road to healing for both individuals and couples.

The sexual addiction movement gained momentum in 1983 with the publication of Dr. Patrick Carnes's *Out of the Shadows*. In it, he identified three levels of behaviors associated with sex addiction. *Level One* behaviors are common and generally sanctioned by society, or at least tolerated. These include but are not limited to masturbation, affairs, pornography, use of escorts and prostitutes, anonymous sex, sexual seduction, and cybersex. *Level Two* behaviors, though often considered more of a nuisance by the legal system, always involve the victimization of someone. Exhibitionism, voyeurism, unwanted solicitation, spousal sexual abuse, sexual predation by people in power, and stalking all fall into this category. *Level Three* behaviors involve the more serious crossing of sexual boundaries and victimize the most vulnerable. These include rape, incest, sexual violence, molestation, sexual bondage, child sexual abuse, and child pornography. It is important to note that though any of the above behaviors can be used compulsively, involvement in any of the above behaviors does not necessarily mean a person is addicted to sex.[2] How do we know if these behaviors are an addiction?

What Is Sexual Addiction?

Sexual addiction is an obsessive-compulsive behavior or excessive sexual behavior disorder that, if left unattended, causes severe distress and despair for the individual or partner. It occurs when a person uses one or more sexual behaviors as a "fix" or drug, and in ways that result in negative consequences. Consequences may be relational, emotional, physical, financial, legal, occupational, social, and spiritual in nature. In the process, a physical dependency on the biochemical or mood-altering experiences of arousal, satiation, and fantasy occurs. There is usually marked tolerance and continued involvement in spite of negative consequences. And, like other addictions, sexual addiction becomes an unconscious habit, a compulsive ritual that is no longer a choice, and a psychological and biological attachment to the stimulus that provides the pleasure. Withdrawal symptoms occur when the sexual stimulus is removed, and preoccupation begins to interfere with life. There are mood changes related to sexual activity or recovering from sexual activity. The addict experiences a high level of denial or rationalization around the out-of-control or self-gratifying sexual behaviors. Denial causes the addict to distort reality, ignore the problem, blame others, and give numerous justifications for the behavior.

And, recall what you learned in chapter 2. We have three distinct brain circuits—sexual arousal, romantic attraction, and emotional bonding—each fed by a unique chemical concoction, and sexual arousal is but one of them. These three drives can and do operate together or alone. Sexual arousal can be sexual arousal and nothing more. The sexual object does not have to be a love or romantic partner and often is not. You can love someone and be in lust elsewhere. Since we can not easily peek into the brain of a person, a history of negative consequences is the best indicator that a problem exists.

It is conservatively estimated that 3 to 5 percent of the population suffers from sexual addiction, and it is on the increase in the adolescent population.[3] The youngest person I referred to inpatient treatment for sexual addiction was only fifteen years old. And 40 percent of those who use sex compulsively on the Internet are now women.[4] It is time for us to take this problem seriously. If we do not do so, the future love relationships of many are at high risk.

Recognizing the warning signs can be helpful to prevent an addiction from developing or to get help to stop it. The majority of sex addicts seek help *after* they have been intervened on or have had serious consequences. The challenge is to remove the shame associated with this problem so a person concerned about her sexual behaviors will feel free to reach out for help. And though I believe sex addiction to be a symptom of a deeper problem, we enter the door of healing at the behavioral level.

Twenty Signs of Sexual Addiction/Compulsivity

Here are some of the warning signs either observable to others or happening within the person using sex compulsively.

1. use of sex to fix, escape, or cope
2. negative consequences due to sexual behavior
3. mood changes related to sexual activity
4. inability to stop, even with negative consequences
5. planning, obtaining, and recovering from sexual activity becomes increasingly time-consuming
6. risk losing a relationship or job
7. guilt and shame because of behavior
8. pursuit of high-risk or destructive behaviors
9. a predictable cycle
10. tolerance or need for more to get the same high
11. at odds with family or spiritual values
12. deny, rationalize, defend, or minimize behavior
13. sexual cravings
14. preoccupation
15. living a double or secret life
16. use sex to feel or not feel past trauma
17. sexualize others
18. violate trust of others
19. inappropriate sexual behaviors
20. use and abuse others for sexual gratification[5]

Use of Sex to Fix, Escape, or Cope

The use of sex can be a way to escape from problems, reduce stress, and fix inner loneliness. In fact, a major problem underlying sex addiction is emotional loneliness caused by a fear of intimacy. Karen's story illustrates how she began to medicate her loneliness with both alcohol and sex, starting in her childhood.

❧ Karen's Story ❧

"At the age of eight, I discovered alcohol. My mother unwittingly showed me how drink can alter a person. On Sundays, she would cook the lunch and drink sherry. She would go from an unavailable, hassled mother of four to someone who almost seemed to love me. This was the key. If I wanted to be loved, then alcohol was the elixir I'd been searching for. I secretly began to siphon sherry into an empty shampoo bottle and smuggle it out of the house.

"At first, the sherry seemed to fulfill some of my needs. It lifted my mood, it made me more daring, and it certainly made me popular with the other kids. But it never filled the gap that I so longed to have filled. I still craved the love and attention of my parents and needed to be special in their eyes. I was miserably lonely.

"By the early age of ten, I thought I'd found what I was looking for. In the arms of a forty-year-old man, I was convinced I was valued and cared for. I spent all the hours I could on his farm, and in return for sexual favors, I learned to drive tractors, milk the cows, feed the calves, and a million other things that ordinary kids didn't get to do.

"Around the age of thirteen, it was as if my world fell apart. I discovered my hero-figure farmer had also been having sex with my best friend. My sense of betrayal was overwhelming, and what little trust I had in people was more or less shattered. I was devastated, not realizing I had been sexually abused.

"However, all was not lost, for now I had two potent weapons in my arsenal—sex and alcohol. I knew stuff other kids didn't know, and I did stuff other kids didn't do. When I put alcohol and sex together, I thought I was invincible.

"And so began my downward spiral into sex and alcohol addiction. I would use them together or individually; it really didn't matter as long as I achieved the desired effect. Eventually, I realized that any emotion or feeling could be altered, and I thought I had life fixed. Whatever had happened to me in the past, whatever it was that I was lacking, whatever it was I was searching for, sex or alcohol or my cocktail of the two could fix it all. I didn't see that I was destroying myself and the person I could be.

"Sex and alcohol ruled my life; they shaped who I am and how I coped with the world, and they held me locked in a desperate looking-for-love limbo. Last year, at the age of forty-eight, I finally had enough of my brokenness and checked into a treatment center. Without my crutches of alcohol and sex, I can finally welcome and care for the little girl I banished all those years ago and discover who I really am."

Negative Consequences Due to Sexual Behavior

A person using sex addictively often fails to recognize or minimizes the negative consequences that sexual acting out can bring. Some of these have been mentioned before:

- depression, low self-esteem
- scandal, date rape, violence
- feeling objectified
- lust substituting for love
- sex as a power play
- confusion about healthy sexual intimacy
- emotional stress and illness
- sex as a consumer product, prostitution
- relationship problems
- loss of productivity
- exploitation
- spiritual emptiness
- inability to focus
- use of other addictive substances
- feelings of betrayal
- breakups and divorce
- increase in HIV and other STDs, unplanned pregnancies
- isolation
- emotional, physical, and sexual abuse
- loss of innocence and self-respect

- sexual harassment
- avoidance of real needs
- sacredness of sexuality is lost
- loss of trust and feelings of safety
- therapeutic failure if not identified
- suicidal ideation

Sixty percent of those who use sex compulsively have faced financial problems; 58 percent have engaged in illegal activities; 83 percent have had concurrent addictions, such as to alcohol and other drugs, to food, or to gambling; and 70 to 75 percent have thought of suicide. Partners of sex addicts do not fare any better as they go into depression, have emotional difficulties, develop psychosomatic problems, and get deeper into their own compulsive behaviors.[6]

Mood Changes Related to Sexual Activity

When sex is used as a drug, there are mood alterations in the brain. A study that included brain scans completed by Dr. Mark Laaser and Richard Blankenship at the Amen Clinic showed that 67 percent of sex addicts had problems in the thinking part of the brain, and 50 percent had problems in the brain area that gets stuck on negative thoughts and behaviors. The study also showed a high association between the mood and anxiety parts of the brain that contribute to emotional extremes.[7] Sex addicts suppress the feelings associated with the behavior—fear, guilt, and despair—and become agitated as the disease progresses. The behavior that was intended to help medicate old and new pain creates even more.

✍ Dena's Story ✍

Dena was introduced to sex at six years of age, when she was repeatedly molested by a babysitter. Like most children in such a situation, she knew what was happening was wrong, and to make sense out of it, she concluded that she was responsible: something in the way she presented her fondness for the sitter had caused the sexual abuse.

Afraid and ashamed, she told no one. She lived with this "dirty" secret and depression her entire childhood. Her body was tense with the anxiety of being found out. Often, she felt alone and different. As she approached adulthood and sexual feelings surfaced, she tried to shut them down. It did not work for two reasons. One was that it was impossible, and two, her depression deepened. She stepped out of her numbness to experiment sexually. She began to notice that she got a high not only from the sex, but also from the attention she received. For those moments, her depression disappeared.

A life of promiscuous and high-risk sexual escapades began. Just as it was in her childhood, her sexual experiences had no connection with caring or love. In time, her fear and shame of sex came back, accompanied by a vague sense of emptiness. When the feelings of being "dirty" returned, she thought the answer was to settle down with one man and start a family. Knowing the art of seduction, she had her pick of men and chose one with status and money. The marriage, position, and money seemed to work for a while, but always there was a vague sense of emptiness. Slowly, she sank into a depression as memories of her past surfaced. Her solution was to sexually act out. It had worked before; why not now?

She turned to online affairs that became real-life affairs. This time, she not only had the sex and attention, she had the rush of keeping it all a secret. Her multiple affairs occupied her life for two years. The time consumption and weight of keeping a secret exhausted her. She was getting physically ill, and her depression and shame resurfaced. But these feelings were not enough to stop her, and in fact, the depression and shame propelled her to more acting out. When she was eventually caught in the act, she was shocked into reality. She went into treatment and is now on medication for chronic depression and anxiety, is discovering the power of her early trauma, is grieving her loss of innocence, and is working to restore her marriage.

Inability to Stop, Even with Negative Consequences

If you ask recovering sex addicts if they have ever tried to stop, they will tell you, "Yes, and hundreds of times." When sex is used as a drug, the urges to use seem impossible to stop. Sex has crossed the line into an addiction when the brain says, "Give me more of that feel-good experience, and I do not care how you do it or what happens to you."

❧ Don's Story ❧

Looking back at his recent relapse, Don said: "What a tragic story. I allowed myself to be psychologically raped. I was willing to give up everything, including my marriage and health. I should have known better, having been in treatment before. I watched myself step into the cycle, and I would say, 'Just one more time.' One became a hundred times. After each sexual escapade, the depression would kick in, and I would look for another opportunity to act out to get away from it. I felt powerless.

"The first step into my relapse was going online to find prostitute ads. I was just looking. That led to scheduling a time to meet. I felt excitement as I wondered what games we could play to make it interesting. The secrecy and naughtiness accelerated the excitement I felt. I would push thoughts of my wife aside. I was so deluded that I told myself it was less dangerous to have the prostitute come to my home. In my crazy thinking, I did not think about the possibility that the person I brought in could case my house, or that having anonymous sex could bring me a sexually transmitted disease. I did not think that I was desecrating our home or that my wife would find out. It did not seem to matter, as I could not stop. One of the prostitutes used heroin, so I tried it. It would make the sex more exciting. I could not stop and see straight, and I kept going. It was like I was in the middle of a lake and not able to swim. I was drowning, and I needed saving. This was beyond any ability to stop. As odd as it sounds, the saving grace was discovering I had a sexually transmitted disease and a wife still willing to work with me."

Planning, Obtaining, and Recovering from Sexual Activity Becomes Increasingly Time-Consuming

As sexual desire becomes obsessive, more and more time is spent increasing the addict's relationship with sex. Yes, sexual addiction—any addiction—is a relationship. This relationship becomes more important than anything else. When involved in planning, obtaining, and even recovering from the sexual behavior, there is an illusion of security. Once again, addiction is a habitual and predictable attempt to fulfill unmet needs, dull pain, avoid fear, fill our loneliness, and perpetuate our personal stories. The intensity becomes a substitute for emotional intimacy with people. Sex becomes confused with nurturing and comfort. To feel secure means to feel sexual. Yet this contributes to more loneliness, which leads to more use of sex to soothe the self. Recovery becomes possible only when a person discovers that the addiction did not fix the inner brokenness; it created more brokenness.

Referring to his addiction, one person told me that though his sexual acting out consumed 1 percent of his life, it occupied 50 percent of his brain. I added that because it was a secret life that his partner was not aware of, it was in his brain 100 percent of the time, hovering over him like a dark cloud.

Risk Losing a Relationship or Job

What seems most crazy to outsiders is that addicted people are willing to throw all good sense out the window and risk losing a career, a reputation, and a person they love to satisfy their sexual urges. When in the throes of an addiction, the possibility of such losses is put out of sight and out of mind so an urge can be fed.

✥ *John's Story* ✥

"I met my wife five years ago. We married two years later, and I had every intention to have a great life with her, not realizing I did not have all the skills to do so. In my family of origin, we never talked about anything personal, so I carried on the family tradition and never talked about the struggles we had. I was afraid to be emotionally honest because, in my mind, she might leave. As I stuffed my feelings and needs, the tension and pressure built up.

"I found one way of making myself feel better in the power of sexual release. My old addiction began to surface, and I secretly sought out women who would admire me, confide in me, and need me. What was so unbelievable to me is that I was with a person I deeply loved and intended to be with forever, and yet I was seeking sexual experiences with others knowing I was risking losing her. I could not stop myself and unknowingly left clues for my wife so she would catch me and stop me. I felt relieved when my secret was finally out in the open. And I was scared to death she would leave. She is hanging in there with me so far, but it is really up to me to restore the broken trust between us."

Guilt and Shame Because of Behavior

Let me distinguish between shame, guilt, regret, and remorse. *Shame* is a debilitating feeling. It goes deep to people's core and is experienced as a disintegration of self, a sense of total vulnerability, and loss of power at that moment. People feel raw and naked. Often, people shame others for who they are or things they have no control over (for example, when an audience laughs at a person who trips while walking across the stage). When shamed, people are not able to separate *who* they are from *what* they did.

Guilt is something people feel when their behavior is identified as terribly wrong. The terrible wrong may have been getting an A- in school. Or, it may have been reaching out for a hug and being frowned at or pushed aside. After a while, people do not need others to inflict guilt and shame. They do it to themselves. When people use sex as a remedy and begin to move away from their own values, they experience intense guilt and shame. These feelings then push people into denial or rationalization; they simply cannot admit they have a problem for fear others will view them in a negative way, which would bring even more guilt and shame. Shame and guilt also confirm any warped belief about self that they developed in childhood, when they did not know better.

As healing occurs, sex addicts own the out-of-control behavior and feel *regret* or *remorse* for the actions, rather than guilt or shame. Whereas guilt and shame are generated from the outside as people imagine how others may view them, regret and remorse come from the inside, from the heart. Sex addicts do not like their behavior because it goes against their own goodness and because it causes harm to self and others. They regret that they stepped out of personal integrity. They feel remorse because they hurt others with their behavior. It takes tremendous courage for sex addicts to own the self that they have come to loathe and to take responsibility for their actions. This gets easier as they mature in recovery, increase self-esteem, and develop compassion for human frailties. There is a big difference between a sarcastic "I am sorry you feel that way" and a heartfelt "I am truly sorry, you did not deserve how I treated you."

Pursuit of High-Risk or Destructive Behaviors

Sex addicts often blot out the risk they are taking as they step into dangerous territory. They are into the thrill, freedom, and power they feel using their sexuality in dark ways. For some, the high is in the secret life, the risk-taking, and living on the edge of being found out. The thrill thrives on fear and arousal. They may need to be found out both to stop a behavior and to embarrass themselves into getting help.

ᥱ *Gordon's Story* ᥱ

"My sexual addiction behaviors followed a common pattern of escalation. Most of my life, I used masturbation and limited pornography. Later in life, I started going to adult video stores. I hid this behavior because I was afraid of what my wife and employer would do if I were caught. It was a new experience that took me out of my comfort zone.

"To enhance my experience, I looked for massage places that gave full-body massages with 'happy endings.' The challenge of anticipating and finding new places and seeing how far a masseuse would go became as exciting as the actual visit.

"I read an article about street prostitutes, and my interest was piqued. It took a long time for me to risk picking up a prostitute for the first time. I was afraid, but I did it anyway, stepping into a very dangerous behavior and a very dangerous neighborhood.

"I became more confident and enjoyed the thrill of making the pickup, driving while engaging in sex, or finding a parking place and driving the prostitute back to her area. Doing all this while avoiding the police was dangerous *and* exciting. My secret life was totally out of character with my other life. I am amazed that I could move so easily and totally from one life to the other. I tried stepping out of my risky behavior, but I could not. Sexual addiction is powerful and real.

"Then one day, my illusionary life crashed. I got careless, and after picking up a prostitute and driving down the block, I noticed a police car right behind me. I was given a ticket for solicitation of a prostitute, which was hitting the bottom for me.

"I don't know how my wife stayed with me. I had caused so much pain for my wife, to the point of her considering suicide. When I started recovery and began feeling hopeful, she started a grieving process, as if someone had died. I am ever grateful for my wife staying with me during this devastating time. We are each fortunate to have found skilled professional help, as well as many people who have provided help and supported us so we could rebuild the trust that was lost."

A Predictable Cycle

Patrick Carnes has identified a very predictable cycle the individual sex addict goes through.[8] Most are unaware of the cycle until they stop and look back at their behavior. It is essential to understand the subtleties and the unique way individuals experience each step.

The Addictive System
Patrick Carnes, Ph.D.

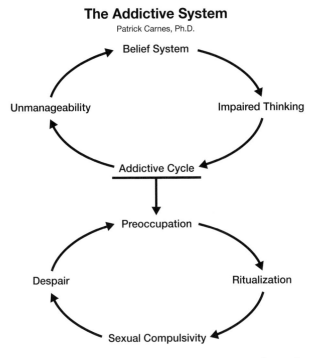

1. *Preoccupation*—creation of a trancelike state similar to the limerent state one feels when newly in love. The addicts' moods begin to alter as they fixate on their excitement-arousing behavior. They imagine spending hours searching for sex on the Internet; they fixate on meeting someone at a pickup bar.
2. *Ritualization*—the predictable routine that intensifies the trance and adds arousal and excitement. Stepping into the ritual, addicts do not have to waste time thinking about what comes next; it is automatic. Putting on specific makeup and putting on a favorite provocative outfit, or turning on the computer before entering the cyber world of pornography or to meet someone, lets addicts know they have just stepped into the game. There is a chemical outpouring that then propels the addict into the next step, acting out.
3. *Compulsive sexual behavior*—the sexual behavior that is the end goal of the first two stages. At this point, a sex addict cannot

stop. The chemical and mental buildup and the intensity of the drive demand getting to the end product to experience relief. But shortly after reaching the goal, there is a letdown.

4. *Despair*—the feeling of hopelessness, powerlessness, and emptiness that follows; the crash. This crash is biological as well as psychological. A person cannot sustain the drug high, and the behavior did not fix anything. Realizing that they have not been able to stop the behavior, addicts may experience shame, start the cycle again to get away from the pain, concoct a story that justifies the behavior, turn to another addiction, make another self-promise to stop, or become suicidal.

The first two stages are not always taken seriously by the person engaged in them. Those who are not addicted can stop at this point. The person addicted to sex cannot. And each time the cycle is repeated, it becomes more intense and ingrained. It is important to note that hitting despair is a psychological payoff of bad feelings supported by the addict's core beliefs or decisions: "I am bad and unworthy," "I am helpless," "I will prove I am unlovable."[9]

Tolerance or Need for More to Get the Same High

The term for needing increasing amounts of a substance or experience to get the same high is *tolerance*. As the behaviors escalate, so do the consequences.

✎ *Joe's Story* ✎

He couldn't believe it was happening to him. Severely depressed, Joe sat in my office in a state of shock. His wife had a court injunction against him. He was considered dangerous and was not allowed to see his wife or child.

"It started out innocently enough," Joe said. "We both enjoyed it. It began with playful spankings. They thrilled us both. But it did not stop there. I wanted more. I thought she did, too. It escalated from there to painfully humiliating sexual acts. I stopped for a while when she was pregnant. But the power and depth of desire took over, and I forced the issue soon after the birth of our baby. I would not hear her pleas and forced my will on her. I got off on my power as I chained her to the bed and inflicted more and more pain. It was as if the devil himself possessed me. She was a mother now, and that came first to her. I would not stop and let her nurse the baby. He was crying for her, and still I could not stop. She almost died, and it was as though I did not care."

At Odds with Family or Spiritual Values

The following story speaks to how the misuse of sex can put us at odds with core values.

✕ *Ted's Story* ✕

"I am well known, and no one would guess my story. I was respected, sought after, constantly adulated. Being in the limelight has its benefits, and it has its pitfalls. My deceit was spiritual, and my duplicity was progressive. I am a spiritual teacher. I had children and a beloved partner, and I lived in integrity for a long time. Perhaps hitting fifty made me feel some inner urgency to cross my own line. My life was a smorgasbord of feminine energy. I had many beautiful and not-so-beautiful but needy women in my life. It was like being in a candy store and being told I could have anything to eat.

"The shift happened without my realizing it. I failed to notice that I began to get a rush from the adoration, and I missed it when it was not there. I began to want the high, and all the while I continued my spiritual practice. I rationalized: 'Spirit has no limits,' 'Love is meant to be expressed to everyone,' 'No one owns my body,' 'I am healing, not harming.'

"I became involved with many women. It was bliss, it was lust, and it was divine. I was so immersed in my spiritual deceit that I am surprised I survived to tell the story. The crash was inevitable. I began feeling depressed. I knew something was wrong, but I was in too much denial to see clearly what it was. I arranged to do a spiritual retreat where I could sit still until I had absolute clarity.

"I got what I was looking for. I was shown my self-deceit; I was shown my future if I were to continue gratifying my lustful urges; I was shown forgiveness. I wept on and off for three days. I had caused a lot of damage. I hurt people who really did love me and whom I could trust. I violated the trust of my students. I had fallen out of grace and certainly love. I had become unsafe to myself.

"One thing I have learned is how easily we can manipulate even our spirituality to be self-serving. I look around now and see so much deceit. I really see the male of our species in deep trouble. They are made war heroes, made sports heroes, and placed in power positions. Yet seldom do they have the networks of other men to say, 'Stop deceiving yourself. What you are doing is wrong. It hurts you. It plays with others' hearts. It kills the spirit inside. And it is not love!'"

Deny, Rationalize, Defend, or Minimize Behavior

For many of the reasons mentioned—soothing oneself, getting a high, filling loneliness or boredom, getting out of a depression, having a private fantasy world, reducing stress, feeling alive, coping with pain—people will initially do anything and everything to keep their addiction alive. They will openly deny that a problem exists, they will minimize the consequences of their acting out, and they will get angry or defensive when you get close to the truth or challenge their behavior. They will even make the problem about you. As the behavior escalates, they will often withdraw or seem distant and cold. They carry on an internal dialogue that goes something like this:

"Everyone is doing it; it's no big deal."
"I deserve it."

"No one is really getting hurt."

"Oral sex is safe."

"A chat room is just a game."

"Sex is my most important need."

"My partner is not satisfying me."

"A cyber relationship won't get me in trouble."

"Guys need a sexual outlet."

"Sex is good for my health."

"I am lonely, and it helps me feel good."

"I like the thrill."

"I was used, and now it is my turn."

"If the men enjoy my seduction, it is harmless."

It usually takes an intervention or a big fall before sex addicts give up the defenses and become willing to look at the problem. Even then, they are in too much shame to recognize and own the extent of the damage. That comes farther down the road.

Sexual Cravings

The Funk & Wagnalls dictionary defines *craving* as a "natural or morbid yearning or appetite; intense longing." Craving has an element of urgency to it—an impulse so great that if the craving is not fed, something awful will happen. Some sex addicts describe craving as a physical ache or compelling need experienced in their body. Why does a craving go from natural to morbid, from a normal sex drive to sex addiction? There are many reasons:

1. genetics
2. physical and emotional stress
3. hormones
4. changes in the brain because of drug use
5. nutritional imbalances
6. psychological and physical trauma

Preoccupation

For many, the preoccupation with sex, often under the influence of alcohol or other drugs, can lead to self-disgust and suicidal thinking. Such was the case with Tess, the youngest client I have referred to inpatient treatment for sexual addiction.

❧ *Tess's Story* ❧

It was a mother's distress call. Her fifteen-year-old daughter, Tess, had become very despondent and was talking about not wanting to live. Tess was doing some cutting on her arms. Her mother asked if I could meet with Tess and make an evaluation and possible referral to a hospital or treatment facility. Tess asked to speak to me in private. She presented a tough exterior, yet I could see the little girl in her. She was scared and sad. She had been working on her self-esteem for quite some time and had been making good progress. I asked her why the sudden change. She reported that she had gotten involved with a group considered outsiders. At first, she felt comfortable with them because they were similar to her. She started out having a good time. But things changed.

One of her friends took her to her boyfriend's apartment, where Tess met a couple of guys who wanted to have sex with her. They were older and experienced, and she felt wanted and excited. It was her first sexual experience, and it felt awful. "They did degrading things to me," she moaned. "But that is not the worst part. I kept going back for more. And it has been going on for months and months, and I can't stop even though I want to. It is like a drug. I think about it all the time. I think about it—I get really excited—I have sex—and then I hate myself. I believe I am pregnant, and I don't know what to tell my mom and dad." This tough young woman broke into tears. "I wish I could just die. As sick and risky as this behavior is, if these guys call, I don't know if I will be able to say no."

Living a Double or Secret Life

Sexual addiction can be considered a dissociative disorder. This means that addicts can separate one part of their personality from the other, or they can psychologically remove themselves from an experience they do not want to deal with and keep it in a separate box. If a well-known politician's sexual secrets are exposed to the public, the response is often "How could he (or she) be so stupid?" When the same happens with a couple in therapy, the question of the partner is "How can he say he loves me if he has this other life?" The answer to both questions is that the acting-out person has two selves—the addict self and the healthy self—as well as the ability to keep them separate.

The addict's secret life is supported by lying to self and others. Telling lies helps cover the shame. And though telling a lie is uncomfortable, the addict believes it is the lesser of two evils, fearing that telling the truth will only make matters worse. Truth telling will mean having to stop the behavior, face withdrawal, take off the image mask, hurt the partner, and feel shame and guilt. The difficulty is that a person not only obsesses about getting the "drug"—in this case, the sex—but also obsesses about how to keep the secret.[10]

✺ *Conrad's Story* ✺

"I kept my sexual addiction from my wife for fourteen years. I had sex with her best friend the first year of our marriage, I had affairs at the office, and I even introduced my wife to some of the people I had affairs with when we were at office gatherings while keeping my other life with them a secret.

"We were in a couple's support group where she and I touted honesty and closeness. With our children, we looked like the perfect couple, and we were. I had a way of compartmentalizing my two lives. It was like switching the sex addict on and off. When I was with my wife and family, I was totally there. When I was in my addiction, I was totally there. Keeping the two parts of me separate allowed me some false inner peace. I did not have to worry about anyone's feelings, and I could keep from feeling my guilt.

"Then I started meeting women online. It seemed safer. But my wife came across my e-mails to a woman I planned to meet in another city. She was stunned and angry. Rightly so. I promised I would stop, but the habit was too ingrained, and I continued. Now that my wife knew about my addiction, it was personally more difficult to keep the addict separate from the husband and father, and so I resorted to conscious lying. My affairs became less exciting, as I feared I might get caught again, and I was also prone to more guilt.

"The duplicity started to eat at me, and I finally wanted to stop it. I went into treatment, and I discovered how important it was for me to integrate the two parts of myself. My addict part had been around a long time and, oddly, had become like a friend who had outgrown his usefulness and needed to be educated. I needed his energy to accompany me in positive ways so I could live a life of integrity. He has met everyone in my life now, and so there are no more secrets."

Use Sex to Feel or Not Feel Past Trauma

As explained in chapter 3, when we experience fear that accompanies trauma, our bodies instinctively react with a fight, flight, or freeze response. It may not be safe to fight or leave, and so we freeze. The problem is, as said before, we do not allow our bodies to thaw out later because they would shake, like all healthy animals' bodies do after a shock. Showing fear seems taboo in our society. Our only option is to store our fearful memories in our bodies. But this pent-up energy does not simply go away. Sex is often an attempt to release such energy or to replay an earlier trauma. We may not even be aware of our childhood traumas, yet we continually re-enact them, attempting to get a new ending. We bond with the traumatic event or person who betrayed us. And, without thinking, we look for the familiar through the following behaviors:

- engaging in thrill-seeking sexual behaviors
- feeling sexual when frightened

- looking for danger
- bonding with abusers
- having difficulty being alone
- having high-risk sex
- using sex to escape
- doing to others what was done to us sexually
- obsessing over the abuser
- anticipating being hurt

For recovery to occur, a person must get to the fear trapped in the body and release it. *Many sex addicts use sex as a means to feel because they have trouble feeling, or to block feelings that might trigger a past trauma and flood them.* The bottom line is that a traumatized person needs to learn that it is safe to have emotions and sensations, learn how to read them, and then take appropriate action to get a need met. It's also important to learn that, when a need cannot be met and emotional pain is produced, that pain can be tolerated. Chronically overwhelmed with emotions, trauma victims have lost their ability to use emotions as guides to figure out what they need, let alone figure out how to get the need met. In addition to or in the process of healing the residue of past trauma, a recovering sex addict must also become a careful observer of her current interior life. When a recovering addict learns how to live an emotional life in the present with ease, it is easier to tolerate any triggers from the past and deal with them in a healthy manner, rather than self-medicating with the drug of choice—sex.[11]

Sexualize Others

In our society, it seems we are groomed to explore and brag about sexual encounters, line up which men and women are the sexiest, and learn the skills of seduction. When people use sex compulsively, they become victims of their own preoccupation with these skills. Everyone they are introduced to, every anonymous person they encounter or observe, is a sexual object. More than noticing or appreciating an attractive person, they scrutinize the person for possibilities.

The intoxication is similar to the first stages of romantic love. The trancelike state of the search, the hunt, the suspense, and the potential conquest is addictive in itself. Going to a large gathering is ripe with possibilities; logging on to chat rooms is ripe with possibilities. Sexual arousal intensifies, and the mood is altered simply in the anticipation or fantasy. Adrenaline pulses through the body as the heart quickens, the pupils dilate, and the body arouses. Just thinking about the possibilities can be enough of a high. Everything and everyone is viewed through the lens of the sex addiction.

✺ Jerad's Story ✺

"I looked forward to attending out-of-town business meetings. Without my wife present, I was a free man. New cities were places where I could fill my cravings. The juices started as I planned what I would wear and groomed myself. Then I would hit the hotel bar lounge and scout for someone to feed my appetite for the night or the duration of my trip. I turned on my seductive self. I would charm several people until I met one who played the same game. I now know that the arousal of the hunt was more important than the actual sex. Sometimes I felt obligated to follow through with the sex and really did not enjoy it."

⌒

Violate Trust of Others

In addition to violating self-trust, sex addiction often creates a breach of trust that is so deep, the partner of the sex addict usually wonders if he can ever trust again. Some even consider suicide. When the compulsive or addictive behavior has been kept a secret and the behavior surfaces, the partner goes into shock. Many trauma symptoms appear as the partner wants to run, numb out, or attack. "How can I ever get over this?" "How can I ever get back the safe feeling I had before?" "Why am I not enough?" Despair, rage, and grief are experienced as the partner attempts to understand and not personalize the other partner's behavior. Where there is a good base foundation of love and with the understanding that trust can only be rebuilt with time, couples are encouraged not to make any hasty decision to leave, but rather commit to the relationship for one year. Whether trust is restored or not is predicated on whether or not *both* do their personal work. Here is one partner's story.

✎ Cynthia's Story ✎

"Three years after we married, John sat me down and told me that during one of his appointments with a female client, he had touched her inappropriately. It had only happened once, it didn't mean anything to him, and he didn't consider it to be a big deal. In my wildest imagination, I couldn't think of anything he could have told me that would have shocked me more. I was devastated. This couldn't be the man I had married. This couldn't be true. But the woman was reporting him, and he was going to have to resign his position.

"He insisted again and again that there had been this one woman only. He couldn't understand why I was so hurt. He reiterated many times that he wanted to be married to me and that he loved me above all else. What more could I want? Then one morning, as we were eating breakfast together, he said to me, 'There were others.' And then I listened as this man described what had been going on. My world crashed that day. Yet as the crashing was happening, I could now make sense of what I'd been struggling with the past year. This wasn't about one woman, this wasn't about me, and this wasn't about our marriage. I didn't know exactly what it was about, but I knew it was big. I stepped into a deep, dark hole of despair and feared I would never come out, or, if I did, I knew I would never be the same.

"John immediately got help. I agreed to stay in the marriage long enough to see if I could rebuild trust and the safe feeling I once had. I continue to get triggered very easily. If he is late, I get anxious. If I see one of his clients, I wonder if he was sexual with her. If we are around attractive women, I wonder where his mind is. Some of the simplest things, like going to a wedding, make me cry. I am hypervigilant and look for ways he is being dishonest. As much as I do not want to obsess, I do. I have been told that time and work on both our parts can help us get through this. I do want to believe that John loves me, and from time to time, I see glimpses of the man that I married. But I worry that I may never be able to trust him again."

⤻

Inappropriate Sexual Behaviors

Sometimes a sex addict is hard to identify because her behavior is covert. Often, our intuition picks up the signals. After a while, if you know what to look for, you can spot a sex addict anywhere. Many sex addicts use sex as the theme of jokes and humor. They do a lot of teasing with sexual innuendos or make direct comments about people's sexual anatomy that make others feel uncomfortable. They give too many hugs, touch in ways that do not feel right, or invade people's physical boundaries. They might follow you, brush up against you, or try to seduce you. They show off body parts and take pleasure in your enjoying them. They are great at double entendre—words or phrases that have two meanings, one of which is sexual. They are quick to pick up a sexual meaning and point it out to you. If someone says, "She got off just in time this morning," a sex addict might coyly or jokingly suggest "got off" referred to sex.

As the disease progresses, these behaviors become even more inappropriate and direct. In a partnership, you get the sense that you must do more and more to thrill your partner. The key word here is *must*—implying that this is not a mutually satisfying arrangement and you feel like a sex object.

Use and Abuse Others for Sexual Gratification

Sex hormones start raging in our adolescence, and for many adult sex addicts, the problem began there. Healthy emotional and sexual development stops at the age the person first used sex as a drug.

Greg's story tells us how his first profound sexual relationship, rather than being a good one, reinforced early childhood trauma and set the neural tracks that would be repeated in his adulthood.

❧ *Greg's Story* ❧

Greg blurted out in the middle of our session: "I think I am addicted to sex. I carry this awful secret inside of me. I run on fear. I do not trust people, and I have these crazy outbursts of anger. It is as though I get possessed, and I say and do things I regret later. I use women for my own gratification. I keep sex separate from my heart."

As I guided him to the roots of the problem, Greg remembered being five years old and sitting in his mother's lap. He remembered leaning in close to her. "I love the way she smells like flowers. I love the way she rubs my hair and scratches the back of my neck. I like her voice. She tells me I am a big boy. I know I'm not. I am sad, but I cannot be sad because she is sad. I have to take care of her. Dad is gone away again, but when he comes home, she forgets about me."

He remembered more. At seventeen, Greg met the most breathtaking person he had ever met; she was twenty-five. She introduced him to sex, but no one could know. When he was with his mind-blowing friend, Greg felt five years old again: "I love the way she smells," he said. "I love the way she rubs my hair and scratches the back of my neck. I like her voice. She tells me I am special. This must be what love is—the touch, the closeness, the anticipation, the sexual high."

Then suddenly, his electrifying friend was gone. She said she fell in love with someone her own age. Greg felt abandoned once again by a woman he thought loved him. In his pain, Greg promised himself, "Never again; I will use women like they used me." From that day forward, use he did. Women fell into his seductive charm. Living on the brink of love became a way of life. Sex became a way of life. No fear, no hurt, and no heart. On occasion, the loneliness and self-disgust would surface, but he would quickly soothe it with sex, drugs, and alcohol. Then one day, he collapsed into a depression. Greg was so far away from himself that it scared him into reaching out for help.

Moving On

I am not suggesting that everyone experiencing sex, romance, and love is addicted or is using them compulsively. I have put a lot of emphasis on how relationships can become a compulsive need and even addictive. Sex, love, and romance do not come with a warning label. We know much less about when and how love, romance, and sex become an addiction than we know about eating disorders and alcohol and other drug abuse in any age group. By now, however, you know how and why love, romance, and sex can go awry and can recognize some of the warning signs that these wonderful experiences are being used to fix our brokenness.

Now, let's move on and talk about the upside of love, romance, and sex. We will look at signs of healthy belonging, then describe a path from addiction to love, and conclude with self-help tools to assist you on your journey.

III

Hope for Tomorrow

Healthy Belonging

Love one another, but make not a bond of love:
Let it rather be a moving sea between the shores of your
souls.
Fill each other's cup but drink not from one cup.
Give one another of your bread but eat not from the same
loaf.
Sing and dance together and be joyous, but let each one of
you be alone,
Even as the strings of a lute are alone though they quiver
with the same music.
Give your hearts, but not into each other's keeping.
For only the hand of Life can contain your hearts.
And stand together yet not too near together:
For the pillars of the temple stand apart,
And the oak tree and the cypress grow not in each other's
shadow.

KAHLIL GIBRAN, The Prophet

Our Need for Others

If you recognize symptoms of addictive love or unhealthy dependency in yourself or your relationship, you aren't alone. In our struggle to end our sense of isolation, pain, and irrelevancy, we often find ourselves snared in a web of needfulness.

We do need other people. Recall that we have three biological drives—

lust, attraction, and attachment—that ensure it. We need to experience and share love in order to bloom to our fullest. As Erich Fromm said, "The affirmation of one's own life, happiness, growth, freedom, is rooted in one's capacity to love—in care, respect, responsibility, and knowledge."[1] We turn now from a diagnosis of the ills that can plague a relationship to focus on the signs of healthy love.

In our evolution as human beings, there is a developing spiritual awareness that we are linked with other people in a very profound way. Each individual's uniqueness contributes to the greater whole of humanity.

If we think of ourselves as individual energy systems, we realize we can choose to inhibit our energy or use it in either destructive or constructive ways. Even love can be a form of energy that we suppress or exercise. Scientists have discovered the atom and its component parts. They now strive to categorize the substance that causes the particles of the atom to adhere together. Some teachers of physics suggest that love is also a tangible force, a power. This concept views love as a power as real as electricity, a divine mortar that cements the universe together—an electromagnetic force that draws the particles of the atoms together and takes form. It makes sense to know more about how we love—whether it is immature love aimed at ego enhancement and need fulfillment, or a mature love that has evolved over time.

To "be in love" means to "stand in the middle of love" and have the courage to put love into all of our relationships. A love relationship is not a neat little package. It is alive. It needs to be fed, protected, and educated. That means we need to learn how to enter a relationship, how to be in a relationship, and how to let go of a relationship.

We can learn what a loving relationship looks like and develop skills to help form and maintain such a relationship.

Twenty Signs of Healthy Belonging

The signs of a healthy love relationship are the opposites of love, romance, and sex addiction. Let's take a look at some of them. A relationship that exhibits healthy belonging

1. allows for oneness and separateness
2. has healthy boundaries
3. creates a feeling of safety
4. brings out the best qualities in ourselves and others
5. accepts endings
6. is open to change
7. is vital and alive
8. encourages true intimacy
9. is not afraid to show feelings
10. gives from the heart
11. accepts differences and limitations
12. encourages self-sufficiency and self-esteem
13. knows what love is
14. accepts and respects commitment
15. has a bottom line
16. has a high level of trust
17. experiences healthy sexuality
18. has a realistic view of romance
19. cares with detachment
20. affirms equality and personal power of self and other

Allows for Oneness and Separateness

Although mature lovers may describe their closeness as oneness, they also have a clear sense of being separate individuals. That is, *both oneness and separateness are experienced, and they are not contradictory.* This allows for a state of euphoria denied to addictive lovers, who are obsessed with the relationship at the expense of the self.

In addictive love, we feel we are being consumed, while healthy love allows for individuality. A healthy relationship allows each person to change and grow in separate ways without one feeling threatened. Such freedom is possible because of the respect and trust in a partner. Individual thoughts and feelings are accepted, not suppressed. Body and mind can remain relaxed when differences and conflicts arise because differences are acceptable and resolution of conflicts is considered a part of normal, everyday life. A person doesn't feel he has to take care of the other's feelings, and he is self-directed enough not to panic when the loved one is mentally preoccupied elsewhere.

Has Healthy Boundaries

Healthy boundaries are necessary to experience oneness and separateness. Think of a healthy boundary as anything that distinguishes you from someone else, in thoughts, words, feelings, and actions. So often, a client will come in and say, "I do not know who I am anymore," or "I have to get back to myself." One client said, "I am learning to be me and have a relationship. That way I can find out who I *am* in a relationship versus who I *should be* in a relationship."

Healthy boundary skills include the following:

- owning and protecting the child within you
- stepping aside from a situation and observing it before acting
- knowing what you want and need and expressing it
- taking the time you need to react to others' perceptions and not swallowing whole
- knowing your limits and stating them
- thinking about what people are asking of you and being free to say no
- saying so if you feel invaded
- not personalizing others' criticisms of you
- trusting your intuition
- developing the uniqueness that distinguishes you from others

Creates a Feeling of Safety

An important sign of a healthy relationship, whether with a friend or a romantic partner, is feeling safe in it—safe to be you, safe to be honest, safe to ask for what you need, and safe to disagree. When we feel safe, our hearts and bodies are relaxed and open. When feeling safe, we experience a sense of warmth, zest, and desire to reach out to and be with another person. Feeling safe is a prerequisite to trusting someone, and trust is the foundation of a healthy relationship.

Here are five characteristics that tell us someone is safe to trust.

1. *Acceptance (unconditional positive regard):* "I may not agree with you or like how you do or say things, but my caring for you is unwavering."
2. *Openness:* "I will take risks with you and respectfully share who I am, what I feel, what I think, and what I do."
3. *Reliability:* "You can count on my being there and my support for you will be strong."
4. *Congruence:* "I will work to make my words and actions match."
5. *Integrity:* "I will honor my word to you. If I fail you, or me, I will own it and make my apology."

When one's thoughts and actions do not match, acknowledging the inconsistency can make them congruent. For example, saying, "I love you, but I have problems expressing love," puts a person into congruence.

The following story speaks to how a feeling of safety is destroyed and how it was restored by living the qualities necessary to trust.

✨ Cynthia's Story Again ✨

"When John first told me about his sexual addiction, I fell apart. Suffice it to say that I got so low I considered taking my own life. I had to ask myself if I loved him. I had to ask myself if I was willing to work on myself. Then I had to ask if I was willing to allow the relationship some time. The answer to all three was yes.

"Although initially my joy and passion for the relationship were shaken—not to mention my commitment to it—I knew the importance of respect and openness. I had said I loved John without conditions, and this was to be the test. And I knew that to trust again, our words and behaviors had to match. I was wise enough to know I could not restore trust alone.

"We agreed to be brutally honest with each other, as scary as it was. We identified why we stayed in denial for years, and we saw how *our* dishonesty blew up in our faces. Listening to each other's pain and story was, oddly enough, creating a feeling of safety.

"More than a year has passed since the unraveling of his life and mine. As we slowly crawl over the addiction hurdle, I am able to separate John from his behavior most of the time. Although this doesn't excuse his acting out during our marriage, I can still treat him with the respect and love of a committed relationship. And this to me seems to be what true love is about—loving no matter what if both are willing to grow from a broken promise."

Brings Out the Best Qualities in Ourselves and Others

This is a rather subtle, but very visible and wonderful, aspect of mature love. In fact, it invites us to a higher quality of life, for it urges from our depths the highest human qualities: respect, patience, self-discipline, commitment, cooperation, generosity, and humility. One advantage of feeling the pleasure chemicals in a new love relationship is that it seems to bring out the best in us. We are more fun, talkative, engaging, romantic, considerate, and giving. We listen to what others have to say, we apologize when we hurt someone, and we are generally nicer.

In other words, if you feel special, serene, and good about yourself when around the object of your affections, and these feelings are there more often than not, this is a healthy relationship. We all have our bad days and say and do things we later regret, but if the relationship is safe and supportive, we do bounce back, make our amends, and get on with life. The better our self-esteem, the easier it is to own our shortcomings and not project them onto others. The challenge is to remember what you were like when you were newly in the relationship and that these are *your* qualities to develop even after the high begins to wane.

Accepts Endings

The death of a relationship is painful, but mature people have enough respect for themselves—and sometimes their partners—to cope when love is over. Mature people know how to let go of unsalvageable relationships, just as they are able to survive crises in healthy ones. Even in their grief, they do not doubt they will love again someday. We can survive pain, though there's no denying its power over us.

I've witnessed strong people break down and cry when they are sexually betrayed by a lover, even when they may themselves have cheated on their partners. Upon learning that his wife was having an affair, one man said to me: "I have never felt so much pain in all my life. I honestly don't know if I can live through it. The funny thing is, I never thought about love before all this happened. She was just there, being my wife and helper, raising the kids. God, I feel terrible. I never, ever want to go through this again."

The tragedy in his last sentence is that he was programming himself to never again be open to love. In order not to lose such vital openness, a wounded lover must transcend the natural tendency to react with anger, fear, jealousy, and panic. We have the power to surmount pain and grief, and to once again forgive and love.

It sounds difficult, and it is. It takes one's spiritual side to overcome the strong, self-destructive rule of pain and anger. In time, mature people are able to accept reality—even when it hurts—and move on to the next chapter in their lives.

The following story reveals an important fact: *Being single is sacred, too.* Often, a person will remain in an intensely destructive relationship to avoid the pain of ending or the fear of failure. Though we have a responsibility to honor commitments and do what we can do to heal our half of the relationship, we must not be shamed into staying in relationships at all costs. *We must learn to differentiate when a person leaves or stays in a relationship for the right reasons from when a person leaves or stays for the wrong reasons.* There is a difference. A healthy person knows when enough is enough, when it is time to let go.

❧ *Charlie's Story* ❧

"After ten years of marriage, I found out my wife was having an affair. I was too weak to confront her about it. Whenever I brought up our relationship problems, she responded with stares filled with cold rage, from which I turned away. I went into a deep depression. I dragged her along to a marriage therapist, and though I tried to follow his behavioral prescriptions, I kept getting more depressed. Then came the day on which I decided to end my life. I was half an hour from carrying it out when something moved inside me; for the first time, I looked deep into my soul and found depths and strength there I'd had no idea existed. The depression slid away. I sought out her lover, confronted him, and threatened to ruin his career publicly if he didn't get out of our lives. He got out.

"Yet my marriage didn't improve. My wife's rage kept escalating as she was unable to control me. She began demanding that I take her on extravagant vacations that we couldn't afford. She found more and more faults to blame me for. Then something happened that broke my passivity. I had a vivid dream of being tied down while she castrated me. The dream woke me up!

"I quietly began making arrangements to stay with friends. Then I confronted her, telling her my soul was dying in this relationship and I would be leaving for a few weeks to find out whether I wanted to come back. Within ten days she filed for divorce.

"So at age fifty-eight, I am in divorce proceedings, financially impoverished, but more at peace than I ever remember being. I am surrounded by caring, supportive friends, and each day is new and beautiful."

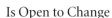

Is Open to Change

Life is a series of changes, yet many of us cling to familiar people and things, disregarding our inner desire to grow as individuals and in our relationships. Openness to change can be risky—it can even lead to breakups—but without it, a relationship will lose its vibrancy.

Often, one partner continues on a growth spiral while the other clings stubbornly to the familiar and seemingly safe. That may mean trouble.

⁓ *Grant and Barbara's Story* ⁓

Grant and Barbara met and fell in love in college. They were alive with the excitement of discovering and sharing new ideas and experiences. After they married, their lives slowly began to change—and then, suddenly, everything came to a standstill. Grant worked outside the home; Barbara was a homemaker. Their upper-middle-class lifestyle, so different from their college ideals, featured a hectic social life and a quest for material possessions. Grant embraced his role as provider, loyal company man, and consumer. Barbara acted as a faithful companion and supporter of her husband's career.

They had been married for about twelve years when boredom and restlessness began to drive a wedge between them. Barbara, approaching middle age, entered graduate school and once again began to be moved by new ideas and experiences. She was eager to share it all with Grant, but to her bewilderment, he resisted her and belittled her schoolwork. Frightened, Barbara ceased talking to him about her experiences. Meanwhile, Grant had extramarital affairs and began to drink too much. It was clear they had drifted apart. Their relationship was devoid of warmth and excitement. At that point, recognizing that their marriage was in peril, they sought counseling.

At first, Grant and Barbara saw the problem as one of communication, but they found it was much more profound. Because they had neglected individual growth in favor of intense social involvement and competition for business and status, their spiritual sides had stagnated. They suffered from the strong but vague sense that something was missing. Through counseling, Grant and Barbara learned that without openness to change and exploration, a relationship is like a body that is never exercised—it loses flexibility and power; it weakens and may even die.

In *The Bridge Across Forever,* Richard Bach wrote: "Boredom between two people . . . doesn't come from being together physically. It comes from being apart mentally and spiritually."[2]

Is Vital and Alive

There is a delicate balance between our need for stability and our need for adventure. We want, even crave, the feeling of being "home," feeling anchored in our relationships. As we have learned, the biological drive to attach to someone is wired into our brains. We seek familiarity, a sense of place not unlike what we needed as a child. On the other hand, we also long for the freedom to move and to explore. Healthy belonging is always a combination of the drive for bonding and the drive for adventure.[3]

Not only do we as individuals need to experience vitality, passion, and excitement, but a relationship needs these, too. Our bodies as well as our psyches want some of the feel-good chemicals we had at the beginning of a relationship. As you give up the melodrama, heated arguments, and dramatic sexual encounters found in addictive love, you will need to replace them with something else. And, how we live is creating memories in our partners' brain circuitry, too. To quote Daniel Amen, M.D., "If you want to be a positive force in your partner's brain, it is important to plant the seeds of excitement, happiness, novelty, and joy rather than boredom, anger, or insecurity."[4] Well said.

Tips for keeping a relationship vital include the following:

- Balance commitment with spontaneity.
- Create romance.
- Do something completely unexpected.
- Do something amazingly thoughtful.
- Revisit and imprint memorable moments.
- Have an adventure.
- Never become boring.

Encourages True Intimacy

The great gift of a healthy love relationship is the experience of emotional intimacy. Recall Dr. Eric Berne's definition: Intimacy is a "profound exchange of thoughts, feelings, and actions in the here and now." It can be verbal or nonverbal. It invites the expression of affection and positive feelings. Intimate relationships give us stability and remind us of our need of others. A validation that a relationship is blooming is the exchange of deep connection that fulfills the drive for bonding. While physical, sexual, and romantic intimacy contributes greatly to a love relationship, if emotional bonding is not there, one feels emptiness and a longing to connect, and sometimes an actual ache in the heart.

A bond is a natural result of any moment of real intimacy. It is the emotional fondness that survives romance and precedes sexual intimacy.

Because mature lovers are not shackled by childhood fears and inhibitions, their relationships feature true, intense intimacy. Fear of love's risks inhibits intimacy; trust and the willingness to take risks invite it. True love seems contradictory: Those who are self-contained and independent are better able to deeply, tenderly love another. Because their love is not obsessive or dependent, they are free to be interdependent, complementing their partners. That is, those who are free as individuals also are free to be intimately close in love and are willing to be known. In healthy belonging, partners work to create an atmosphere of trust, respect, and safety that sets the stage for emotional intimacy. Relationships that permit us to be who we are nourish closeness and allow us to grow from conflict. Free to be imperfect, we can take risks that, paradoxically, encourage perfection. We are then more likely to stay in our relationships and learn the lessons that love relationships can teach us.

ℵ *Dawn and Dale's Story* ℵ

"My husband and I are two accomplished, articulate adults. In our respective work worlds, we are both recognized as exceptional communicators, readily able to build consensus among diverse groups. Not so at home. The inability to communicate on an intimate level created distance and loneliness for me and, I think, him. That got us to therapy, where we realized we had to learn more than communication skills; we also had to learn to be comfortable with emotional intimacy. That meant looking at what in our backgrounds prevented it. It's unfamiliar and uncomfortable for me to feel so clumsy, and sometimes even incompetent, as we work to more deeply communicate with each other. In order to more openly talk with each other, we first had to more honestly listen to and process what our own body, mind, and spirit were telling us.

"We expected learning the language of emotional intimacy would stretch us. We'd need to develop new levels of candor, compassion, vulnerability, and trust. We'd need to become more intentional in our communication, to actually make time for it; we'd need to be more active and reflective listeners.

"We're certainly stumbling as we venture into previously avoided topics and emotions. Only by trial and error are we discovering which words and actions have different meanings and triggered responses for each of us. We're creating our own verbal shorthand, so simple phrases can relay more complex messages without the long-winded explanations initially needed to make them understood. We're learning to acknowledge what we do gain from our still-awkward and often tear-inducing conversations. Most important, we're exploring ways to emerge from emotionally intense discussions in ways that keep us connected and confident about our shared future."

Is Not Afraid to Show Feelings

Recently, a client asked why in the world he should get in touch with his feelings. The answer I gave him was that without ownership of his feelings, there would be no emotional honesty, and without emotional honesty, there would be no emotional intimacy. He was, like so many are, too afraid to show emotions, too afraid to discuss emotions, and too shut down because of earlier trauma to know what he was feeling.

Feelings can be tricky. And not all feelings are legitimate. There are three types of feelings:

1. *Reactive*—a feeling that makes sense for a given situation. We feel it, figure out an action plan or feel the feeling, and let go. We are not attached to the feeling. For example, we feel sad when a relationship ends.

2. *Rubber-band*—a feeling that is out of proportion to what is happening, and we do not understand why. It is related to some feeling-loaded event in the past that we stuffed inside and forgot about. In relationships, rubber-band feelings are called *triggers* or emotional soft spots. We feel scared when we meet someone who reminds us of the person who sexually abused us in the past, for example.

3. *Racket*—our favorite bad feeling. When a reactive feeling such as sadness was disapproved of, we found a substitute feeling that was acceptable to those around us, such as self-righteous anger, shame, inadequacy, loneliness, anxiety, and even false happiness. A core belief system, such as "I am bad," keeps the racket alive.[5]

In a healthy relationship, we have the ability to self-regulate our moods, control our impulses, delay gratification, persist despite frustration, motivate ourselves, and have empathy for others. Reflect back to the adult problem-solving diagram in chapter 2. We have the ability to read our feelings, distinguish between the three categories of feelings, think about our feelings, and act on them. We feel sad, we think about why we are sad, we acknowledge the want or need, we give it a voice and let go. If the need or want is met, we feel relief. If not, we grieve the loss and get on with life. Asking directly for what we need or telling someone what we feel is one of the biggest challenges I have encountered as a therapist working with couples.[6]

Gives from the Heart

When we give from the heart, we experience giving and receiving similarly. Pleasure obtained in giving to the one we love is as intense as that gained in receiving from him or her. In healthy love relationships, we give more easily and without expectations.

❧ *Betsy's Story* ❧

Anger and frustration often mark a turning point for a giver who gives to get. At this point, a giver may quit such egocentric giving in frustration and begin to be more honest with a partner. A client's husband once called me and said, "Geez, I don't know about this therapy. My wife, Betsy, is driving me up a wall. She's angry all the time and refuses to do a thing for me." I said, "It's only a phase, and someday you'll understand."

Weeks later, he called me to say, "You were right. She's back to her old self." In truth, the woman, who had been "giving to get," wasn't back to her old self; she was very different. She was learning to give to her husband, to do things that pleased him, not because she expected anything in return, but because she truly loved him and was experiencing the joy of giving for its own sake. Betsy's anger and frustration over the failure of giving to get had been a natural phase—one in which some relationships flounder. She had to learn to say no before she could say yes freely. Giving from our hearts, on the other hand, is a profound experience that encourages us to expand our giving to others.

A person has reached emotional maturity when he knows what it means to give with a pure and unselfish heart. If you feel relaxed, energized, alert, and free when you give to others, you are experiencing true giving. Even if someone does not accept the giving, you know you have done your part. And you are not afraid to give more than you receive.

Accepts Differences and Limitations

Though it may sound simple enough, one of the most difficult parts of love is learning to accept ourselves and others as we and they are. This does not assume that one partner likes everything about himself or herself or the other. Nor does it mean unacceptable and hurtful behaviors go unattended. It is always important to confront any abuse that occurs in a relationship. Acceptance does mean that we respect the unique personality traits and another person's view of the world. In mature love, we attempt to walk in the other's shoes to see what it is like in their reality. Each person in a relationship has a unique story and a unique personality, and therefore we cannot all view life the same way.

The best romances are based on realism. In mature love, we adjust our beliefs to what is real, rather than try to twist reality to fit what we want a person or the relationship to be. Life and relationships are filled with choices. The relationships that fail are those in which one person is unwilling to accept the other's limitations or worldview. Pushing, pulling, and power struggles then override joy and love. So often the very thing that drew us into a relationship at the beginning becomes an aggravation. It is important to remember why these differences were attractive and not lose sight of that. We can only invite a person to change, not coerce them. And even then we must leave the challenge to change up to them. Healthy love does so.

Encourages Self-Sufficiency and Self-Esteem

Fromm writes: "The most important step is to learn to be alone with oneself without reading, listening to the radio, smoking, or drinking . . . This ability is precisely a condition for the ability to love."[7] Mature love occurs when we realize we are substantial alone, that we no longer need as we needed in infancy and childhood, that we have qualities within us that make us complete. In a healthy relationship, both individuals have a sense of self-esteem and well-being. They trust themselves and others; they love themselves unconditionally without guilt.

A healthy relationship nourishes good self-esteem in each person. Lovers celebrate the good fortunes, the successes, and the talents of the other. They compliment and encourage each other, and there is no place for inflated egos. I once heard *humility* defined as a gentle acceptance of oneself. Mature lovers seem to express this quiet self-confidence alone and with each other.

While we can affirm each other's worth and goodness, we cannot give each other the self-esteem we lack. Others may put you on a pedestal, and you may be tempted to stay there and enjoy the view. This is a very dangerous place, for what goes up eventually comes down.

Knows What Love Is

In mature love relationships, we no longer "crave" unconditional love from our partners. We no longer need it from others because *we are* unconditional love. We understand that unconditional love is a state of being that comes from within us—not the other way around. The paradox is that when we stop searching for or holding back our unconditional love, we are often surprised to find someone loving us just that way. Perhaps it is because when we experience ourselves as unconditional love, we give the safety that invites others to more openly share their love with us.

ℐ❧ *Steve and Alisa's Story* ℐ❧

"What is love?" I asked my clients Steve and Alisa. The question took them by surprise.

Each paused. Steve answered first. "I do not know if I can describe it. I know when I am in it. The way it shows up in our relationship is as a feeling of closeness, even in quiet times. It is a meeting of the minds, a strong connection, and a friendship. There is respect. Mostly, though, it is the safe feeling I have to be myself when I am with Alisa."

Alisa went next: "Love is much bigger than our relationship. I agree with Steve. I have never felt as safe as I have in this relationship. I know I feel scared of getting hurt at times, but we talk a lot. What I have learned from the awful stuff in my past is that relationships are not the problem; they are the places where problems show up. Likewise, they are not love, but a place we can experience it or not."

Accepts and Respects Commitment

If I do my thing, and you do your thing
And we don't live up to each other's expectations
We might live, but the world will not survive.
You are you, and I am I together, not by chance
Joining hands, we will find each other beautiful
If not, we can't be helped.

CLAUDE STEINER

In addictive love, commitment often is experienced as a "loss of self." In mature love, the opposite is true; self-esteem is enhanced. We experience commitment as expanding ourselves. We go beyond narcissistic self-gratification to share with, give to, and sacrifice for our beloved ones. Commitment accepts, without resistance, the importance and value of the other person in one's life. This is unlike addictive love, which uses commitment as an excuse for hurtful behaviors, e.g., "I have a right to sex—you are my wife." There is a genuine concern for and commitment to the well-being of the other person. We consider how our actions will affect our relationships. We recognize that autonomy is not always doing "what I want when I want it," but rather taking responsibility for our lives in ways least hurtful to ourselves and others. Autonomy includes boundaries and limits, and mature lovers mutually define the boundaries of their relationship to enhance their commitment. Our commitment expresses our deepest values and transcends our fears.

At the base of many relationship problems is a person's having suffered a betrayal in earlier commitments. Such betrayals can be healed with a new experience of commitment. The commitment is not made to a person, nor is it focused on outcomes, and it makes no guarantees. Rather, it says, "I am committed to the process of being with you and becoming the best me I can be. I will do my part to maintain the connection even as the form of our relationship changes." As we commit to the changing process of love, we are more likely to be there for another.

Has a Bottom Line

The ordinary bumps and scrapes, the growing pains of a relationship, are inevitable. We try to do it right, and we make mistakes. We flounder. We try to put together a hundred-piece relationship puzzle with only a handful of the relationship puzzle pieces. Most of us will experience some pain in love relationships. The questions then are: "How much should I put up with before I draw the line? When does a relationship have more disease than health?" The answers lie in *progression*. A healthy relationship is green and growing; an unhealthy or addictive one is not. Does being emotionally honest result in hurtful or attacking behaviors? Is emotional hurt followed by mental, physical, or sexual injuries? When we speak up in an unhealthy relationship, the other person will try to shut us up, calm us down, be defensive, try to fix us, condescend, judge, analyze, attack, push us away, cry, or leave. Healthy relationships stay with the discomfort, state a bottom line, and try to work through the problem without too much damage.

Mature love operates with care, concern, *and* tough love. An example of a bottom line is this statement: "I want to stay in relationship with you, and what is essential for me to stay is that you commit to getting treatment for your sexual addiction. I know that, as an addict, you cannot promise to never act out again, but I need to know you are committed to the process." It is important that our bottom lines be realistic and not a setup for failure to the relationship.

Has a High Level of Trust

An important indication of true love is the ability to trust one's memory of the absent lover so we can accept and enjoy our time alone.

Although we may want to be with our romantic lovers or partners, we are confident they eventually will return. In the meantime, memories of good feelings are enough to satisfy us. Separation anxiety and obsessing about the one we love are replaced with a strong connection with self and life. We like our own company and know how to fill the time and space. And we know the difference between self-intimacy and isolation.

As one lover said to another: "How I feel about you in our separate times is so different from what I've known before. I want to be with you, I think about you, I feel your presence, and I eagerly look forward to our time together. I trust our bond, and the anxiety and longing are gone. Perhaps it is because you trust our absence, too."

I do not wish to sound naïve. Because of the many betrayals of trust we have likely experienced in love relationships, most of us work very hard to heal and open ourselves to trust once again. This is perhaps the greatest challenge love offers.

Experiences Healthy Sexuality

We are sexual beings. Being sexual is a good thing. Yet sex is often confused with nurturing, sensuality, and sexuality. To remind you, sex is biological. It is a function of the lower brain. Sexuality is about growing into a whole human and preparing to share sexuality with another in good and exciting ways. It is using all three brains—instinctive, emotional, and rational.

Healthy sexuality is about a person's ability to value their body and sexuality, not use or abuse it. I remember telling my children that, as they were entering their adult bodies, they would have new sensations and feelings that could be both frightening and exciting. These were sexual feelings and a very special gift of life. It was important to accept, protect, and treat the gift of sexuality respectfully as they explored relationships.

For many, because of being abused sexually, being taught that sex is bad, or other cross-wiring, there is a tendency to spend energy on either denying sexual urges or rebelling and acting on them. When sex is a part of the relationship, it is by mutual desire, has agreement to the limits and boundaries, and is without the slightest hint of manipulation or commitment testing. When newly in love, we generally respond with lustful feelings first, romantic sensuality second, and then move to bonding. When there are problems in a sexual relationship or if there has been a sexual betrayal, the process is reversed. Self-healing precedes bonding, bonding precedes sensuality, and sensuality precedes being sexually intimate. Many want to do it in reverse order and create more problems. Healthy sexuality

- accepts when partners want differing amounts and kinds of sex
- does not personalize a no
- does not compare self to what is presented in the media
- knows that sex is about bonding two people into a loving couple
- understands that sex comes from inside two people
- does not use sex to fix an urgency, low self-esteem, or loneliness
- does not judge performance
- understands that many people are sexually cross-wired because of distorted information and sexual trauma
- takes responsibility for whatever sexual experience is brought into the relationship without shame and is willing to learn and grow

❧ Ward's Story ❧

"Before I had a chance to discover sex as an appropriate expression of desire, care, and connection, through less-than-ideal circumstances I experienced it as a way to distract, manipulate, and control.

"Sex became one of many dysfunctional ways I engaged in pursuit of immediate gratification at any cost. A moment of relief from the confusion and discomfort of life on life's terms was all I seemed able to attain or sustain. Having no constructive relationship to its use, sex has always magnified the challenges for any attempt at an intimate union. It is only now as I enter my fifties (some twenty years into Twelve Step recovery) that I have managed to sit still long enough and go inside deep enough to right the course. I am successfully reclaiming the composure necessary for healthy sexual intimacy—first and foremost with myself. Perhaps now even others may have a shot as well. It was always in there, I just had to go back and get it."

Has a Realistic View of Romance

Romantic love has an important place in our lives. It is a courtship time and includes flirtation, a romantic glow, and profound intimacy. It is a time to learn about the passion *and* safety of our senses—touch, sight, sound, smell, taste, movement—and sharing them. In healthy love, we are willing to let the fires of romance glow without attempting to hang on or use them as a fix. We also let them smolder because we know keeping that high is unrealistic, remembering the chemical high must give way to something better. It is only after the high wanes that the thinking brain is able to turn on and help assess the relationship's real merits.

In a mature love relationship, a lover transitions from a romantic high to a more sane friendship without being afraid that the relationship is ending. While the relationship may end, it was not given up so that one partner may chase another high, but for reasons that make sense. Red flags that may have been ignored when experiencing the newness of a relationship become more evident and are discussed or taken as a sign to move on and explore another relationship. It is not uncommon to hear, "What in the world did I see in that person?"

In healthy bonding, the partners create romance in their lives to keep passionate living and loving alive. Like fire carriers in the Native American tradition, partners must keep the coals burning, knowing that once the coals are out, it is difficult to start a fire. How do we keep the levels of dopamine going? In addition to what I said about keeping a relationship vital, there are other things that work as well:

- Variety, variety, variety—excitement triggers arousal.
- Be mysterious—uncertainty triggers elevated dopamine.
- Create a romantic mood—it triggers old good-feeling memories.

- Pleasure the senses via touch, taste, smell, sound.
- Have good sex—it produces a flood of chemicals.
- Laugh and play—it produces feel-good chemicals and brings out the child in us.
- Be exciting and keep your own chemicals going.
- Do novel things—adrenaline makes the heart grow fonder.
- Have a good, fair argument and get rid of grievances—anger produces arousal chemicals and resolve produces bonding chemicals.
- Know what invites romantic feelings in your partner.
- Be a sensual person—a relaxed body invites closeness.
- Have a lot of good emotional intimacy—it produces bonding chemicals.

Love is a canvas furnished by Nature and embroidered by the imagination.

VOLTAIRE

Cares with Detachment

Maturity brings the knowledge that we can care, listen, and respond to others' feelings, but we cannot "fix" or remove all ill feelings in others. Therefore, a sense of caring detachment is a healthy sign in a relationship. The partners say, "I care what you feel and I'm here for you," but not "Let me feel your pain for you," or "Let me help you feel better." Caring detachment is not indifference. You remain present to a person's pain, you are attentive, you let the person know you hear or support her, and you do not feel guilt or discomfort when you cannot do more. And you never push the other person to stop feeling bad in order to make yourself comfortable, because the message translates into "Don't have feelings or needs," and the pain only gets bigger. Sometimes this is difficult to do when you have caused the pain and disappointment or violated the trust.

Affirms Equality and Personal Power of Self and Other

In mature love, lovers recognize each other as equals; they are not caught up in psychological games and one-upmanship. Healthy competition allows each one to grow without attempting to exert power over the other. And, confrontation stops pain; it does not inflict it. When two people are content and free as individuals, they are much more likely to have a content and free love relationship. No longer lost in denial, they acknowledge the draw of power plays and consciously work toward power sharing. Projecting shortcomings onto others is replaced with giving permission to be authentic and passionate about life. Personalizing others' behaviors is replaced with setting clear boundaries that offer protection and frame individuality.

Power is viewed, then, not as a measurable commodity, but as an unending source of life energy. It is our personal vitality, vigor, passion, and intensity that command a life-changing presence. It is a statement: "I am here with you as an emotional and spiritual equal." Unlike power plays that leave us with an ugly feeling, power sharing "enlightens" us. We feel lighter. We are more lighthearted! We are easier to be around. Relationships are nourished. Love merges with power as we penetrate the illusion of disparity and seek healing.

Power Sharing

The transition from childish omnipotence to power sharing seems to be an endless struggle. Yet, with practice, sharing in ways that empower us and affirm the power of others will become more natural. Here is a list of power-sharing behaviors that support healthy love:

- being free to state beliefs, values, and thoughts, and to be heard and respected
- being free to express needs, wants, and feelings, and to ask for support and love
- being free from ego-driven expectations and outcomes
- participating cooperatively to empower people in a positive way

- celebrating another's intelligence, knowledge, and other gifts; letting go of jealousy for what another has
- being willing to come out from our deepest selves and interact intimately with others, to give and receive
- expressing personal power in a steady and reliable way—being trustworthy and following through on promises
- giving of oneself in an emotionally supportive way without overnurturing—just being there is enough
- compromising—agreeing that we are emotional equals and each can share taking the lead
- mutual problem solving and decision making—examining together how to do things more effectively
- owning and sharing mistakes guilt-free; making amends to ourselves and others
- giving direct, clear answers to questions and requests
- taking actions that support equality and win-win positions—no one-up or one-down situations
- accepting others where they are—respecting another person's being while we confront improper behaviors
- treating others with respect and sensitivity, especially when they are vulnerable
- having a solid sense of identity and acknowledging the need to share ourselves with others
- listening, discussing, suggesting, and inviting, rather than telling, bribing, or threatening
- expressing anger and disappointment without the expectation of change—letting go
- stopping verbal, emotional, and physical abuse in potent and respectful ways
- being assertive and not passive or aggressive
- sharing in making decisions and living with the outcomes
- being willing to yield or wait, and accepting that we will not always get what we want
- stating positions clearly, and then respectfully letting go while trusting that the outcome will be positive

In conclusion, mature lovers welcome the need to love and risk vulnerability. They have faced their aloneness and know the joys of sharing. They know they no longer need people to survive as they once did in childhood, that life is harsh at times, unfair at times, and yet continues to be good.

You have known the experience of love. Each time you re-experience it, tell yourself, "This is love, this is real, and I will experience it over and over again."

> *I Am! And You Are! And Love;*
> *Is All: That Matters!*

RICHARD BACH, The Bridge Across Forever

From Addiction to Love

The highest expression of civilization is not its art but the supreme tenderness that people are strong enough to feel and show toward one another.

NORMAN COUSINS, Human Options

"What is REAL?" asked the Rabbit one day, when they were lying side by side near the nursery fender, before Nana came to tidy the room. "Does it mean having things that buzz inside you and a stick-out handle?"

"Real isn't how you are made," said the Skin Horse. "It's a thing that happens to you. When a child loves you for a long, long time, not just to play with, but REALLY loves you, then you become Real."

"Does it hurt?" asked the Rabbit.

"Sometimes," said the Skin Horse, for he was always truthful. "When you are Real you don't mind being hurt."

"Does it happen all at once, like being wound up," he asked, "or bit by bit?"

"It doesn't happen all at once," said the Skin Horse. "You become. It takes a long time. That's why it doesn't often happen to people who break easily, or have sharp edges, or who have to be carefully kept. Generally, by the time you are Real, most of your hair has been loved off, and your eyes drop out and you get

loose in the joints and very shabby. But these things don't matter at all, because once you are Real you can't be ugly, except to people who don't understand."

"I suppose you are Real?" said the Rabbit. And then he wished he had not said it, for he thought the Skin Horse might be sensitive. But the Skin Horse only smiled.

"The Boy's Uncle made me Real," he said. "That was a great many years ago; but once you are Real you can't become unreal again. It lasts for always."

MARGERY WILLIAMS, The Velveteen Rabbit

Viktor Frankl developed a school of existential psychiatry after suffering harrowing experiences as a prisoner in Auschwitz during World War II. He has written of a revelation he had during his darkest days in the concentration camp: "I saw the truth as it is set into song by so many poets, proclaimed as the final wisdom by so many thinkers. The truth that love is the ultimate and highest goal to which man can aspire. The salvation of man is through love and in love. I understand how a man who has nothing left in this world still may know bliss . . . in the contemplation of his beloved . . . Love goes very far beyond the physical person of the beloved. It finds its deepest meaning in his spiritual being, his inner self."[1]

Obsession with another person is not love; attachment to romance or sex is not love; nor is true love anything like addiction. Love and addiction are separate entities that can resemble and be mistaken for each other. Our challenge is to move from addictive love to healthy belonging, for there we experience most profoundly the meaningful inner self Frankl described.

The Way Out

What can you do if you discover you are in an addictive relationship or becoming attached to the high of romance or sex?

First, remember that most relationships have addictive elements or unhealthy dependency. None of us had all of our needs met in childhood. Our parents, being human, failed us at times. Their failures become our weaknesses when we blame them or demand from others what we failed to get. And we likely experienced trauma in one of its forms.

Second, keep in mind that on some level, addictive love is perceived as crucial to survival—thus, it won't easily be given up.

Third, remember the psychological reasons for your addiction are as unique to you as your fingerprints. Only you can discover what purpose they serve; only you can find what fears keep you from letting go. If you are unable to let go of an unhealthy relationship, if you find yourself moving from one romantic relationship to another, or if you are using sex compulsively, it's time to seek outside help.

Fourth, work toward intimacy with yourself. When we know that we are complete by ourselves, we are ready for healthy love relationships. Self-sufficiency and self-knowledge can be the keys to love and freedom.

Fifth, remember that moving from addiction to love is a process. Just as there was a way into dependent behavior, there is a way out. There is hope. In knowing the difference between addictive love and healthy belonging, in understanding that process, you can learn acceptance of yourself and others; thus, your chances of achieving fulfillment in love increase.

Out of Addiction and into Healthy Love: The Process

I experienced the ending of a marriage in 1980. To that date, the relationship had been the most significant one in my life, and ending it was very painful. I never thought it could or would happen to me. In my personal journey afterward and in my journey through therapy with others, a clear process with definable stages in and out of such relationships emerged. We went through consistent stages, and as I began clarifying those phases, change became less painful and more acceptable—even welcome. It became much easier to know if a person was staying in a love relationship for right or wrong reasons, or leaving a love relationship for right or wrong reasons. Knowing the difference became critical to knowing what to do and when to do it. There was a sense of relief in knowing the process and in preparing for a positive outcome. Trusting the process became necessary to successfully complete the process. Whether one was currently in or out of a relationship did not matter. Whether one was addicted to romance or sex did not matter. One could be involved in the process.

My therapy with couples changed. Getting out of addiction and into healthy love was an "inside job." Attempting to change a relationship without altering the individuals' internal beliefs proved futile. Stopping an addiction without healing the underlying trauma led to more frequent relapse. Initial therapy sessions had been settings for power struggles, and I was required to be the judge and referee. This never worked, and I ended up feeling drained—a victim.

I had learned from my own unhealthy dependency that I had drawn certain people into my life and had behaved in predictable ways. I had needed to examine my fear of separateness, my fear of having needs, my fear of closeness. I learned I was only responsible for changing myself. I had brought people and situations into my life that fit who I had been at the time. Although I had found others' behaviors unacceptable at times, I had to wonder what part of me needed this pain, and why. As I changed, I began inviting healthier people and relationships into my life. And though it was not always easy, I let go of those I needed to let go of.

I began working with couples in a more effective way. I saw that who they each were in the relationship made perfect sense. I diffused their power plays by asking them each to journey alone awhile, to discover who they were and how the discord in their relationship made sense to them psychologically. Some were angered by this suggestion and insisted it was the relationship that was in trouble, that it was their partner's acting out that was the issue, or some other problem. Those who risked the inner journey and stayed with the process learned the key to love is inner freedom.

In the model I have described, there are seven stages in moving from addiction to love.

1. denial
2. discomfort

3. confrontation
4. psychological separation
5. resolution of self
6. belonging
7. reaching out

Denial

In this stage, the relationship often seems to be normal. If a romance or sexual addiction is present, its impact is explained away. Perhaps we endured considerable emotional, spiritual, or physical abuse or neglect from a partner, and later denied or rationalized it. We could have a tendency toward dependency with someone who might harm us. In the new relationship, the euphoria of infatuation masks danger signals, but the relationship follows a definite pattern. Giving is often motivated by what others expect or is experienced as losing; fear of true intimacy is dealt with melodramatically, ensuring a level of excitement that substitutes for authentic closeness. Many—perhaps all—of addictive love's signs are present, but they are ignored or denied. *Suppression* is a hallmark of this stage.

Here are some beliefs, expressed in common maxims, which support this stage:

"All couples go through this."
"It's better to be in a bad relationship than none at all."
"I took him (or her) for better or worse."
"That's life."
"Always see the good in people."
"I don't have it so bad."
"I have a right to act out."

Addictive lovers fear the truth about themselves. Sometimes only a lack of information keeps a person or couple in this stage. However, with the right information, one or both partners will begin to move out of this stage.

Sadly, many couples stay locked in this stage, believing this is all there is or the best they can get. Or, if not entrenched in this stage, many couples return to denial when they are faced with the challenges the process of healthy love requires.

Discomfort

In this stage, one or both partners become aware that something is missing, that something is wrong. Inner voices say:

> "This is not enough."
> "Something is not quite right."
> "What's wrong with me? I should be happier."
> "I wonder if she (or he) still loves me? I wonder if I still love him (or her)?"
> "Is this all there is? I feel bored."
> "I feel oppressed; I've got to get out."
> "I don't quite believe her (or him)."

In the first stage, we suppressed problems and tried to adapt to the relationship, but in the second stage, agitation makes such denial impossible. Such *agitation* is caused by blocked energy that needs to be expressed in the intimacy and creativity denied in addictive love. At this point, it's a challenge to identify the problem and to resolve it.

Because in this stage our relationships remain primarily addictive, or we are not ready to own the addiction, most people begin looking outside themselves and their relationships for solutions or comfort; they may turn to alcohol, food, affairs, work, exercise, religion, gambling, or other processes that hold the potential of becoming obsessions. Although such obsessions may provide initial relief, they don't satisfy a person's longing because they become yet another misguided, addictive attempt to develop self-esteem, find meaning in life, or cover the pain we feel but have not yet clarified.

A person may become aware of recurring emotions, behaviors, and frequent unhappy feelings. Generally, one person, feeling fearful and guilty, begins to move out of the addictive relationship. At this stage, the problem has not been defined, so frustration, confusion, depression, and anxiety are common. Often, one or both partners return to the first stage in resignation to relieve themselves of fear and guilt.

Confrontation

Our desire to grow is accepted. Life may have knocked on our door with an event that shakes us up and wakes us up, so we are now willing to see the disease of our unhealthy dependency on love, romance, or sex. That major life event may be a depression, a separation, a book, treatment for an addiction, a brush with death, an illness, a major life change, a caring confrontation by a friend, or the wisdom of experience. Suddenly, problems in the relationship are confronted by one or both individuals. However, in keeping with the relationship's addictive quality, the emphasis tends to be on changing each other to rebalance the relationship. Because one person is threatening to leave, the alarming symptoms escalate. There is more melodrama; accusations, denials, and anger, all of which mask fear or shame, prevail. Both partners try to control the situation, in the form of threats, physical abuse, or overadapting in an effort to placate the other. There may be much literal and figurative pushing and pulling.

At this point, a couple may return to a previous stage, decide to separate or divorce, or seek counseling. If they enter therapy, the partners often want the therapist to change the other partner or address symptoms of trouble in the relationship, such as sexual problems or lack of communication. Mundane psychological how-tos—how to have sex, how to communicate, how to fight—do not work! They miss the point: there is much more going on psychologically that both people need to wake up to than just the surface or behavioral problems in the relationship or a presenting addiction.

Secretly, the individuals may fear they failed or did something wrong; they may suffer from guilt or despair. Suppressing these unpleasant feelings, they often place blame elsewhere and become angry. This stage, then, is characterized by *crisis*. It involves much interaction—in fact, too much interaction—that is so negative it compounds the problem. This is the stage where domestic abuse is likely to occur. Homicide, suicide, violence, illness, and other escalations may also be parts of this stage.

Psychological Separation

If the partners possess enough insight and are committed enough to their relationship, one or both of them move into this stage. If one is single, it is important to experience this stage to ensure healthy love relationships in the future. To be sure, this stage is crucial, time-consuming, and often resisted.

Psychological separation is necessary if people are to move from obsessive dependency into healthy, mature relationships. In this stage, we become willing to let go of our addiction or the expectation that a relationship must fulfill our private fears and needs. We are now willing to begin an inward journey of self-discovery and to confront private myths, illusions, and self-promises that contribute to love, romance, or sex addiction. Through self-discovery or with the help of therapy, we learn to ask and answer questions such as the following:

"Who am I?"
"How did I get where I am today?"
"What private promises did I make to myself when I was younger?"
"What am I afraid of?"
"Why do I fear separation?"
"Why do I fear closeness?"
"What false attempts have I made to alleviate my fears?"
"What do I believe about women? men? love? power?"
"How is my addiction a friend?"

Because psychological separation involves a need to be emotionally detached for a time, the individuals may appear to be egocentric; when in a relationship, they often are unable to feel or express love for the other during this difficult time. *But this is temporary.* Experiencing self-intimacy is important during this period. *Distance,* or *detachment,* is the hallmark of this stage.

Sometimes a physical separation also takes place, although this is not necessary if the individuals give each other the freedom to journey through this stage without terrible tensions. It is easier to accept distance if one realizes one's partner is doing what he or she must in order to develop a capacity for love. Understanding that being distant is a part of the process allows one not to feel guilty.

Until people have a sense of who they are, like who they are, and have healed their wounds and dealt with their fears, they are not psychologically free to love fully. In the meantime, when in a relationship, it is important that a commitment be made to the relationship until one or both partners have the clear understanding of themselves that will allow them to assess the relationship from a new, healthier viewpoint. When one is single, it is wise to complete this stage before entering another relationship. People need to learn to be friends and parents to themselves—a prerequisite to having good relationships with others.

Healthy support systems—friends, family, or support groups—can help affirm self-exploration and change. Because the partners have backed away from each other psychologically during this time, it is a very difficult period. Stress can make it harder, and outside support is needed. In fact, during this time, some people revert to old, familiar ways, because self-exploration can be terrifying. If the partners call on their greatest strengths—compassion, patience, tolerance, acceptance, and caring detachment—they'll make it through.

Resolution of Self

At this stage, individuals have answered the question "Who am I?" Through a long, sometimes difficult process, individuals have gained a sense of self-identity, self-esteem, and the knowledge that "I am enough alone." They know what they need and want, what is important, and what is not. They have uncovered the fears and negating beliefs that contributed to problems in their love relationships, and, for the most part, have healed or changed them. It is important that people allow for the necessary time to *integrate* such large changes into their lives and personalities. I once heard that it takes the body six months to incorporate a change into the nervous system.[2] A compulsive need to get results now must not run interference with the process.

People in this stage develop an appreciation for their talents, interests, creative potential, passions, and pursuits. They find a sense of healthy detachment and an awareness of their capacities for intimacy and love. They are comfortable while alone and feel a sense of inner peace. To others, it may seem as if they have matured and accepted reality. They seem to recognize that life consists of new experiences and lessons that provide many options. Life involves choice, action, and consequences—and that fact is no longer terrifying.

It is not uncommon for resistance to appear with questions to test our sincerity. "Are you sure you want to change?" "How do you know it will be better?" "What if people do not like you anymore?" "I miss the high." Sometimes we resort to old behaviors to answer these questions and feel like we have relapsed. Sometimes a person does relapse.

We go back and forth between the old and the new. It usually does not take long to realize that we cannot go back to the way it was. We are different.

Once an individual has resolved the inner questioning and gained this self-reliance, it is time to examine how the addiction was self-serving and to evaluate his relationship from a new perspective to decide whether it should continue. If a person has already left a relationship or been deserted, she now begins to trust that love is possible in the future. We may even surprise ourselves with a feeling of gratitude for the painful lessons learned. We are ready to forgive the person or addiction we considered our nemesis.

Belonging

If the individuals have made it to this stage, they possess a new freedom and ability to love maturely whether single or partnered. They discover that being in a love relationship is not the only way to belong—they can also be part of families, have friends, and belong to support groups. Belonging comes from inner beliefs that say, "I belong in this life and with meaning"; "I can belong and still be me"; "I can have passion and belong." *Separate and close* characterize this stage.

If couples therapy continues, it now focuses on "we." For the partners are now ready to experience the essence of each other, and there can be a high level of intimacy. Though they see themselves as unique and different from each other, they know that their new closeness allows for individual differences, that the relationship complements and coexists with individual freedom. Giving is spontaneous; there is physical, emotional, and spiritual bonding. Commitment is characterized by a desire not only to give to the other, but also to serve the other without expecting something in return. A new realism allows for faults, failures, and disappointments. There is equality, and power plays diminish. There is a willingness to live with uncertainty and the knowledge that a relapse is always a possibility when there has been an addiction. The three entities of every relationship—"I," "you," and "we"—can now coexist peacefully. It is understood that any relationship is a living process.

Reaching Out

In this stage, people move from focusing on themselves and their relationships to a more *universal giving* and experiencing. Content with themselves and with others, they now have more creative energy, physical stamina, and spiritual strength to help them give and respond. Since they no longer depend on love relationships, sex, or romance to provide most of life's meaning, they are free to seek additional meaning in life. Adversity now provides opportunities to be more, to experience more. A mature love relationship serves as a springboard to expand our energy and our interest in the world. Our primary love relationships are the fueling docks that help launch us into life to do what really matters—share our uniqueness with life. But one need not be with a lover to feel energetic or nourished. Love expands from an exclusive relationship to universal love that reinforces the belief that love does, indeed, make the world go 'round. Imagine what the world might look like if we were all free to share love and power!

Stages one, two, and three include characteristics of addictive love. To end a relationship here without awareness of that truth is addictive in itself, and we will carry the scars of the relationship with us, repeat history, or carry the anger and pain for years. For these reasons, when a sexual addiction is present, couples are asked to commit to the relationship for a year and do stages four and five before considering leaving. When someone has left an unhealthy romantic relationship or been left, he is encouraged to move through the next two stages before entertaining another relationship. Stages four and five reflect independence. They are "I" stages that often seem narcissistic. Here we learn what we were supposed to learn in late adolescence and early adulthood: autonomy, spontaneity, and the capacity for true intimacy. Stages six and seven reflect healthy belonging: interdependency alternating with healthy primary dependency.

Going through these stages is not always smooth. We may be in stage six one day and in stage two the next. As we climb upward, we spend more time in the higher stages. Keep in mind that one person in a relationship can stay in a lower stage as another moves through to stage seven. We can only be where we are ready to be. Those in a higher stage are challenged to be more patient. Couples therapy is a struggle in the first three stages, but quite simple in stage six after people have done their individual work in stages four and five. Then there is a sense of understanding and openness to new ways of being together. To further complicate matters, thinking about this from a holistic viewpoint, we can be in all seven stages at the same time. We have the potential of each stage within us at all times. Thus, the choices we make in our love relationships do make a difference. With knowledge and experience, we do become wiser.

From Addiction to Healthy Love: A Story

What follows is the story of Carly and Dave, a couple in their thirties who moved successfully from an addictive relationship to a healthier, more mature relationship; from victim and grandiose roles to mutual provider and receiver positions (discussed in chapter 4). Following their situation was inspirational and educational for me as a therapist. There were times when the relationship seemed doomed and therapy seemed to be of little help. The pain and isolation Carly and Dave felt during their ordeal, which also included elements of romance addiction, were often great, yet they trusted that change was possible, and they were willing to spend the necessary time and energy to improve their marriage.

✣ *Carly and Dave's Story* ✣

Carly and Dave needed to let go and discover who they were as individuals. Only then could they come back together and choose each other again—not because of need, but because of new love, respect, and desire for each other. Observing Dave and Carly confirmed my belief that many potentially good relationships end too early because of addictive qualities that mar them. Sometimes, love simply needs to grow up.

✣ *Carly's Story* ✣

"In a four-year period, my husband and I changed our residence three times to enhance his career. Although I had a choice in these decisions, I acted out of fear and duty rather than free choice. As I started looking for a job after our third move, I was angry and depressed. I thought, *Stop, Carly. What do you want from your life? You're living through him.* I had always been a happy person before; I wanted that contentment back.

"I got the name of a counselor and began to find out why I wasn't content.

"I began to learn that I thought Dave's and most other people's feelings and needs came before my own. I also gave others the kind of power I had granted to my parents as a child. Thus, my life fit well with Dave's, who believed his needs came first and that he had to do the thinking and decision making for both of us.

"I also discovered that because anger had not been expressed in either of our families, we weren't truly honest with one another when a problem arose.

"If I did bungle something, I thought something was wrong with me. Dave was also very concerned with perfection and was very critical of any mistakes I made. I was avoiding life to avoid Dave's reactions.

"When I shared my discoveries about myself with Dave, he listened, but he didn't understand or accept all of them. At the same time, I was feeling more and more oppressed in my marriage. Something seemed to be missing. If I were single, I thought, I could spend more time with my friends, with people I liked whom Dave didn't like. I wanted more intimacy.

"Unexpectedly, I became pregnant. Dave did not want children, and said, 'I don't know if I want to share you after all the time we've spent together and things we've done, just the two of us.' But abortion was not a choice for me.

"After we decided to continue with the pregnancy, Dave went on a business trip. When he returned, he told me he had been attracted to a single woman he had met on the trip and that he, too, had been feeling restless and unsatisfied in the marriage.

"This was the first time he had been seriously attracted to another woman since he and I had started dating fifteen years before. He kept saying it was only a friendship, yet he didn't know how he felt toward me any longer. He seemed to have a strong need for the friendship with Rita, the other woman, and in my gut, I didn't trust that their relationship was just a friendship.

"I finally became strong enough to ask Dave to end the relationship with Rita. He was reluctant to do so, but about a month after my request, he severed his ties with her. He was angry at me, which was a new experience for me. Because I had always attended to his feelings before my own, I felt guilty that I was asking him to end the relationship, yet I knew his affection for Rita was interfering with our marriage and working against changes we were making in our relationship.

"Months passed in which Dave struggled with his feelings about me and the marriage. In my emotional turmoil, I lost the baby. Then one night we got into a terrible argument, and Dave said things that hurt me deeply. Something inside of me changed; I told Dave I could accept that he didn't know how he felt about us, but I would not accept his biting comments. I told him I didn't want to hear them again. I guess I was at the point where I'd decided I was ready to get on with my life, with or without Dave. I was tired of his lack of commitment. He needed to decide if he was in or out of the marriage so we could either really work together on improving what we had or go on with our lives separately. At this point, Dave made his decision. He decided he was committed enough to give 'us' time to improve our relationship.

"Nevertheless, for the next six months, I felt a great space between us, and Dave didn't feel very close to me. A lot of games we'd played had ended. I started to spend more time with close friends and realized that what I had heard in counseling was true—that you can't depend on one person to meet all your needs. I found when I was with friends, I'd laugh and have fun. I also spent time alone during this time, trying to develop my spiritual side. All of these helped me regain my balance. I asked Dave to go to therapy for himself, and he did.

"We began to share what we were learning about ourselves in our individual counseling. It was open, honest communication. Sometimes it was very difficult to bring up something that was painful or uncomfortable, but I was learning we could be close, even through pain and anger. We were told that feeling distant was a normal part of ultimately growing together again, and though it scared us, we stuck with each other through this time. After Dave began to understand why he still didn't feel close to me, I started to notice a change for the better in him.

"The therapist suggested then that we start to look at the 'we.' Although I trusted her, I felt some resistance in my gut to doing so. But we began to study the relationship and to ask how we could improve it and purge it of the unhealthy dependency. We identified how we replayed history with each other, how we pushed each other's buttons, and why we became so defensive.

"Now things were definitely starting to improve between us. It was as I had always heard but never before experienced: when I quit looking for unconditional love, it was there. I felt happy about myself, and my happiness was much less dependent on Dave or anyone else than it had ever been. Dave began to honestly share feelings with me, and I felt he respected my thoughts and feelings more than he ever had. He showed a willingness to really listen. I also was more open to him, knowing now I could say no, and therefore, I was more willing to take suggestions or advice from him. He began to do things for me and to compliment me in a most pleasing way.

"Our marriage isn't perfect, and I know achieving intimacy is a long, difficult process. It's exciting now because we can laugh, joke, and have fun with each other, yet we also are free to be angry, and we don't always have to 'make everything okay' when it isn't. We also can be separate from each other; if one of us is feeling down, the other can be supportive but not become depressed also. And we know we can have close, separate friends and still be close to each other.

"When I began counseling for myself, I had no idea where it would lead. I just knew I wanted to be happy again. The entire process with myself and with my marriage has been very painful at times. Yet, it has also been exciting and rewarding. I feel I rediscovered parts of myself I had lost touch with. I've also developed new parts of myself to become more of a complete person. I have a real, growing, honest, spontaneous relationship with my husband that feels very good. I love him much more freely than before. It was well worth the risk, work, and time to reach this point. And now we're looking forward to the birth of our first child."

ℐ Dave's Story ℐ

"Looking back now, I can see it was a crisis, although at the time it didn't seem that way. It just seemed as if things kept getting more and more complicated until finally there was no room to move. Still, I don't think I would have sought counseling as a solution. It was Carly who suggested it.

"For most of the time Carly and I had known each other, our relationship wasn't especially healthy. We didn't know that, of course. We thought everything was fine, operating under the same system that had brought us together back in school.

"I was the one who had to be strong, be in control, be special, and be one-up. When we went to a party, I had to get the laughs. When we were going to go somewhere for the weekend, I was the one who decided where we'd go. I remember at that time a lot of my humor demeaned Carly.

"I also was the peacemaker, as I had been while growing up in my family (or had thought I had to be). Carly and I rarely fought or even had serious arguments because I thought that was wrong. As a child, I swallowed my feelings a lot. It wasn't okay to feel. Big boys don't cry. I had never had an intimate talk with my mom or my dad. In our family, we laughed things off. If it was negative, we'd bury it. As a result, I couldn't even ask for the simplest things—a back rub, time alone, sexual intimacy.

"But I found someone who took care of all that for me—without my even asking. When we were trying to decide what to do for an evening or weekend, Carly would wait to see what I wanted to do, then go along with it. She offered to rub my back; she got real value out of taking care of me. Of course, I didn't know that. I just knew that for some magical reason, I was getting taken care of. But there was no intimacy or shared feelings.

"Then things started to change. I suppose it began when Carly started therapy. She started changing her part of our system. No more demeaning humor, she said. She quit taking care of me so much. She began to have her own friends, her own life. I was no longer the one in control. The time I remember most vividly was the first time she got really mad at me. I knew things were no longer the same.

"I remember criticizing Carly for being dependent on me; that bugged me. Yet, at the same time, I'm sure I was beginning to feel scared that she was no longer dependent on me! It was a very mixed-up time for me. It doesn't surprise me now, looking back, that I began to want to pull away from Carly then.

"The crisis that led to our seeing a therapist grew out of a business trip I'd made where I became strongly attracted to Rita. I didn't know how to deal with the feelings I had for this woman. I was strongly attracted to her, but I knew I couldn't act on those feelings. She was also attracted to me, and we decided to keep in touch on a friendship basis.

"It became clear to me in the days following the trip that my feelings for Rita were more than friendship, and I fantasized about somehow being able to be with her in the future. For the first time, I found myself questioning whether I wanted to spend the rest of my life with Carly. Did I love her? Did I love her for the same reasons I had fallen in love with her fifteen years before?

"I found myself constantly caught in the middle, trying very hard to build a new friendship by long distance with Rita, and at the same time trying to assure Carly that everything was all right. It was one of the most uncomfortable times in my life. What bugged me most was that Carly couldn't understand my desire for the friendship. I thought she was being restrictive and jealous, and we had lots of discussions and arguments about that.

"Well, things just kept getting worse for Carly and me. I was always in the middle, trying harder and harder to make Carly and my new friend understand why the other felt the way she did. As I learned later, this 'middleman' position was a familiar place for me, for I had always tried to make everyone happy.

"I thought about separating from Carly; I even thought about divorce. I didn't find either very acceptable, but nevertheless, they were options. I'm not sure why I didn't exercise either of them. For one thing, I was probably too scared. And somewhere, beneath all this mess, I think I believed we'd gone too far just to give up.

"By this time, I'd begun weekly group therapy sessions. I had almost no emotional connection to Carly. I had said I was committed to the relationship, and I was. I had decided I would give it about the only thing I felt I could—time. And I also had agreed to begin looking at myself and my role in our marriage. At first, I merely used sessions to deal with my anger and sadness about not being able to continue my new friendship. But in spite of that, I began to find out why I was the person I was, and that was fascinating.

"Still, times weren't easy. I still wanted to pull away from Carly, even more so when I started discovering something about myself and having more of a sense of myself. All my life with Carly, it had been 'us.' Before therapy, I had focused on Carly and thought about how she should be different, but now I was looking almost entirely at myself. Now there was a 'me' again that I liked. That part of me wanted to go off on my own and not slog through all this muck of trying to rebuild a relationship.

"I think the one way therapy helped most was to confirm my belief that things could be better in time. We aren't talking weeks here. I was in group therapy for more than a year. Finally, very slowly, I began to feel closer to Carly again. I mean very slowly. There had been so many times when I didn't think I could ever feel close to her again.

"It was intriguing to see us beginning to have a healthier relationship again. It sure wasn't puppy love or romantic infatuation or anything like that. Carly wasn't instantly a new woman, nor was I a new man. But we both knew ourselves a lot better than we ever had before, and we both had learned a lot about how to have a healthy relationship. I didn't have to feel in control anymore; I began to let go in many situations where I once would have had to be in charge.

"The whole process has been amazing to me. It is ironic to think that in order to become a healthy couple again, two people have to travel separate ways for a while. They don't have to be physically separated—and I'm glad we weren't. But they have to be psychologically distant before they can come together again. Until each is willing to step aside and examine his or her role in the relationship, I think it's almost impossible to change. But I feel that making that separate, inner journey and bringing what I learned from it back to our new relationship has been the most meaningful and rewarding experience of my life. *We* are feeling good again. The closeness has come back; I think it's safe to say we're in love again—in a much different way than we used to be."

～

Sometimes, We Need to Let Go

Sometimes, our relationships cannot be salvaged, and we must be willing to say good-bye to them. When we feel vulnerable to the thought of life outside a particular relationship, we often hang in there and attempt to control it instead. In such situations, we must discern whether we are there to satisfy addictive compulsions or a passion that emanates from our deeper truth—the heart, soul, body connection discussed in chapter 8. While passion can be an important part of healthy love, the compelling high must not pull us off course. The pull of sexual or romantic attraction can be so strong that we begin denying the obvious—that the relationship cannot work except as mutual addiction. Attraction can come with lightning speed, trumpets, and cymbals that defy all words and suggest a mystical connection. Sometimes it is. On the other hand, it can also be a magnetic pull to self-destruction.

ℐ✤ Dan's Story ℐ✤

Dan's story is of a type I have witnessed many times. Yet, I also know that we do not see what we need to see and let go of people we need to let go of until we are ready to see and let go. Sometimes, as in Dan's case, one needs to get "sick and tired" before one is willing to move on in one's process.

At first, Dan was reluctant to seek help for his addictive relationship because he was a successful counselor and felt he should know all the answers. He saw himself as a strong, independent, handsome man with high self-esteem, and it was hard for him to admit he felt otherwise. He had relied on himself for a long time. But Dan learned that real strength came through his inward odyssey and discovery of things that kept him in an unhealthy relationship.

When Dan first sought help, his life seemed out of control. He was physically abusive when angry, he drank too much, and he suffered from high blood pressure and migraine headaches. It was clear that if he didn't change, he would continue on a self-destructive course. He came into therapy to regain control of his life.

Unlike Carly and Dave, Dan needed to leave his relationship in order to move ahead with his life, something he initially could not imagine doing. His theme, like the themes of so many others trapped in addictive love, was "I can't imagine living without her."

"To begin, I think I must go back to my childhood and to my relationship with my father. I don't think I ever felt loved by him even though I worked hard to get it. Although I now believe my father did, in fact, love me, I don't think he found the words very easy to say or the feelings very easy to display because I do not recall my father ever telling me he loved me.

"I carried this striving for love over into my adult relationships. I believed I needed another's love to affirm my right to live. I also think this need to be loved led me to marry at the very young age of nineteen. This marriage was a mistake from the start, but I stayed in it for twelve years. I did so mainly because of insecurity; I felt I was not a lovable person.

"When the marriage—in which I was extremely unhappy for years—became absolutely intolerable, I filed for a divorce. Shortly after the divorce, I met Ann, also recently divorced. In a short time, we became friends and lovers. But this relationship was extremely addictive romantically and sexually.

"Both Ann and I had feelings of not being able to live without the other. Shortly after starting to date, we moved in together. Very early in the relationship, it seemed Ann and I allowed the relationship to consume and control us. We spent little time outside the relationship and maintained few outside interests. We feared losing each other. We were completely obsessed with our relationship, each of us expecting the other to meet all our needs, never realizing just how impossible such a thing was.

"The relationship became extremely painful for me when Ann started to see other men, reinforcing my belief that I was not very lovable. Although this caused me great pain and anxiety, I stayed because I was addicted to the relationship and did not know how to get out 'without dying,' as I would have said then. I feel the most addictive aspect of our relationship was that we demanded unconditional love from each other no matter what our behavior was and no matter how much we did to destroy the relationship.

"I think that at this time I kept telling myself I could change Ann if I loved her enough. I *had* to change her because I could not live without her! I was not a whole person without my relationship with her. This very addictive relationship became more and more destructive for me, and I think for Ann, too. The destructiveness of our bond began to affect me; my drinking increased, and my behavior became more and more self-destructive.

"Finally, because of my behavior, someone whom I greatly respected asked me to take a serious look at where I was heading and to try to bring my life under control. At this time, I realized my explosive anger, my bad feelings about myself, and my unhealthy relationship with Ann were things I was unable to stop by myself.

"So I sought help from a therapist. I feel this is where I realized many things about my life, and I soon realized I had to end my unhappy, addictive relationship. I finally was able to do so after a number of therapy sessions. I truly believe that had it not been for my entering therapy, this addictive relationship would have subsequently destroyed me, if not both of us.

"As I began to be good to myself, changing my beliefs about my worth and accepting that my parents had loved me the best they could, I began to open myself to women who were capable of love and intimacy. I learned I was the one who feared the hurt and pain of rejection, who had believed it wasn't safe to be close, and who substituted melodramatics for intimacy. I had unconsciously sought out a woman, Ann, who could not love me intimately, supporting my belief that I was unlovable or a disappointment to others. It was great to discover I actually had a choice.

"Since that time, I have made some big changes in my life, such as moving to a new area. Admittedly, this was one of the hardest decisions I've ever made. Since my relationship with Ann ended, I've had occasion to see her, and I sometimes feel pulled toward her. Then I remind myself that I don't want to go down that street, so why go there?"

⌒

Carly, Dave, and Dan have come a long way. And they did so by living the process one step at a time. If you see a bit of yourself in their situations, read on. You, too, can learn how to put love and freedom simultaneously to work in your life.

If you bring forth what is within you, what you bring forth will save you. If you do not bring forth what is within you, what you do not bring forth will destroy you.

The Gospel According to Thomas

Helping Yourself Out of Addictive Love

The highest goal a therapist can have for clients is to instill in them the knowledge that solutions to their problems lie within, then to pass on tools to help guide people to those powerful inner answers. This chapter attempts to provide you with skills that will allow you to act as your own therapist and to address your relationship problems in a helpful, hopeful way.

We've discussed the roots of addictive love, described its characteristics, and studied the process of moving from troublesome dependency to mature, fulfilling love. As we've seen, the roots of addictive love run deep, and the road out is often long and rough. So long and rough, in fact, that you may be asking yourself: "Why bother? Isn't any love better than no love at all?"

Why expel addictive love from your life? There is an extremely good answer to that challenge: *addictive love is limiting*.

It limits your ability to feel content.

It limits your ability to function and to live up to your potential.

It limits your openness to new experiences.

It limits your ability to enjoy and live in the present.

It limits your energy for creative pursuits.

It limits your personal power and your freedom.

It limits your ability to accept others.

It limits your willingness to face your fears.

It limits your spontaneity.

It limits your level of consciousness and your spiritual potential. It limits your capacity for intimacy and your ability to truly love.

You must decide for yourself what choices you'll make for your life. You surely do not have to change, but if you do decide to change, make sure you're doing it for yourself. Once you decide to forgo addictive love, once you stop seeing life in melodramatic black and white and start seeing it in true, complex colors, it may be difficult or impossible for you to retreat to your old way of thinking or behaving. You'll find you can invite—but not pull or coerce—others in your life to come along with you. If they resist, you'll do well to be patient and compassionate. You may even find that your decision to give up addictive love means you'll have to end your troublesome relationship completely, a decision that surely will cause you some very natural grief.

Fulfillment never comes easily; there are no guarantees that your choice to change will bring you instant happiness. As this book's descriptive sketches have illustrated, some who risked change grew into healthier love relationships, while others found they had to let go of their relationships and get new starts in life and love.

Once you decide to free yourself from addictive love, you agree to let go of your desire to be controlled or to control another; you cease to manipulate others to get what you need and want. The urge to manipulate others is a powerful one, and in giving it up, you'll no doubt experience some grief. But in the long run, such suffering will be far less than the pain you may have inflicted on yourself or another via an addictive relationship.

This chapter is dedicated to those who opt for healthier, happier love. If you feel uncertain about how you wish to proceed, you may want to experiment with the exercises that follow; see what you can learn about yourself. If you wish, for whatever reasons of your own, to maintain the status quo in your troublesome relationship, you may want to stop here. You're being honest, but remember, the decision against change is yours—so give up blaming others for your relationship troubles or addiction. You must remember that you've relinquished personal power and growth to addictive love.

You may doubt the statement that most, if not all, love relationships harbor some elements of addictive love. To you, I suggest doing the following exercises before you decide it can't be true. The exercises are based on the premises that much of who we are is not in our conscious awareness most of the time, and that awareness precedes change.

Change = awareness + action. These exercises are designed to help increase awareness and motivate action.

I have designed the exercises based on my experience as a psychotherapist and workshop leader; some are combined with my personal knowledge. I have found that the exercises are helpful for people who wish to purge their lives of addictive behavior. Although all therapy is basically self-therapy, these exercises are usually done with professional guidance. In the event you find it difficult to use them on your own, or if moving through them elicits information or feelings that make you uncomfortable, don't hesitate to seek professional support.[1]

Some of the exercises may require a great amount of thought and time. They are not designed to be completed hurriedly, which will be obvious as you move through them. The time and thought you put into them will probably grow into a self-help process that could span several months. Some exercises will mean more to you than others do. Though their purpose is serious, they are designed to be fun or stimulating.

Good luck on your personal journey toward self-discovery. My hope is that you will discover at least one personal insight that alters your life for the better; my wish for you is more joy, freedom, wisdom, and love.

The Self-Help Method

Listed here are seven basic steps that will help you move from addictive love to healthy love:

1. *awareness:* admitting that addictive love plays a role in your life
2. *assessment:* discovering the extent of your addictive love
3. *decision:* using your personal power to move out of addiction
4. *exploration:* examining your personal fears, myths, and trauma history

5. *reprogramming:* letting go of the old; embracing the new
6. *renewal:* moving toward mature love
7. *expansion:* developing personal uniqueness and the ability to truly love yourself and others

Awareness Exercise:
Admitting That Addictive Love Plays a Role in Your Life

The fact that you chose this book, and perhaps others similar to it, indicates that you already know your love relationship has addictive aspects. Without such an admission, you might still be trapped in the denial stage, where there is no fertile ground for the seeds of change to grow. The information in this book is designed to help you move from awareness that a problem exists into the next important steps: recognizing your dependency problem and gaining control over it.

Exercise 1-A: Recognition

Remember the first time you heard the term *addictive love.* Now, read the questions that follow, then close your eyes and visualize your responses.

What did you think and feel when you first heard the term?
What made you decide to read a book about addictive love?
Were there feelings of hesitation about reading it?
What fears, if any, were a part of such resistance?
How do you hope to be different after reading this book?

Assessment Exercises:
Discovering the Extent of Your Addiction

The following exercises can help you evaluate yourself or your relationships for signs of love, romance, and sex addiction. It is assumed that the fewer addictive characteristics, the higher will be the quality of your relationships and life.

Exercise 2-A: How Does Your Relationship Rate?

With a love relationship in mind—past or present—carefully read first the signs of love addiction, then those of healthy love. Score your relationship for each love addiction characteristic based on the following scale: 0 = never; 1 = rarely; 2 = sometimes; 3 = often; 4 = almost always; 5 = always. Then score yourself for healthy love.

Love Addiction	*Healthy Love*
__ Feels all-consuming	__ Allows for individuality
__ Has difficulty defining ego boundaries	__ Experiences and enjoys both oneness with and separateness from partner
__ Has elements of sadomasochism	__ Brings out best qualities in both partners
__ Fears letting go	__ Accepts endings
__ Fears risk, change, and the unknown	__ Experiences openness to change and exploration
__ Allows little individual growth	__ Invites growth in both partners
__ Lacks true intimacy	__ Experiences true intimacy
__ Plays psychological games	__ Feels freedom to ask honestly for what is wanted
__ Gives to get something back	__ Experiences giving and receiving in the same way
__ Attempts to change the partner	__ Does not attempt to change or control the partner
__ Needs partner to feel complete	__ Encourages self-sufficiency of partner
__ Seeks solutions outside of self	__ Accepts limitations of self and partner
__ Demands and expects unconditional love	__ Does not insist on unconditional love
__ Refuses or abuses commitment (antidependency)	__ Can make and respect commitment
__ Looks to partner for affirmation and worth	__ Has high self-esteem and sense of well-being
__ Fears abandonment upon routine separation	__ Trusts memory of beloved; enjoys solitude
__ Re-creates familiar negative feelings	__ Expresses feelings spontaneously

Love Addiction	Healthy Love
__ Desires, yet fears, closeness	__ Welcomes closeness; risks vulnerability
__ Attempts to "take care" of partner's feelings	__ Cares, but can remain detached
__ Plays power games (one-upmanship)	__ Affirms equality and personal power of self and partner

Now, add the scores for each list and divide by twenty to get a numerical average for each. Does your relationship exhibit more symptoms of trouble than of health?

Think about troubled relationships with other people, such as friends, co-workers, or relatives and do the same.

Exercise 2-B: Romance Addiction Assessment

With a current or past romantic relationship in mind, read carefully the signs of romance addiction, then score your relationship for each characteristic based on the following: 0 = never; 1 = rarely; 2 = sometimes; 3 = often; 4 = almost always; 5 = always. If you are not in a romantic relationship but live in fantasy of it, score yourself on the following signs as well, using the same scale.

Signs of Romance Addiction

- __ 1. obsession
- __ 2. intense jealousy
- __ 3. possessiveness
- __ 4. depression and melancholy
- __ 5. dependence on intoxicating feelings
- __ 6. heightened anxiety
- __ 7. romance interferes with life
- __ 8. living on the edge of perfected love
- __ 9. exaggerated fantasy life
- __ 10. choice of entertainment is romantic, dramatic, or euphoric
- __ 11. stalking the love object
- __ 12. chasing the illusion
- __ 13. lured by intermittent reinforcement

___ 14. longing for reciprocation
___ 15. withdrawal symptoms when the love object moves away
___ 16. friends and family express concern
___ 17. hanging on to the unavailable or abusive
___ 18. outcomes are disappointing
___ 19. distortion of reality
___ 20. melodrama

Now, add the scores and divide by twenty to get a numerical average.

Note: If your average score for romance addiction is 2.5 or higher, I suggest doing the exercises in this book and retaking the test. If your score is still 2.5 or higher, talk to a counselor who understands romance addiction. If your average is 2.4 or less, focus on the exercises in this chapter and work to lower your score.

Exercise 2-C: Sex Addiction Assessment

To know whether or not you are using or abusing your sexual expression or leaning toward using sex compulsively, review and score the following signs of sex addiction. If you are in a relationship and questioning whether your partner is using sex compulsively, score him or her. It just may save a life. Score for each sign based on the following: 0 = never; 1 = rarely; 2 = sometimes; 3 = often; 4 = almost always; 5 = always.

Signs of Sexual Addiction/Compulsivity

___ 1. use of sex to fix, escape, or cope
___ 2. negative consequences due to sexual behavior
___ 3. mood changes related to sexual activity
___ 4. inability to stop, even with negative consequences
___ 5. planning, obtaining, and recovering from sexual activity becomes increasingly time-consuming
___ 6. risk losing a relationship or job
___ 7. guilt and shame because of behavior
___ 8. pursuit of high-risk or destructive behaviors
___ 9. a predictable cycle

___ 10. tolerance or need for more to get the same high
___ 11. at odds with family or spiritual values
___ 12. deny, rationalize, defend, or minimize behavior
___ 13. sexual cravings
___ 14. preoccupation
___ 15. living a double or secret life
___ 16. use sex to feel or not feel past trauma
___ 17. sexualize others
___ 18. violate trust of others
___ 19. inappropriate sexual behaviors
___ 20. use and abuse others for sexual gratification

Now, add the scores and divide by twenty to get a numerical average.

Note: If your average score for using sex compulsively is 2.5 or higher, I suggest doing the exercises in this book and retaking the test. If your score is still 2.5 or higher, talk to a counselor who understands sex addiction. If your average is 2.4 or less, focus on the exercises in this chapter and work to lower your score.

Exercise 2-D: Relationship Connections
Study the following list illustrating the different areas of contact that connect you and your partner or a previous partner. Now, on a 0-to-10 scale, with 10 being the highest, rate your love relationship.

Area of Contact	*Rating*
• *Physical* (degree of attraction, affection; quality of sexual relationship, physical nurturing)	____
• *Emotional* (degree of expression, communication, support between partners, emotional trust)	____
• *Social* (mutual compatibility with friends, family; quality of social life)	____

- *Mental*
  (quality of ideas/information exchange; mutual problem
  solving; acceptance of changing ideas and opinions)   ____
- *Behavioral*
  (quality of partners' treatment of each other and
  conflict resolution; support for individual differences)   ____
- *Spiritual*
  (mutual values and attitudes; support for individual
  development)   ____

If there are one or more zeros, the relationship probably is addictive; if your scores are fours or less, the relationship probably needs attention.

Exercise 2-E: How Do I Love Me?

Your self-image plays a significant role in your relationships—the higher your self-esteem, the better your relationships are likely to be. By going through the process of answering these questions, you will become more aware of your own level of self-esteem. Using a scale of 0-10, 10 being high, rate yourself on the following questions:

1. How much do you like yourself? ____
2. As a child, how much did you think or feel your mother liked you? ____
3. As a child, how much did you think or feel your father liked you? ____
4. As you grew up, how much did you think or feel your peers liked you? ____
5. How much would you like to like yourself? ____
6. How much do you look to others for approval? ____
7. How much do you think or feel your partner likes you? ____
8. Have you ever liked yourself more? If yes, what was the score, when, and why? _____
   _____
9. Have you ever liked yourself less? If yes, what was the score, when, and why? _____
   _____

Exercise 2-F: Power Plays

The following are power plays that often appear in addictive relationships. To the left of each power play, write "yes" or "no" based on whether you have experienced that symptom in your relationship. Note how many "yes" and "no" answers you have.

Since power plays are characteristic of addictive love, any "yes" indicates some degree of trouble in the relationship. The more times you wrote "yes," the more attention you'll want to pay to the presence of harmful manipulation in your relationship.

Common Power Plays

_____ Giving advice but not accepting it

_____ Having difficulty in reaching out and in asking for support and love

_____ Giving orders; demanding and expecting much from others

_____ Trying to "get even" or to diminish the self-esteem or power of others

_____ Being judgmental; using put-downs that sabotage others' success; faultfinding; persecuting; punishing

_____ Holding out on others; not giving what others want or need

_____ Making, then breaking, promises; causing others to trust us and then betraying the trust

_____ Smothering, overnurturing others

_____ Patronizing, condescending treatment of others that sets one partner up as superior, the other as inferior; intimidation

_____ Making decisions for others; discounting others' abilities to solve problems

_____ Putting others in no-win situations

_____ Attempting to change others (and unwillingness to change self)

_____ Attacking others when they are most vulnerable

_____ Showing an antidependent attitude: "I don't need you"

_____ Using bullying, bribing behavior; using threats

_____ Showing bitterness or self-righteous anger; holding grudges

_____ Abusing others verbally, emotionally, sexually, or physically
_____ Being aggressive and defining it as assertiveness
_____ Needing to win or be right
_____ Resisting stubbornly or being set in one's own way
_____ Having difficulty admitting mistakes or saying "I'm sorry"
_____ Giving indirect, evasive answers to questions
_____ Defending any of the above behaviors

Decision Exercises:
Using Your Personal Power to Move Out of Addiction

You've assessed your love relationship, and if you found signs of trouble, you now have a decision to make. If you've discovered that your use of romance and sex are addictive to some degree—perhaps to a great degree—you now must decide whether to maintain the status quo or to work toward change.

Note: If you are clearing out compulsive habits, you may initially feel more compulsive. When letting go of an unhealthy dependency, your feeling of neediness may escalate. When letting go of a romance or sex addiction, you will experience withdrawal symptoms. These are signs that your process is in motion. Make sure a solid support system is in place. And use it!

Exercise 3-A: What Do You Get from Your Addictive Love?

We cling to troubled relationships or sex and romance addictions because they serve us on some level. Perhaps we gain feelings of self-esteem and security; a sense of belonging; sensations of pleasure, comfort, and success; avoidance of fear; or a sense of meaning in our lives. Think carefully about how your relationships or addiction serve or protect you. Taking plenty of time to answer this question, make a list of secondary gains you are receiving from your current relationship with a person, romance, or sex. Try to be honest with your answers.

We introduce now a set of rituals designed to help you concentrate on your addictive relationship and its qualities. You will be making the following statements based on how you have been in your relationship in the past. Place a symbol of your relationship—perhaps a picture of your loved one, or a gift from that person—in front of you. Slowly repeat these words: "I, (your name), now give you, (other person), the power to make me whole. Without you, I am incomplete. You give me (list your secondary gains here) and satisfy my human needs for security, sensation, and power. I relinquish my power to you and will do whatever you ask in exchange for your making me whole. If you try to move away, I will do whatever I can to get you to stay."

Now, introduce a new ritual, one designed to help you reclaim your personal power. Again, place the symbol of the person you love before you and say: "I, (your name), now reclaim my God-given gift of personal power from you, (other person). I now know that I have within me the ability to live a full, complete, and successful life; I now believe that what I need in life (again, list secondary gains) is there for me independent of our bond. I no longer need to try to overpower you. I let go of you easily and gently. I thank you for your attempt to make me whole while I was learning, growing, and claiming my birthright. And while I may choose to be with you as an enhancement to my life, my choice will spring from love, not from fear."

Now, do the same with your addictive relationship with romance or sex, eliminating the last sentence of the preceding paragraph.

Which ritual felt right, and why?

Exercise 3-B: How to Know When It Is Time to Let Go

Look at the following indicators and check off the ones that apply to a relationship you are in or one you are mentally and emotionally hanging on to. It is time to let go if these indicators are present.

1. You or the other starts to pull back.
2. You stop feeling safe in the relationship.
3. When the chemical high or excitement wears off, you see that you and the person are truly not compatible.
4. The person is not willing to build a deeper friendship or relationship.
5. You recognize a pattern of choosing the wrong people.

6. You are putting more energy into the relationship than the other person is.
7. When you bring up problems, the other person becomes defensive or withdraws.
8. You are blamed for the problems in the relationship.
9. You are stagnating.
10. You find the person boring.
11. Your intuition knows it is time to move on.
12. The other person says it is over.

Exercise 3-C: Letting Go

Letting go is one of the most difficult of life tasks. If it is important to let go of a relationship, here are some suggestions that can help you.

1. Find support people you can reach out to. Ask them to remind you why it is important to let go of this relationship or addiction *now*.
2. Live one day at a time saying to yourself: "I can do today what I might not be able to do for a lifetime," or "I will live today with a peaceful heart."
3. Use stop techniques instantly, such as telling yourself: "This thought, feeling, behavior is not in my best interest, and I will stop obsessing instantly."
4. Do deep breathing, physical exercise, and meditation several times a day.
5. Remind yourself that you made the right decision for you and that you will not give in to the compulsive self. Tell yourself: "I have everything I need to get beyond what I fear," or "It is in my best interest to let go of this relationship now."
6. Create new routines to fill in the spaces that remind you of the past.
7. Find something you feel passionate about and do it.
8. Clean out any reminders—pictures, gifts, music, etc.—of the person, at least for now, as they are likely to trigger pain and obsession. Sex addicts remove all triggers or stash.
9. Find ways to give to others. Put your caring to work in other places.

10. Hang out with family members and friends that you like being around and who are free of judgment and advice giving. You simply need a place to be right now.

11. If pain comes up, accept it knowing that denial will make you sick. Let yourself grieve the loss and do not dwell on it or look back. Remember to use your pain wisely as you tell yourself: "This is healing pain, and I will grow from it."

12. If your symptoms worsen or go beyond two weeks, call a therapist immediately.

Exploration Exercises: Examining Your Personal Fears, Myths, and Trauma History

Once you've decided to reclaim your personal power from an unhealthy attachment to romance and sex, or you're ready to relinquish pseudo-control over your partner, it is important to explore the complex roots of your addiction.

Often, we say we want one thing, yet we continue to work for another. That occurs because, on an unconscious level, what we have makes perfect sense to us. Therefore, it is crucial—and no simple task—to explore your own unconscious fears and myths, and to discover the personal reasons for your choices. Many addictive behaviors spring from forgotten or suppressed traumas that occurred during childhood or adolescence. Though such experiences may have been spirited away from our conscious minds, they greatly affect the decisions we make and the impressions we hold of the past.[2]

The following exercises are designed to launch you into self-discovery. Until we understand our own conscious and unconscious beliefs, we'll remain emotionally tied to habitual behaviors—even those we may want to change. It is one thing to try to *stop* a behavior; it is quite another to *understand* it. That requires discovery of how the behavior evolved.

Exercise 4-A: Impasse Dialogue

The paradox of personal change is that we have a strong urge to grow, yet we often fear and resist change. The most important relationship is the inner one. At times, the consciously chosen new decision, affirmation, or behavior will provoke the old, unconscious belief system, and an inner conflict will emerge: "I want to let go of this relationship, but I do not want to risk change." If this occurs, you experience a mental impasse internally that makes it impossible to resolve a problem externally. You feel confused, agitated, or hesitant. One marvelous way to resolve the inner war is to write a letter to yourself until the dialogue is resolved. Here is one way to help you do so.

1. Write a letter from the part of you that fears intimacy or resists change to the part of you that desires close, loving relationships and is ready for change. Let that side tell
    A. why I, the fearful or resistant part, am here
    B. where I came from; what experiences, traumas, and lessons led to my beliefs and behaviors
    C. how I perceive myself as a friend and protector
    D. what I need in order to change
2. Now, respond from the part of you that is ready for change and mature intimacy:
    A. thank the fearful or addictive self for what it has provided
    B. say why it is important to change now
    C. say what might happen if change does not occur
    D. say how needs will get met in healthy ways

Exercise 4-B: Learned Solutions
The next questions can help you study your social education and the role it plays in your current relationships.

1. Write down the most significant problem in your relationship.
2. Answer the following:
    A. If your mother had this same problem, how did she or how might she have solved it?
    B. If your father had this problem, how did he or how might he have solved it?
    C. Would their solutions be effective?
    D. Which parent are you most like?

Exercise 4-C: Learned Responses

In your imagination, create a scene in which the significant grown-ups in your life are gathered—a family reunion, a family celebration, etc. As a child, observe the grown-ups carefully. From your observations and intuition, what are you beginning to believe about love, relationships, power, men, and women? Complete the following statements based on what you experienced.

1. Love is _____

2. Relationships are _____

3. Women are _____

4. Men are _____

5. Relationships should _____

6. Power is _____

7. Sex is _____

Examine your conclusions. Do they support healthy or addictive love? Have any of these beliefs come true in your adult relationships? How would you change any of these beliefs/conclusions to support healthy love?

Exercise 4-D: Coping with Relationship Problems

The following exercise can help you understand your own deeply held myths and beliefs.

Read through the entire exercise until you understand it. Relax by taking several deep breaths. Close your eyes and guide yourself through the exercise. Don't attempt to force images into your mind's eye; let them come to you at their own pace. Remember, images can be words, visions, feelings, or all three. (If you wish, you may enlist a friend to help guide you through the exercise.)

After you have imaged your responses, write them down. (If you have more than one bad feeling, take one at a time and repeat the exercise for each one.)

Think of the unpleasant feeling you have experienced most often in your current relationship—anxiety, loneliness, fear, rejection, anger, or boredom, for example. Now, recall the most recent scene in which this feeling prevailed.

In your mind's eye, observe the scene as though you were observing it on a television screen. Who is there? What's happening and not happening? What's being said? What are you thinking or saying to yourself about yourself, others, and your life? As the scene unfolds, pay special attention to your negative thoughts. What is it you need in this scene that you aren't getting? How do you take care of yourself as it occurs?

Now, return to a time in your childhood (preferably early childhood—age six or under) when you experienced the same bad feeling. Let the scene appear on the TV screen. Again, don't force this scene into your mind; let it emerge gradually. If you have difficulty visualizing it, create a scene in which a parent or another significant adult is present. Observe the scene and become aware of details. Again, notice who is there, what is and isn't happening, and what's being said. Notice why you are experiencing the bad feeling. Are you taking care of that feeling? What do you want or need during this experience that you aren't getting? What are you doing to take care of yourself? What is your secret response to the scene as you are present in it? What do you begin to believe about yourself, others, and life based on what's going on there?

Now, carefully study the two scenes; scrutinize them for similarities. If, by magic, you could change the childhood scene so you felt better about yourself, others, and life, how might it be different? If the childhood scene *had* been different, how might the recent scene be different? Think about, and then write down responses to, these questions.

Exercise 4-E: Trauma Exercise

Review the four kinds of trauma in chapter 3. List yours. Don't push to remember. Review each trauma and note what impact the trauma has had on you; what you did to cope; how this coping pattern keeps repeating in your life, love relationships, or compulsive habits; and what you are willing to change. If discomfort arises, talk with a therapist.[3]

Here are examples to give you a starting point.

Trauma of omission:

Who/what: My parents didn't talk to me about life, and when I approached them with my problems, they were too busy to listen.

Fears/belief structure/behaviors: I was afraid to trust. I came to believe that I should handle everything on my own and felt lonely.

Coping: Because I had locked my hurts and frustrations inside, I drank to deal with the pain.

How this trauma gets triggered in relationships: I feel unimportant when someone does not figure out my needs.

Willing to change: I will stop abusing alcohol. I will take a risk and talk about feelings.

Trauma of commission:

Who/what: My first-grade teacher reprimanded me in front of the class and said that I wouldn't amount to anything.

Fears/belief structure/behaviors: I began to fear people in authority, believed I would not succeed in life, and felt inadequate.

Coping: I became very quiet. I figured if I didn't say anything, I couldn't say anything stupid.

How this trauma gets triggered in relationships: When someone important to me doesn't listen to what I have to say or interrupts me, I feel stupid.

Willing to change: I will work on character defects, rather than giving them power over me.

Shock trauma:

Who/what: When I was six years old, I had surgery that was frightening. No one explained it to me.

Fears/belief structure/behaviors: I felt afraid and abandoned and decided I had to be strong.

Coping: I tried to be brave by pretending I was never afraid. In relationships, when afraid, I dismissed it.

How this trauma gets triggered in a relationship: When someone gets mad at me for something I did, I feel weak inside and then I clam up.

Willing to change: I'm willing to acknowledge my fears and ask questions until I feel safe.

Post-traumatic stress disorder:

Who/what: I witnessed my best friend in school get hit by a car and die. I still have nightmares about that day.

Fears/belief structure/behaviors: If I don't have other close friends, it won't hurt if something happens to them. I keep my distance and feel like an outsider.

Coping: I stay frozen. I haven't made many close friends since then.

How this gets triggered in a relationship: When someone wants to get close to me, I feel cornered and tense up or remove myself.

Willing to change: I will finish my grief and attempt to make new friends, knowing that I may one day lose them.

Reprogramming Exercises:
Letting Go of the Old, Embracing the New

Listed here is the necessary process in moving from addiction to love.

1. Face the facts in your life and honestly examine your own role in your relationships.
2. Acknowledge resistance to change that stems from fear of not getting your secondary needs met.
3. Stop looking for "magic"—external solutions to your problems.
4. Look inward to examine fears, self-promises, and archaic beliefs that may support addictive beliefs and behaviors.
5. Reprogram the negative experiences.

To develop true openness to mature love, it is important to change the internal beliefs that hold you in dependent behavior. For lasting results in behavior change, internal inhibitions and false beliefs must be transformed from the inside out. As you try to learn why your current relationships make sense to your unconscious self and how to improve those relationships, keep in mind that you are the sum total of all your thoughts and experiences. Those thoughts and experiences produce results even when you're not aware of them. Therefore, when you gain some control over your internal "program," changes come easier and last longer. You should also understand that relinquishing an archaic belief might cause you great sadness and emotion. But that grief eventually will end, and the sadness will pass as the void is filled.

Exercise 5-A: Learning to Be Your Own Parent

What is self-parenting? It is the art of becoming a wise, loving, protective mentor to yourself. Now that you've grown up, you have the ability to grant yourself those messages and pieces of information you may have missed in childhood and adolescence. This exercise is designed to guide you toward the wonderful independence that self-parenting provides.

Read carefully through the exercise. Take several deep breaths until you feel relaxed. Close your eyes and imagine you are a newborn baby. Feel your innocence and vulnerability; notice the naturalness of your body processes. Now, bring yourself as an adult into the scene and embrace the newborn you; hold the child close to your heart and slowly repeat the following: "Welcome; I'm so glad you're here. I've been waiting for you for a long time. I know how to take care of you, and what I don't know, I'm willing to learn. You can have what you need when you need it, and you can stop when you are full. All you need to do is 'make noise' to let me know. I love you!"

Tell the infant (you) what it has a right to—a full, rich life—and what you plan to do to encourage that life. Take as much time as you need.

Tell the child (you) how you feel about child abuse; how you regret all the times you abused it or allowed others to abuse it. In particular, study any abuse you allowed in your love relationship or in your addictions. Again, take as much time as you need to fully feel any sorrow or regret. Remember, abuse can be emotional, mental, spiritual, sexual, or physical.

Tell the infant (you) that you're willing to provide it healthy love relationships from this moment on. And, before setting the inner child to rest, say you will always be there as a wise, loving parent, or that you will see to it that the child is in good hands. (Be specific about the kind of parenting you will provide or learn more about.)

Now, set the child to rest, knowing the child is you and will continue to reside within you. It is now your responsibility to acknowledge the child's needs.

In the days after you do this exercise, you may want to enhance it by placing a picture of yourself as a baby or young child in a place where you will see it many times a day. Several times each day, affirm the child as part of you, and remind yourself that you are the parent, the problem solver. Take good care of yourself. Talk to the child within and tell it what it needs to hear to grow to self-love, autonomy, and intimacy.

Exercise 5-B: Your Future Relationships

This exercise helps you visualize future relationships. Read through it slowly and carefully. Take several deep breaths. Inhale, count to four slowly, and exhale. Repeat five times. As you exhale, let go of discomfort and tension and allow yourself true relaxation—a prerequisite to vibrant imagination. The images you conjure up may be visual images, word images, feeling images, or all of these.

If you've had difficulty with imagining exercises, keep in mind that people imagine in several ways—by listening, by seeing, and by feeling. Start with the style that is easiest for you. With time and practice, you'll soon find you can use all three modes of imagination.

Close your eyes. Imagine a television screen with a DVD player. There are two discs. The first disc begins to play. It is you five years from now without change in your relationships or life. The same problems that plague you now still exist. Take as much time as you need to let this image emerge in your mind's eye. Notice how you look. Notice how you feel about yourself and what you are thinking about yourself, others, and life. Notice who is present in or absent from your life. Check your health; with things going wrong in your relationship, how does your body feel? What are you feeling or thinking as you review these images?

Now, leave that image and imagine that a second disc, one that shows a very different future scene, begins to play. It is five years from now, and this time, things are different. Your life and relationships are characterized by harmony. You've changed the restrictive beliefs you formed in childhood that once kept you from the love you so desired; you've stopped destructive behaviors that held you back. Take as much time as you need to let this image emerge. Notice where you are, how you look, how you feel, and what you think about yourself and others. What are you doing with your life? Who is there and who is not there? Explore your body along with your health.

As you review this new image, what do you feel and think? The images in our minds and the energy in our bodies are closely linked. The images we harbor—in or out of our awareness—contribute to our future reality. Most often, *what we think we are—we become.*

If your relationship is troubled and addictive, you have thus far been acting out the first set of images. They have quietly affected your feelings, choices, and actions. Assuming you want the second set of images to take hold, it is essential that you embrace those images. Think about them several times a day until they are indelibly imprinted on your mind. From there they will be conveyed to every part of your being.

Carefully examine the second set of images. Define them as clearly as possible, allowing them to become more and more distinct each time you review them.

Now, choose a symbol that will serve as a potent reminder of the future you want for yourself and your relationships. This should be a tangible object that you can view or use daily. Look at it often to remind yourself of the bright future you're working toward. Remember, the more you concentrate on positive images, the more quickly your old images will fade and the less power they will hold over your future.

Exercise 5-C: Finding the Spiritual Guide Within

This exercise is based on the premise that each of us contains a higher self characterized by love, wisdom, detachment, compassion, and spiritual intelligence. The spiritual guide within can be our greatest aid in solving life and relationship problems. Sadly, this higher level of consciousness is often subordinated to the lower instincts that give rise to our addictive tendencies. Real, mature love emanates from the higher self, and it is through our development of this spiritual guide that we will find enduring, sustaining love.

Read slowly through the fantasy that follows. Take several deep breaths until you feel relaxed. Inhaling through your nose and exhaling through your mouth, feel your innocence and vulnerability. Do this several times until your body fully relaxes and releases any distracting thoughts or tensions. Close your eyes.

When you feel ready, without hurrying yourself, imagine you are with a wise, caring, compassionate guide, spiritual teacher, or witness.

Ask the guide what you need to do or let go of to make your future of choice reality. Wait for the answer; if it is clear, thank the guide. If it isn't, continue communicating with the guide until the answer is clear. (Be sure the response comes from a wise, spiritual mentor and not a punitive, parental figure.) Thank the guide for direction and understanding, and know you can return for wise answers anytime you wish. Realize that this detached, compassionate guide is within you. Before you leave the guide, give it a gift—something that symbolizes what you're willing to give up to have the happy future relationship you so desire.

Exercise 5-D: Affirming the Positive

You are no doubt familiar with the concept that positive thinking helps effect change. This idea is not new; it stems not only from modern psychology but also from ancient spiritual teachings that included the idea of prayer as creative visualization. The seeker is urged to avoid thoughts of failure and despair and to replace them with messages of faith, such as "All things are yours" (1 Cor. 3:21), "As a man thinketh within himself, so is he" (Prov. 23:7), and "No longing remains unfulfilled" (Kahlil Gibran).

On a scientific level, this positive process is described simply as action and reaction. An individual is the total of all her thoughts. Such thoughts determine action and affect results even when one is not conscious of them. The thoughts one radiates may be either positive or negative.

The following affirmation technique is a synthesis of ideas from many schools of positive thinking. It has worked well for me personally and for my clients. Let's define *affirmation* as a specific positive thought you create in response to a current need or goal.

Here is our affirmation exercise:

1. Define your desire (in this case, a relationship desire).
2. Think back to the parental message you needed as a child that could permit or affirm this desire.
3. Write the affirmation fifteen times, always including your name: five times in the first person, five times in the second, and five times in the third. (Example: "I, John, deserve love." "You, John, deserve love." "He, John, deserves love.")
4. Listen for any negative responses or feelings you experience while doing these affirmations; if there are any, write them down.
5. Continue to refine your affirmation so it fits comfortably against the negative responses. When it is as you want it, repeat it fifteen times.
6. Imagine your life as if the affirmation had become reality.
7. Release the thought; let your energy flow into pursuits that will turn it into reality.
8. Live your life as though the affirmation is reality. Create or respond to situations that can help you make your desire a reality.
9. Move through this exercise several times a day until the desire has become reality or the new belief feels natural to you, or both. You may switch from writing your affirmation to saying or thinking it.

Exercise 5-E: Putting the Negative to Work for You

Addictive relationships are propped up by core beliefs within our Child ego state that were born of emotionally painful experiences. As children, when we were upset, we told ourselves such things as, "Men (women) are dangerous"; "I'll never get what I need in life"; "People always hurt me"; "I'll never get close again." Such messages, formed in an emotional state, are automatically recorded in our neurology and become part of the foundation of our future reality. Addictive relationships allow us to repeat earlier life pains, and old emotions and myths will surface again and again. At such times, without realizing it, we tend to roll out the negative self-programs we gave ourselves as children. Thus, we often say, "I knew this would happen"; "This proves I should never love again"; "I'll never be this vulnerable again."

We programmed ourselves while we were in an emotional state. It makes sense that an opportune time for reprogramming ourselves for positive relationships is during periods of deep emotion, including painful ones. If you are struggling with an addictive relationship, you may well be feeling such emotion.

Knowing about beliefs formed during profound states of emotion, *you can make use of your current pain—rather than fearing it— as an opportunity to prepare yourself for future healthy relationships.* When your heart is broken, you can tell yourself: "This pain will end, and I will learn to love in healthier ways. I am determined to stop my destructive patterns of behavior because I deserve a healthier, happier love life."

Exercise 5-F: Use Your Pain Wisely and Make It Your Friend

Though the following exercise may not be pleasant, since it involves concentration on pain or unhappiness you usually suppress, its use is certain to be followed by relief. Keep in mind, as you move through this exercise, that bringing bad feelings to the surface usually helps vanquish them.

1. Allow yourself to remember a pain that has troubled you by recalling a life scene where the feeling was present.
2. Listen carefully to negative core beliefs and behaviors associated with that pain.
3. Even as you are conscious of your pain, say to yourself: "I now release myself from the old belief that kept me stuck."
4. Give yourself a new message—an affirmation—that supports mature love.

5. Recognize that your pain has provided you with an opportunity for healing.

6. Trust that the pain eventually will go away. Let go and believe in a better future.

Renewal Exercises: Moving toward Mature Love

You've gained an understanding of how you've contributed to your tendency toward addictive love. You've explored your inner beliefs and begun to free yourself to love in wonderful new ways. You've learned that since you expect and demand less from love, you may get more from love.

When you give up self-limiting beliefs, you experience a high level of energy that brightens your outlook and your life. At this point, you are ready to let go of unhealthy relationships and patterns and move forward.

Exercise 6-A: Forgiveness

I. Self-Forgiveness

While it is important that we become able to forgive others who have hurt us, we must also be willing to fully own up to the wounds of the heart that we have inflicted on others. Just as it is true that we can only love others to the degree we love ourselves, it is also true that we can only forgive others to the degree we can forgive ourselves. No one wants to admit that he has behaved as outrageously as others have toward him. Though we intended to love in good and noble ways, because of our own injuries or role models, we end up saying or doing things we promised ourselves that we would never, under any circumstances, say or do. Until we fully own up to such infractions, we continue to project them onto others.

We must be willing to go back in time and review our relationships and, with full honesty and accountability, be fair witness to our own abusive, hurtful, and injurious behaviors, release each of these events, and connect to the depth of regret or remorse that leads to healing. Changes in our behavior occur when we fully acknowledge that we do not like what we have done because it goes against our own goodness, and when we feel the inner consequences of that acknowledgment.

Leaving denial can be the most healing step we take to attract healthier relationships into our lives. Done right, this exercise helps a person heal very deep heart wounds. Self-trust can be restored.

Read through the steps of the exercise. Create the time and space in which you can give this exercise full attention. Don't expect to get it done in one sitting. With full honesty, it may take hours, or days, to complete. Often, we see what is most obvious first. The subtle nuances generally appear later.

1. Relax physically with deep breathing. Clear your mind.
2. Take time to shift into your higher self, or witness, as described in exercise 5-C. Separate your witness from the self who hurt or betrayed others.
3. Let compassion emanate from your heart. Extend this feeling to the imperfect self.
4. Staying in your witness self, go back in time and recapture each hurtful experience. With honesty, acknowledge the ways you hurt others and the times you even enjoyed getting even.
5. Take one person at a time. Note how that person reacts to your hurtful behavior. As you are ready mentally, send love to the person.
6. Feel the regret and sorrow of each of your actions without self-blame. Observe and release the experience without judgment. Imagine the life energy trapped in that experience coming back to you.
7. Transform the experience by forgiving yourself. Trust that you have learned an important lesson. Note the freedom that you now feel.
8. Empower the experience by clarifying the lesson learned. Make a commitment to do what you can to stop the hurtful behaviors.
9. Make your amends to others as it feels right and as others are available to you. If you are not able to make amends to a person

directly, visualize a dialogue between your higher self and his or her higher self. Or, write a letter that can later be burned or buried.

10. Feel gratitude for the lessons learned and the opportunity to grow. Acknowledge that we are all players in the game of life.

Now, you are ready to forgive others. You may even find it possible to forgive those who remain in denial and who continue to hurt you. As you forgive them, you may experience what seem like miracles as people you never dreamed would ever own their part of hurtful relationships come to you to make heartfelt amends.

II. Forgiveness of Others

One of the ways in which we cling to old, unhealthy ways is by harboring resentments, accusations, guilt, and anger. It is always best to let go of such feelings and try to forgive yourself and others for past mistakes and wrongs. When this comes with difficulty, which it often does, try to separate a person's actions from her personhood. Even if you can't accept people's actions, you may be able to forgive them. Learning to forgive is a process that necessarily involves the release of anger and resentment.

1. Make a list of the people you need to forgive; look particularly at past loves.

2. As you review the list, pick out those people whom you still feel angry with. (Be honest; conning yourself may hurt future relationships.)

3. Write letters to each. Because you will not be sending them, you can fully express your anger. The anger does not have to be rational at this point because you already know that you, too, contributed to the situation that made you angry. Keep in mind that anger is a poison that separates you from others; you are expressing it in order to clear yourself for acceptance and forgiveness. It is nature's way to fill empty vessels; before we are free to say no to the expression of anger, we need to be free to say yes to it. Say yes for now.

4. Acknowledge that you cannot change what has happened in the past. Acknowledge that clinging to anger and resentment keeps you in an addictive cycle that excludes healthier love relationships. By letting go of old anger, you create a vacuum to be filled by new, better feelings.

5. Work to accept reality—what's happened has happened. Acceptance does not mean that you must like a person or his behavior. What lessons did you learn from the experience?

6. Now it is time to forgive. Take time out each day to sit quietly and forgive each person you've been out of harmony with in the past.

7. Make forgiveness a daily habit in your present relationships.

(*Note:* If you find you have difficulty forgiving a person, simply say, "I cannot humanly forgive this person, but my higher self will help me forgive and let go of resentment, for that is in my best interest.")

Exercise 6-B: A New Family Tree

As we give up addictive relationships, we acknowledge that one person cannot possibly meet all of our needs. Ideally, we are supported by a network of others, a large extended family. To assess your own network of support, you may want to create a new kind of family tree and see how many of its spots are filled for you.

1. Make a list of significant relatives and friends you have had or wanted to have.

2. Define the needs each fulfilled or the needs you wanted each to fulfill.

3. Evaluate your current situation to see how many of those people and roles are present.

4. Choose people in your present life who complement or fill those roles. (You can ask nonrelatives if they are willing to serve in the symbolic role of a sister, brother, etc.)

5. Work toward filling in your family tree and strengthening your network of support and love.

Exercise 6-C: Wellness Affirmation

To enter into and sustain a healthy love relationship, or sustain sexual boundaries, one must be complete in oneself and living a life of wellness. *Wellness,* in our context here, means knowing how to meet one's needs and not looking outside oneself for completeness.

Read slowly the following affirmations, personalizing them by inserting your name. If an affirmation feels out of sync, it is an indication that you may need to explore the disharmony, for it hints at a vulnerable spot in your relationship or life.

I, _____, now know what my real needs are and how to meet them.

I, _____, now am freely and effectively expressing my feelings to others.

I, _____, am acting assertively and in ways that consider the feelings and freedom of others.

I, _____, am enjoying my body by means of good nutrition, adequate exercise, and physical awareness.

I, _____, am engaged in activities that are meaningful to me and reflect my inner values.

I, _____, am creating and enjoying close, intimate relationships with others.

I, _____, am responding to challenges in life as opportunities for growth in strength and maturity.

I, _____, am creating the life I want rather than reacting to whatever happens.

I, _____, am using physical signals to bring into my life improvement and increased self-knowledge.

I, _____, am enjoying a sense of well-being even in times of adversity.

I, _____, know my own inner emotional and physical patterns and understand them to be signals from my inner self.

I, _____, trust my own personal resources as the greatest strength for living and growing.

I, _____, am experiencing myself as a wonderful person.

I, _____, am creating situations that help me realize my personal
    worth.

I, _____, believe there is abundance in life for me.

I, _____, am experiencing gratitude for life.

Exercise 6-D: Intentional Relationships

Take the lessons from your relationships and the insights you
learned in the book, and make a list of what you want in friends and
in a romantic partner, current or future.

1. Make two lists—one for best friends and one for intimate
   friends.
2. List the "Absolutely Necessary Qualities." (Example: He is
   honest.)
3. List the "Important Qualities." (Example: She returns my
   calls.)
4. List the "Nice But Not Necessary Qualities." (Example: He
   likes cats.)
5. List the "Bottom Line Qualities." (Example: I will *not* associate
   with anyone who controls with anger.)

Review your list with a mentor that you trust and ask if you
missed anything. If you agree with your mentor's suggestions, add
them to your lists. Now put yourself in places that echo your lists.

Exercise 6-E: Improving Your Relationship

This exercise is for those who choose to remain in their relationship.
When partners in a troubled relationship begin to work toward self-
discovery, and then make a commitment to their relationship, there
are many things they can do immediately to help improve the relationship. These actions are closely linked to their new individual autonomy and self-esteem.

Remember, it is important to focus on the positive in yourself,
others, and your life, and to build on what is already good in a love
relationship. Of course, this does not mean problems should be dismissed. It means you and your partner can enhance what is good—
and perhaps ease some problems—by letting each other know what

is important to each of you. Listed here are some exercises to work on in your relationship.

1. Do what you see lacking. That is, rather than complaining about what your relationship lacks, work to fill the void and to communicate your values and desires to your partner. To truly work, this must be done without expectations; learn the joy of unconditional giving.
   A. If you feel ignored, acknowledge yourself and your partner.
   B. If you want a gift, give your partner something special.
   C. If you want a back rub, offer to give one.
   D. If you feel lonely, reach out to your partner and to others around you.
   E. If you want excitement, be exciting.
   F. If you want support, be supportive.

2. Encourage your partner's growth. Let your partner know all of the ways he or she encourages you and helps you grow. Express your appreciation for all of the good things your partner gives you. Ask your partner how you can be more helpful and supportive.

3. Commit yourself to positive change. Tell your partner how you're willing to change for the benefit of the relationship. (Be sure these changes spring from free choice, not from a forced promise. Free choice is experienced as voluntary yielding; a forced promise generates rebellion later.)

4. Make use of rituals—symbolic, repetitive actions that provide a sense of security and grounding to the child within each of us. Relationship rituals serve to affirm the importance of your bond. For example: A couple with jobs that involved travel wrote notes to each other to be opened on days they were apart. They found this ritual added meaning to the times they were separated.
   A. Think of a ritual that meant something to you as a child and adapt it to your adult life.

    B. Look at your current relationship. What rituals are developing? If they feel good, hang on to them.

    C. Work to create pleasant new rituals that help affirm your bond to your partner.

5. Make giving special. When you no longer expect and demand, the gifts and favors you are given have special value. Here's an exercise that has worked well for many couples.

    A. Make an uncensored list of the things you want from your partner. This list can cover all kinds of things, including sexual wishes.

    B. Exchange lists.

    C. Once a week, choose something from you partner's list and spontaneously give it to your partner.

6. Create private time. True intimacy blooms when individuals have uninterrupted time together to share feelings, thoughts, dreams, play, affection, and sex. A rule of thumb: An hour of sustained intimacy a day keeps troubles away!

7. Serve each other. When you commit yourself in true love, you agree to an almost spiritual yielding, to nourish your beloved, though occasionally it may mean you choose to postpone your own needs. Ask your partner, "How can I serve you?" The answer you receive will be much clearer than if you try to mind-read, as many people trapped in addictive relationships do. Distinguish between caretaking and caregiving.

8. Nourish the relationship. An emotionally healthy person is able to reach out to others, to embrace the good in others, and to let go of others when the time to let go comes. Work to develop the skills for living listed here.

    A. Express appreciation and thanks.

    B. Give spontaneously.

    C. Ask for what you need.

    D. Learn to listen.

    E. Be flexible.

    F. Accept disappointment and "no" from others;
        let go when you must.

    G. Resolve or manage conflicts as openly and with as little
        hostility as possible.

    H. Communicate honestly, from your center.

    I. Accept reality.

    J. Work to develop humility, objectivity, and a respect
        for life.

9. Bring romance, passion, and excitement back. Review the lists in chapter 8, pages 168 and 179–180.

10. Heart-to-Heart Bonding. Though this is a profound and simple exercise, it is not easy for many partners to do. It is based on the premise that at the core of relationship problems is a violation of trust. The first developmental task we had to complete as children was to trust ourselves, others, and life. When the heart is injured by a betrayal of that trust, we are reluctant ever after to share it fully, even though the more inspired part of us wishes to do so. Only by being willing to be vulnerable once again can we heal that betrayal.

    This exercise has been suggested to partners wishing to renew their heartfelt bond after much hurt and betrayal of trust. I have been amazed at how many well-motivated individuals have resisted doing it. I have learned that if a couple is not willing to be emotionally vulnerable, there are limits to the amount of healing or emotional intimacy that can occur in their relationship. This exercise has also been suggested to couples working toward a sacred sexuality experience when recovering from a sexual addiction. In that regard, becoming comfortable sharing our hearts precedes sexual intimacy.

        A. Create a safe and nurturing environment that will allow for privacy and uninterrupted time. This should be mutually discussed and agreed upon.

B. Position yourselves chest-to-chest to allow each person to feel the other's heartbeat against his or her own.

C. Breathe deeply and relax. Do not speak, but instead share your love from the heart.

D. Feel your partner's heartbeat. Stay with the experience.

E. Observe any fear, distancing, or limiting thoughts without judgment. A broken heart takes time to heal.

F. Continue doing this exercise until it flows naturally and easily, and hearts are in sync.

G. Now, share loving feelings heart to heart.

6-F: Safe Communication and Conflict Resolution

How and when we communicate and do conflict resolution is more important than what we are talking about. Here is an example of a communication contract that can be modified to your situation.

1. Accept that the need to communicate and the need to resolve conflict are a part of life.

2. Establish a designated "safe place" to communicate or resolve conflicts. It should never be in the bedroom, in a moving vehicle, in a social setting, or in front of children or family members.

3. If arguing has occurred in the bedroom, do a cleansing ritual and agree that the bedroom is a place to make love, not war.

4. Schedule a time to meet every week for open discussion. If you know you have this time, you do not feel as desperate to talk at inappropriate times, and you know your emotional need or issue is not going to be dropped.

5. Develop and sign a respectful conflict agreement that goes something like this:
   We agree that we are allies working toward the same goal.
   We agree to keep what is said private.
   We agree that what is said will not later be used against the other.
   We agree to no name-calling, shaming, blaming, sarcasm, or offensive or threatening language or behavior.

We agree to let one person speak at a time.

We agree to listen without interrupting or defending.

We agree to use "I" statements rather than "you" statements. (For example: "When you were late, I felt_____and told myself_____, and what I prefer next time is_____.")

We agree to acknowledge what the other said. A simple "I hear you" is enough.

We agree to limit the time of the discussion.

We agree to a time-out if necessary and openly acknowledge: "I will be back."

We agree not to discuss major problems or push the other for discussion when hungry, angry, low, tired, or stressed out (HALTS).

We agree to stay in the now and not bring up the past.

We agree to stay in our Adult ego state and not personalize what the other is saying.

We agree to seek help if we are getting nowhere.[4]

6. Develop a sense of curiosity and wonderment rather than judgment: "I wonder what happened that he or she is having a hard time listening to me." (Something is likely being triggered, or the way something is being said may be accusatory or discounting.)

7. Bring objectivity, compassion, and humility into the discussion.

8. Separate who a person is from his or her emotions and behavior: "I love who you are, and when you overreact to what I say, I feel frustrated."

9. Use the "sandwich" approach when stating a concern or complaint: start with a positive, put in the negative, and end with a positive. "I love you, I am angry that you are not taking care of yourself, and I really want you to be around a long time."

10. Take responsibility for what you bring into the relationship that sabotages intimacy and use this time to make a heartfelt amend when you had a "slip" into old behavior.

11. Verbally celebrate the positives you see in your partner's and your behavior.

12. Close the discussion with some type of ritual: a hug, a prayer, a kiss, a handshake.

6-G: Four Legs of the Recovery Table for Sex, Romance, and Love Addiction

Think of yourself as a tabletop in need of support. You have had only one leg supporting the table, and it was your unhealthy dependency on or addiction to a person, romance, or sex. There are four legs to the table called recovery, each of which is important: behavioral, mental, emotional, and spiritual. Here are suggestions to stabilize each leg of your table.

Behavioral: A person owns the problem and makes a commitment to stop the behavior, understanding that there are no guarantees that a slip or relapse will not occur. For many, it is living one day at a time.

- Attend a support group.
- Dig out lost passions.
- Mentor someone who needs you.
- Write, paint, dance, sing, garden.
- Try something entirely new.
- Have a celebration party.
- Exercise your body.
- Focus on your relationships.
- Read books for fun.
- Go to places you never had the time to visit.
- Renew old friendships.

Mental: A person educates herself about the problem and looks for unhealthy beliefs, rationalizations, contaminated thinking, and cross-wiring that supported addictive love.

- Clean out the core beliefs that supported the addictive love.
- Listen for negative self-talk.
- Replace the negative self-talk with affirming messages.
- Attend lectures and workshops on positive change.
- Read or listen to self-help tapes or CDs.
- Let go of worry.

- Keep an open mind.
- Screen the messages that come your way.
- Stop rationalizing, scrutinizing, personalizing.
- Stop analyzing and trust insights coming to you.
- Keep your mind active and interested in learning.

Emotional: A person examines the psychological contributions to his behaviors and discovers the story behind them. It is this leg of the table that is perhaps the most difficult.

- Look at what emotional needs the addiction was serving.
- Find healthy replacements for getting these needs met.
- Identify what triggers you and get to the source.
- Go back to the day your addiction started and reclaim those years.
- Learn to become your own best friend.
- Learn to recognize and interpret your body sensations and emotions.
- Use your emotions intelligently—tell others what you feel and want.
- Put out a picture of yourself as a child, and every day commit to that child's care and safety.
- Laugh and play and find ways to have positive emotions.
- Weed out people, places, and things from the past that are no longer useful.

Spiritual: A person recognizes she has been out of personal and spiritual integrity and designs a program for spiritual healing and spiritual practices that help her become more heart centered.

- Define for yourself what *higher power* means.
- Develop a spiritual life that fits you.
- Meditate, spend time in nature, or actively pray each day.
- Practice harmlessness.
- Define your higher purpose.
- Visualize yourself two years from now living purposefully.
- Step into basic trust and wonder instead of worry about outcomes.

- Work with the energy of love and not fear.
- Act with ease, poise, grace, and serenity, which invite trust.
- Give to others where it is not noticed.
- Do a service project.

Expansion Exercises: Developing Personal Uniqueness

He who has a why to live can bear any how.

FRIEDRICH NIETZSCHE

Self-imposed limitations in your relationships not only sabotage those relationships but also keep you from achieving your individual potential. As you gain a sense of well-being, you contribute to the health of your relationships as well. And as your relationships provide you with a wonderful sense of interrelatedness with others, you are free to soar to new levels of awareness, meaning, and creativity you've never known before.

Life has but two directions—evolution and devolution; one is a forward motion, one a retrogression. Contrary to what many think, few people stand still; they are either on an upward or a downward spiral.

When faced with a problem we do not know how to solve, we continue to move in a downward spiral. Each time the problem recurs, our dilemma deepens. But if we work to resolve the problem, we spiral in a progressive, upward fashion. Though we may experience the same problem again later, we'll then examine it with greater understanding and confidence, and it will have less emotional impact.

As we give less control to our problems and more to ourselves, we find we're able to channel our energies in order to find our "place in the sun"—not as designed by our relationships, but as we really are. We each have something unique to contribute to the world, but sadly, because of the restrictions people place on themselves and others, such higher purpose often gets ignored or lost.

An addictive stance means that we look outward, denying and repressing the power of the self, and demand that life give us meaning. Once free of addictions, we realize life does not owe us anything;

rather, it is our responsibility to give meaning to life. Freeing ourselves from past bonds does not guarantee a tension-free life, but it provides a healthy tension that challenges us to move toward an ideal of ourselves. The conquering of despair—the filling of what philosophers call the "existential void"—comes when we create our own lives, *mold* our own selves toward our ultimate potential, and contribute to the world community.

The exercises that follow may help you become more attuned to the higher level of consciousness from which your true purpose emanates. Remember that the higher self you seek to discover is more than the sum of its parts.

Exercise 7-A: The Personal Mission

Imagine yourself as a highly developed being somewhere in the cosmos, contemplating a voyage to planet Earth. You've been assigned to evaluate life on Earth and to use your knowledge and talents to enhance its quality. After much thought, you write out your goals:

My purpose on Earth will be _____.

I'll accomplish this purpose by _____.

I'll know I've succeeded when _____.

Study your answers. What do they tell you about your deepest goals and dreams?

Exercise 7-B: Living Consciously

In addition to the opportunity to discover our ultimate purpose as human beings, life offers us situations that challenge us continually to make sense of it all. A person striving to live fully looks forward to all situations—even painful ones—as opportunities to expand into higher levels of consciousness.

Listed here are some things to do to help you live more consciously.

1. Accept situations as they present themselves; don't shun or deny problems.

2. React to situations openly with your thoughts and feelings.
3. Take responsibility for whatever part you may have played in contributing to a problem.
4. Evaluate the truths such acknowledgment presents about you.
5. Study the choices you have.
6. Answer these questions: What lessons can I learn from this experience? How can I prevent this problem from recurring?

Exercise 7-C: Daily Affirmation

As you begin each day, repeat this affirmation five times. As you repeat it, create an image of yourself as though this affirmation were a reality: *This is a time of divine fulfillment. The fruits of my labor and purpose of my life now unfold in clear, harmonious ways. I will do my part.*

There is so much of life we cannot control; we cannot make someone love us. But much of life is in our hands, and what we do, whom we choose, and how we think will show measurable results. Best wishes on your journey toward self-discovery, self-affirmation, and true love. You have taken the time to get to know yourself and to improve the quality of your relationships and your life. You deserve love and life.

Notes

CHAPTER 1:
The Power of Love

1. Erich Fromm, *The Art of Loving* (New York: Harper and Row, 1956), 59–60.

2. Brenda Schaeffer, *Love's Way* (Center City, MN: Hazelden, 2001), 35–36. *Love's Way* gives a comprehensive description of what love is and is not and shares current research on love and health, types of love, and how the body, ego, soul, and spirit express love.

3. Medieval writings, such as *The Art of Courtly Love* by Andreas Capellanus, demonstrate how a balance of the feminine and masculine characterized the search for a mystical form of romantic love.

4. Charlotte D. Kasl, *Women, Sex, and Addiction* (San Francisco: HarperSanFrancisco, 1990), 41.

5. Stanton Peele, with Archie Brodsky, *Love and Addiction* (New York: Signet, 1975).

6. The *Diagnostic and Statistical Manual of Mental Disorders,* third edition, revised (DSM-III-R) (Washington, DC: American Psychiatric Association, 1987), lists nine criteria for the diagnosis of chemical dependency, at least three of which must be met for diagnosis. Most of the criteria concern behavior. In the DSM-IV (Washington, DC: American Psychiatric Association, 1994), each mental disorder is conceptualized as a significant behavior, psychological syndrome, or pattern that results in distress or disability in an area of functioning, or in a significant increase in risk of suffering pain, death, disability, or an important loss of freedom. The descriptive terms *love addiction, romance addiction,* and *sexual addiction* do not appear in the DSM-IV. These are subsumed in various diagnostic categories, and a complete and comprehensive assessment is necessary. Also, it is possible for a single disorder to fit more than one diagnostic category. In my experience working with people attached to love objects in unhealthy or destructive ways, it is not uncommon to have a diagnosis of depression or anxiety; a personality disorder and physical illness; and substantial relational, financial, or other problems that are interfering with treatment and overall functioning. Ariel Goodman, in a list of criteria for an addictive disorder (1989), suggests that

any behavior that is used to produce gratification and to escape internal discomfort can be engaged in compulsively and can constitute an addictive disorder. Jennifer P. Schneider, in an article in the journal *Sexual Addiction and Compulsivity* (1994), summarized the key elements of any addictive disorder as loss of control, continuation despite adverse consequences, and a preoccupation or obsession. (See also Schneider and Irons [1996].)

7.   Harvey Milkman and Stanley Sunderwirth, "Behavioral and Neurochemical Commonalities in Addiction," *Contemporary Family Therapy* 13, no. 5 (1991): 431.

8.   Helen E. Fisher, *Anatomy of Love* (New York: Fawcett Columbine, 1992), 57.

9.   Dorothy Tennov, in her book *Love and Limerence* (New York: Stein and Day, 1979), described limerence as being a romantically compelled high.

10.   Mark R. Laaser, in *Healing the Wounds of Sexual Addiction* (Grand Rapids, MI: Zondervan, 2004), states that experts in the field of sexual addiction speculate that as much as 10 percent of the Christian population is sexually addicted and that it is time to address the problem so that true spiritual healing can occur.

11.   Patrick Carnes, *Don't Call It Love* (New York: Bantam Books, 1991). This classic book describes various aspects of sexual addiction and the recovery process. It is based on the stories of one thousand people and their families afflicted with the disease and committed to recovery.

12.   In his books *Silently Seduced* (Deerfield Beach, FL: Health Communications, 1991) and *When He's Married to Mom* (New York: Fireside, 2007), Kenneth M. Adams presents an understanding of covert incest. He limits his scope to opposite-sex incest survivors while acknowledging that same-sex covert incest damage is parallel.

CHAPTER 2:
The Roots of Addictive Love

1.   Helen E. Fisher, in her book *The Sex Contract* (New York: William Morrow and Co., 1982), gives an anthropological perspective of how the changing of the female estrous cycle affected human relationships.

2.   John Bowlby, *Attachment and Loss: Separation,* vol. 2 (New York: Basic Books, 1973), quoted in Helen E. Fisher, *Why We Love* (New York: Henry Holt and Company, 2004), 166.

3.   Daniel G. Amen, *Sex on the Brain* (New York: Three Rivers Press, 2007), 68–69.

4.   Patrick Carnes, *Don't Call It Love* (New York: Bantam Books, 1991), 31–32.

5.   Michael Liebowitz, *The Chemistry of Love* (Boston: Little, Brown, 1983).

6.   Helen E. Fisher, "Lust, Attraction, and Attachment in Mammalian Reproduction," *Human Nature* 9, no. 1 (1998): 23–52.

7. Amen, *Sex on the Brain,* 58–63.

8. Fisher, *Why We Love,* 212–13.

9. Amen, *Sex on the Brain,* 73–78.

10. Al Cooper, David Delmonico, and Ron Burg, "Cybersex Users, Abusers, and Compulsives: New Findings and Implications," *Sexual Addiction and Compulsivity* 7, no. 1–2 (2000): 5–30. The entire issue of the journal is dedicated to cybersex addiction.

11. Robert Weiss and Jennifer Schneider, *Untangling the Web* (New York: Alyson Books, 2006).

12. Patrick Carnes, *Out of the Shadows,* 3rd ed. (Center City, MN: Hazelden, 2001), xiii–xiv.

13. Jennifer Schneider, "Effects of Cybersex Addiction on the Family: Result of a Survey," *Sexual Addiction and Compulsivity* 7, no. 1–2 (2000): 31–58.

14. Al Cooper and L. Sportolari, "Romance in Cyberspace: Understanding Online Attraction," *Journal of Sex Education and Therapy* 22, no. 1 (1997): 7–14, reported in Milton S. Magness, "Cybersex: A Profile of Addiction and Recovery," a research paper (2004), 5.

15. Abraham Maslow, *Toward a Psychology of Being* (Princeton, NJ: Van Nostrand Reinhold, 1968) and *The Farther Reaches of Human Nature* (New York: Viking, 1971).

16. Jacquelyn Small, *Transformers* (New York: Bantam Books, 1992), 2, 193.

17. Erich Fromm, *The Art of Loving* (New York: Harper and Row, 1956), 18.

CHAPTER 3:
The Psychology of Addictive Love

1. Several transactional analysis references are utilized in this chapter: Eric Berne, *What Do You Say After You Say Hello?* (New York: Grove Press, 1972) and *Games People Play* (New York: Grove Press, 1964); Muriel James and Dorothy Jongeward, *Born to Win* (Reading, MA: Addison-Wesley, 1991); Stanley Woollams and Michael Brown, *Transactional Analysis* (Dexter, MI: Huron Valley Institute Press, 1978); Claude Steiner, *Scripts People Live* (New York: Grove Press, 1974). Transactional analysis theory takes complex psychological information and presents it in clear, comprehensible language that empowers the client. It has been criticized for the simplicity of its language and its reliance on jargon.

2. Berne, *Games People Play,* 23–28.

3. Berne, *What Do You Say After You Say Hello?* chapter 2.

4. Robert D. Phillips, "Structural Symbiotic Systems" (Chapel Hill, NC, 1975), 24–29.

5. The author's *Corrective Parenting Chart* is a summary of the developmental stages, needs, and tasks of each stage; parental do's and don'ts; problems that occur in childhood and adulthood when needs/tasks are not met; and

corrective measures that can be taken. It is an integration of ideas from the developmental theories of Freud, Erikson, Piaget, and Berne. The chart is available from the author (see page 263).

6. Paul MacLean, *The Triune Brain in Evolution* (New York: Plenum, 1990).

7. Peter Levine and Ann Frederick, *Waking the Tiger* (Berkeley, CA: North Atlantic Books, 1997), 19.

CHAPTER 4:
Love Addiction

1. Robert D. Phillips, "Structural Symbiotic Systems" (Chapel Hill, NC, 1975), 6–22.

2. More on boundaries and the characteristics of healthy love can be found in chapter 8 of the author's *Loving Me, Loving You* (Center City, MN: Hazelden, 1991).

3. Stanley Woollams and Michael Brown, *Transactional Analysis* (Dexter, MI: Huron Valley Institute Press, 1978), 84–92.

4. Stephen B. Karpman, "Fairy Tales and Script Drama Analysis," *Transactional Analysis Bulletin* 7 (1968): 39–43.

CHAPTER 5:
Power Plays

1. Chapter 5 in the author's *Loving Me, Loving You* (Center City, MN: Hazelden, 1991) gives an in-depth discussion on the problem of experiencing power as a commodity. Chapter 2 of that book addresses power bases as they are culturally assigned to men and women and how they tend to lock us in power struggles.

CHAPTER 6:
Romance Addiction

1. Dorothy Tennov, *Letters from a State of Limerence* (Greenwich, CT: The Great American Publishing Society, 2007), 2.

2. E. Hartfield and G. W. Walser, *A New Look at Love* (Lanham, MD: University Press of America, 1978), referenced in Helen E. Fisher, *Why We Love* (New York: Henry Holt and Company, 2004), 25.

3. Tennov, *Letters from a State of Limerence*, 4, 5.

4. Andreas Bartels and Semir Zeki, "The Neural Basis of Romantic Love," *NeuroReport* (2000): 3829.

5. Fisher, *Why We Love*, 9.

6. Ibid., 21–22; 173–177.

7. Ibid., 179.

CHAPTER 7:
Sex Addiction

1. Patrick Carnes, *Don't Call It Love* (New York: Bantam Books, 1991), 31–32.

2. Patrick Carnes, *Out of the Shadows,* 3rd ed. (Center City, MN: Hazelden, 2001), 66–67.

3. This percentage was taken from the Society for the Advancement of Sexual Health (SASH) Web site (www.sash.net) as of August 2008. It is based on the number of sex addicts in recovery. Some professionals estimate that the percentage is closer to 6 to 10 percent, given the shame and secrecy surrounding this problem.

4. Al Cooper, David Delmonico, and Ron Burg, "Cybersex Users, Abusers, and Compulsives: New Findings and Implications," *Sexual Addiction and Compulsivity* 7, no. 1–2 (2002): 5–30.

5. Many of these signs were first developed by Dr. Patrick Carnes. For a more comprehensive assessment, a person can take the Sexual Addiction Inventory (SAI), available through its publisher, Gentle Path Press, at www.gentlepath.com.

6. SASH, www.sash.net.

7. Daniel G. Amen, *Sex on the Brain* (New York: Three Rivers Press, 2007), 125.

8. Carnes, *Out of the Shadows,* 26.

9. Ibid., 19–23.

10. M. Deborah Corley and Jennifer P. Schneider, *Disclosing Secrets* (Carefree, AZ: Gentle Path Press, 2002), 43–47.

11. Bessel A. van der Kolk, "Clinical Implications of Neuroscience Research," *New York Academy of Science* (2006): 1–17. The technical name for trauma victims having trouble relating to their emotions and overreacting or underreacting is *alexithyma.*

CHAPTER 8:
Healthy Belonging

1. Erich Fromm, *The Art of Loving* (New York: Harper and Row, 1956), 53.

2. Richard Bach, *The Bridge Across Forever* (New York: William Morrow and Company, Inc., 1984), 210.

3. Stephen A. Mitchell, *Can Love Last?* (New York: W.W. Norton and Co., 2002), 36–39.

4. Daniel G. Amen, *Sex on the Brain* (New York: Three Rivers Press, 2007), 169.

5. Eric Berne, *What Do You Say After You Say Hello?* (New York: Grove

Press, 1972), 137–39. Rackets are now thought to be a composite of distorted feelings supported by internal beliefs and expressed in external behaviors, as described by Richard Erskine and Marilyn Zalcman in "Rackets and Other Treatment Issues," *Transactional Analysis Journal* 9, no. 1 (January 1979): 51–59.

6. Neuroscientists make a technical distinction between a feeling and an emotion. An emotion is a neural system that signals behaviors needed for survival, and a feeling is our conscious perception of these emotions. I believe that what they refer to as an emotion I refer to as reactive feeling. I use the words interchangeably throughout the book and differentiate between a body sensation and an emotional feeling.

7. Fromm, *The Art of Loving,* 112.

CHAPTER 9:
From Addiction to Love

1. Viktor E. Frankl, *Man's Search for Meaning* (New York: Pocket Books, 1963), 58–60.

2. C. Norman Shealy, *90 Days to Self-Health* (New York: Bantam, 1978), 36, 45. Our central management system, the hypothalamus and the limbic systems, seems to require that habits be patterned and repeatedly programmed to reach the lower levels of consciousness.

CHAPTER 10:
Helping Yourself Out of Addictive Love

1. The self-help exercises offered here were developed by the author for specific workshop modules and in response to client requests and needs. They have been modified for a reading audience, though some may wish to record the exercises on audiocassette tape for greater ease of use. Do as much or as little of each exercise as is comfortable, and seek professional help when needed.

2. What you think may have happened in the past, and your impressions, conclusions, and beliefs about past events, are at least as important as what, in fact, occurred. Past events cannot be changed; sometimes, they cannot even be corroborated. However, how we feel about those events, how we interpret and frame them in our lives, can be changed.

3. Charles L. Whitfield's *Memory and Abuse* (Deerfield Beach, FL: Health Communications, 1995) is a thoroughly documented, groundbreaking work on healing from the effects of childhood trauma. It addresses the psychology of memory, the history of child abuse, ways to verify and corroborate a memory, and methods for sorting true from untrue memories.

4. Some of the items on the list of healthy conflict resolution are an adaptation of the RCA (Recovering Couples Anonymous) list.

Bibliography

Ackerman, Diane. *A Natural History of Love*. New York: Random House, 1994.

Adams, Kenneth M. *Silently Seduced: When Parents Make Their Children Partners*. Deerfield Beach, FL: Health Communications, 1991.

———. *When He's Married to Mom: How to Help Mother-Enmeshed Men Open Their Hearts to True Love and Commitment*. New York: Fireside, 2007.

Almass, A. H. *Facets of Unity: The Enneagram of Holy Ideas*. Berkeley, CA: Diamond Books, 1998.

Amen, Daniel G. *Sex on the Brain: 12 Lessons to Enhance Your Love Life*. New York: Three Rivers Press, 2007.

Bach, Richard. *The Bridge Across Forever: A True Love Story*. New York: William Morrow and Company, Inc., 1984.

Bartels, Andreas, and Semir Zeki. "The Neural Basis of Romantic Love." *NeuroReport* (2000): 3829.

Beattie, Melody. *Beyond Codependency: And Getting Better All the Time*. Center City, MN: Hazelden, 1989.

———. *Codependents' Guide to the Twelve Steps*. New York: Simon and Schuster, 1990.

Berne, Eric. *Games People Play: The Psychology of Human Relationships*. New York: Grove Press, 1964.

———. *Transactional Analysis in Psychotherapy: A Systematic Individual and Social Psychiatry*. New York: Grove Press, 1961.

———. *What Do You Say After You Say Hello?* New York: Grove Press, 1972.

Bly, Robert. *Iron John: A Book About Men*. Reading, MA: Addison-Wesley, 1990.

Branden, Nathaniel. *The Psychology of Romantic Love: Romantic Love in an Antiromantic Age*. Toronto: Bantam Books, 1980.

Buscaglia, Leo. *Love: What Life Is All About*. New York: Fawcett Crest, 1972.

Campbell, Joseph, with Bill Moyers. *The Power of Myth*. New York: Doubleday, 1988.

Capellanus, Andreas. *The Art of Courtly Love*. Edited by Frederick W. Locke. New York: Ungar, 1957.

Capra, Fritjof. *The Turning Point: Science, Society, and the Rising Culture*. New York: Bantam Books, 1982.

———. *Uncommon Wisdom*. New York: Bantam Books, 1989.

Carnes, Patrick. *The Betrayal Bond: Breaking Free of Exploitive Relationships.* Deerfield Beach, FL: Health Communications, 1997.

———. *Contrary to Love: Helping the Sexual Addict.* Center City, MN: Hazelden, 1989.

———. *Don't Call It Love: Recovery from Sexual Addiction.* New York: Bantam Books, 1991.

———. *Out of the Shadows: Understanding Sexual Addiction.* 3rd ed. Center City, MN: Hazelden, 2001.

———. *Sexual Addiction and Compulsivity: The Journal of Treatment and Prevention* 1, no. 1 (1994).

———. *Sexual Anorexia: Overcoming Sexual Self-Hatred.* Center City, MN: Hazelden, 1997.

Clarke, Jean Illsley. *Self-Esteem: A Family Affair.* Center City, MN: Hazelden, 1978.

Colgrove, Melba, Harold H. Bloomfield, and Peter McWilliams. *How to Survive the Loss of a Love.* Toronto: Bantam Books, 1976.

Cooper, Al, David Delmonico, and Ron Burg. "Cybersex Users, Abusers, and Compulsives: New Findings and Implications." *Sexual Addiction and Compulsivity* 7, no. 1–2 (2000): 5–30.

Corley, M. Deborah, and Jennifer P. Schneider. *Disclosing Secrets: When, to Whom, and How Much to Reveal.* Carefree, AZ: Gentle Path Press, 2002.

Cousins, Norman. *Human Options: An Autobiographical Notebook.* New York: W.W. Norton and Co., 1981.

Covington, Stephanie, and Liana Beckett. *Leaving the Enchanted Forest: The Path from Relationship Addiction to Intimacy.* San Francisco: HarperSanFrancisco, 1988.

Damasio, Antonio. *Descartes Error: Emotion, Reason, and the Human Brain.* New York: Putnam, 1994.

DeMause, L. "The Universality of Incest." *Journal of Psychohistory* 19, no. 2: 123–64.

Diagnostic and Statistical Manual of Mental Disorders. 3rd ed. rev. (DSM-III-R). Washington, DC: American Psychiatric Association, 1987.

Diagnostic and Statistical Manual of Mental Disorders. 4th ed. (DSM-IV). Washington, DC: American Psychiatric Association, 1994.

Diamond, Jed. *Looking for Love in All the Wrong Places: Overcoming Romantic and Sexual Addictions.* New York: Avon, 1989.

Eisler, Riane. *The Chalice and the Blade: Our History, Our Future.* San Francisco: HarperSanFrancisco, 1988.

———. *Sacred Pleasure: Sex, Myth, and the Politics of the Body.* San Francisco: HarperSanFrancisco, 1995.

Erskine, Richard, and Marilyn Zalcman. "Rackets and Other Treatment Issues." *Transactional Analysis Journal* 9, no. 1 (January 1979).

Fisher, Helen E. *Anatomy of Love: A Natural History of Mating, Marriage, and Why We Stray.* New York: Fawcett Columbine, 1992.

———. "Lust, Attraction, and Attachment in Mammalian Reproduction." *Human Nature* 9, no. 1 (1998): 23–52.

———. *The Sex Contract.* New York: William Morrow and Co., 1982.

———. *Why We Love: The Nature and Chemistry of Romantic Love.* New York: Henry Holt and Company, 2004.

Fox, Matthew. *Original Blessing.* Santa Fe, NM: Bear and Co., 1983.

Frankl, Viktor E. *Man's Search for Meaning.* New York: Pocket Books, 1963.

Freud, Sigmund. *Sexuality and the Psychology of Love.* New York: Collier Books, 1963.

Fromm, Erich. *The Art of Loving.* New York: Harper and Row, 1956.

Gibran, Kahlil. *The Prophet.* New York: Random House, 1951.

Goodman, Ariel. "Addiction Defined: Diagnostic Criteria for Addictive Disorder." *American Journal of Preventive Psychiatry and Neurology* 2 (1989): 12–15.

Goulding, Mary McClure, and Robert Goulding. *Changing Lives Through Redecision Therapy.* New York: Brunner/Mazel, 1979.

———. *The Power Is in the Patient: A TA/Gestalt Approach to Psychotherapy.* San Francisco: TA Press, 1978.

Grof, Christina, and Stanislav Grof. *The Stormy Search for the Self: A Guide to Personal Growth Through Transformational Crisis.* Los Angeles: Tarcher, 1990.

Grubbman-Black, Stephen D. *Broken Boys/Mending Men.* New York: Ivy Books, 1990.

Guillaumont, A., H.-Ch. Puech, and G. Quispel, translators. *The Gospel According to Thomas.* New York: Harper and Row, 1959.

Ingerman, Sandra. *Soul Retrieval: Mending the Fragmented Self through Shamanic Practice.* San Francisco: HarperSanFrancisco, 1991.

James, Muriel, and Dorothy Jongeward. *Born to Win.* Reading, MA: Addison-Wesley, 1991.

Johnson, Robert A. *He: Understanding Masculine Psychology.* New York: Harper and Row, 1986.

———. *Inner Work: Using Dreams and Creative Imagination.* San Francisco: Harper and Row, 1986.

———. *She: Understanding Feminine Psychology.* New York: Harper and Row, 1997.

———. *We: Understanding the Psychology of Romantic Love.* San Francisco: Harper and Row, 1983.

Kalin, N. "The Neurobiology of Fear." *Scientific American* (May 1993).

Karpman, Stephen B. "Fairy Tales and Script Drama Analysis." *Transactional Analysis Bulletin* 7 (1968): 39–43.

Kasl, Charlotte D. *Women, Sex, and Addiction: The Search for Love and Power.* San Francisco: HarperSanFrancisco, 1990.

Keyes, Ken. *A Conscious Person's Guide to Relationships.* Coos Bay, OR: Living Love Publications, 1979.

———. *Handbook to Higher Consciousness.* Berkeley, CA: Living Love Center, 1975.

Laaser, Mark R. *Healing the Wounds of Sexual Addiction.* Grand Rapids, MI: Zondervan, 2004.

Labowitz, Rabbi Shoni. *Miraculous Living.* New York: Simon and Schuster, 1996.

Lerner, Harriet. *The Dance of Intimacy: A Woman's Guide to Courageous Acts of Change in Key Relationships.* New York: Harper Perennial, 1990.

Levine, Peter, and Ann Frederick. *Waking the Tiger: Healing Trauma.* Berkeley, CA: North Atlantic Books, 1997.

Lewis, Thomas, Fari Amini, and Richard Lannon. *A General Theory of Love.* New York: Vintage House, 2001.

Liebowitz, Michael. *The Chemistry of Love.* Boston: Little, Brown, 1983.

MacLean, Paul. *The Triune Brain in Evolution.* New York: Plenum, 1990.

Magness, Milton S. "Cybersex: A Profile of Addiction and Recovery." A research paper, 2004.

Maslow, Abraham. *The Farther Reaches of Human Nature.* New York: Viking, 1971.

———. *Toward a Psychology of Being.* Princeton, NJ: Van Nostrand Reinhold, 1968.

Mellody, Pia. *Facing Love Addiction: Giving Yourself the Power to Change the Way You Love.* San Francisco: HarperSanFrancisco, 1992.

Milkman, Harvey, and Stanley Sunderwirth. "Behavioral and Neurochemical Commonalities in Addiction." *Contemporary Family Therapy* 13, no. 5 (1991).

Mitchell, Stephen A. *Can Love Last? The Fate of Romance Over Time.* New York: W.W. Norton and Co., 2002.

Myss, Caroline, and C. Norman Shealy. *The Creation of Health: The Emotional, Psychological, and Spiritual Responses That Promote Health and Healing.* Walpole, NH: Stillpoint, 1993.

Needleman, Jacob. *A Little Book on Love.* New York: Dell, 1996.

Paddison, Sara. *The Hidden Power of the Heart: Discovering an Unlimited Source of Intelligence.* Boulder Creek, CA: Planetary, 1998.

Palmer, Helen. *The Enneagram in Love and Work: Understanding Your Intimate and Business Relationships.* San Francisco: Harper and Row, 1995.

———. *The Enneagram: Understanding Yourself and Others in Your Life.* New York: Harper and Row, 1988.

Peck, M. Scott. *The Road Less Traveled.* New York: Simon and Schuster, 1978.

Peele, Stanton, with Archie Brodsky. *Love and Addiction.* New York: Signet, 1975.

Phillips, Robert D. "Structural Symbiotic Systems: Correlations with Ego States, Behavior, and Physiology." Chapel Hill, NC: 1975.

Ponder, Catherine. *The Dynamic Laws of Prosperity.* Englewood Cliffs, NJ: Prentice Hall, 1962.

Ray, Sondra. *I Deserve Love: How Affirmations Can Guide You to Personal Fulfillment*. Millbrae, CA: Les Femmes, 1976.

———. *Loving Relationships*. Berkeley, CA: Celestial Arts, 1980.

Ruskan, John. *Emotional Clearing: A Self-Therapy Guide to Releasing Negative Feelings*. New York: R. Wyler and Co., 1993.

Schaef, Anne Wilson. *Escape from Intimacy: Untangling the "Love" Addictions: Sex, Romance, Relationships*. San Francisco: HarperSanFrancisco, 1990.

———. *When Society Becomes an Addict*. San Francisco: Harper and Row, 1987.

Schaeffer, Brenda. *Corrective Parenting Chart*. 5th ed. 2005.

———. *Love or Addiction: The Power and Peril of Teen Sex and Romance*. Andover, MN: Expert Publishing, 2006.

———. *Love's Way: The Union of Body, Ego, Soul, and Spirit*. Center City, MN: Hazelden, 2001.

———. *Loving Me, Loving You: Balancing Love and Power in a Codependent World*. Center City, MN: Hazelden, 1991.

Scheid, Robert. *Beyond the Love Game: An Inner Guide to Finding Your Mate*. Millbrae, CA: Celestial Arts, 1980.

Schneider, Jennifer P. *Back from Betrayal: Recovering from His Affairs*. 3rd ed. Tucson, AZ: Recovery Resources Press, 2005.

———. "Effects of Cybersex Addiction on the Family: Result of a Survey." *Sexual Addiction and Compulsivity* 7, no. 1–2 (2000): 31–58.

———. "Sex Addiction: Controversy within Mainstream Addiction Medicine, Diagnosis Based on the DSM-III and Physician Case Histories." *Sexual Addiction and Compulsivity* 1, no. 1 (1994): 19–45.

Schneider, Jennifer P., and Bert Schneider. *Sex, Lies, and Forgiveness: Couples Speaking Out on Healing from Sex Addiction*. 3rd ed. Tucson, AZ: Recovery Resources Press, 2004.

Schneider, Jennifer, and Richard Irons. "Differential Diagnosis of Addictive Sexual Disorders Using the DSM-IV." *Sexual Addiction and Compulsivity* 3, no. 1 (1996): 7–21.

Shealy, C. Norman. *90 Days to Self-Health*. New York: Bantam, 1978.

Sipes, A. W. Richard. *Sex, Priests, and Power*. New York: Brunner/Mazel, 1995.

Small, Jacquelyn. *Transformers: The Artists of Self-Creation*. New York: Bantam Books, 1992.

Steiner, Claude. *Scripts People Live: Transactional Analysis of Life Scripts*. New York: Grove Press, 1974.

Tennov, Dorothy. *Letters from a State of Limerence*. Greenwich, CT: The Great American Publishing Society, 2007.

———. *Love and Limerence*. New York: Stein and Day, 1979.

van der Kolk, Bessel A. "Clinical Implications of Neuroscience Research." *New York Academy of Science* (2006): 1–17.

van der Kolk, Bessel A., Alexander C. McFarlane, and Lars Weisaeth, editors. *Traumatic Stress: The Effects of Overwhelming Experience on Mind, Body, and Society.* New York: The Guilford Press, 1996.

Weed, Joseph. *Wisdom of the Mystic Masters.* West Nyack, NY: Parker Publishing Co., 1968.

Weiss, Robert, and Jennifer Schneider. *Untangling the Web: Sex, Porn, and Fantasy Obsession in the Internet Age.* New York: Alyson Books, 2006.

Whitfield, Charles L. *Memory and Abuse.* Deerfield Beach, FL: Health Communications, 1995.

Williams, Margery. *The Velveteen Rabbit.* New York: Doubleday and Co., 1975.

Woollams, Stanley, and Michael Brown. *Transactional Analysis: A Modern and Comprehensive Text of TA Theory and Practice.* Dexter, MI: Huron Valley Institute Press, 1978.

Woollams, Stanley, Michael Brown, and Kristyn Huige. *Transactional Analysis in Brief.* Ypsilanti, MI: Spectrum Psychological Services, 1974.

Resources for Further Information

Brenda Schaeffer
www.loveaddiction.com

American Foundation for Addiction
  Research (AFAR) (for information
  on sexual addiction)
www.addictionresearch.com

Peter Levine and the Foundation for
  Human Enrichment
www.traumahealing.com

The International Transactional
  Analysis Association
www.itaa-net.org

Hazelden
www.hazelden.org

Daniel Amen, M.D.
www.amenclinics.com

CyberSexualAddiction.com (for infor-
  mation on cybersex)
www.cybersexualaddiction.com

Jennifer P. Schneider, M.D., Ph.D.
www.jenniferschneider.com

Patrick Carnes, Ph.D., and
  SexHelp.com
www.sexhelp.com

Helen E. Fisher, Ph.D.
www.helenfisher.com

Robert Weiss and the Sexual Recovery
  Institute (SRI)
www.sexualrecovery.com

The Society for the Advancement of
  Sexual Health (SASH)
P.O. Box 433
Royston, GA 30662
706-356-7031
www.sash.net

Resources for Support

Co-Dependents Anonymous (CoDA)
www.codependents.org

COSA
P.O. Box 14537
Minneapolis, MN 55414
763-537-6904
www.cosa-recovery.org

Love Addicts Anonymous (LAA)
www.loveaddicts.org

Sex Addicts Anonymous (SAA)
P.O. Box 70949
Houston, TX 77270
800-477-8191 or 713-869-4902
www.sexaa.org

Sex and Love Addicts Anonymous (SLAA)
www.slaafws.org

Sexaholics Anonymous (SA)
P.O. Box 3565
Brentwood, TN 37024
866-424-8777 or 615-370-6062
www.sa.org

Sexual Compulsives Anonymous (SCA)
P.O. Box 1585, Old Chelsea Station
New York, NY 10011
800-977-HEAL
www.sca-recovery.org

Recovering Couples Anonymous (RCA)
P.O. Box 11029
Oakland, CA 94611
510-663-2312
www.recovering-couples.org

Index

About the Author

More than a psychologist, author, and speaker, Brenda Schaeffer, D.Min., M.A.L.P., C.A.S., is the friend next door you don't mind telling your secrets to. Described as warm, wise, and down to earth, she radiates the soul and spirit of a sage, the experience of a highly trained psychologist, and a playful curiosity. She believes that daily challenges can be just the thing we need to wake up to a better life. In a convincing and compassionate style, she has guided hundreds of people to become their own best friend. In her published works—including best-seller *Is It Love or Is It Addiction?* (now in five languages); *Love or Addiction? The Power and Peril of Teen Sex and Romance; Love's Way: The Union of Body, Ego, Soul, and Spirit; Loving Me, Loving You: Balancing Love and Power in a Codependent World;* and the Healthy Relationships Series—she shows her gift of putting problems in street-smart language and then giving practical advice on how to solve them. She has appeared on numerous national television and radio shows and has been quoted in other news media. Her experience, knowledge, and realness make her an exceptional speaker and trainer.

Dr. Schaeffer is a licensed psychologist, is a certified addiction specialist, and holds a doctorate in spiritual psychology. She has extensive training and experience in a number of psychologies including, but not limited to, child development, sexual addiction, and trauma. Brenda has served six years on the board of directors of SASH (the Society for the Advancement of Sexual Health), is a member of the International Transactional Analysis Association and the International Association of Enneagram Teachers, and is in private practice in Minneapolis, Minnesota. Her other publications include a meditation CD, *Inner Reflections,* and a developmental chart, *Corrective Parenting.*

Dr. Schaeffer lectures and trains internationally on a wide range of topics and can be reached for private consultation, training, workshops, speaking engagements, or media interviews by one of the following:

Phone: 888-987-6129

E-mail: brenda@brendaschaeffer.com

Web: www.loveaddiction.com or www.itsallaboutlove.com

HAZELDEN, a national nonprofit organization founded in 1949, helps people reclaim their lives from the disease of addiction. Built on decades of knowledge and experience, Hazelden offers a comprehensive approach to addiction that addresses the full range of patient, family, and professional needs, including treatment and continuing care for youth and adults, research, higher learning, public education and advocacy, and publishing.

A life of recovery is lived "one day at a time." Hazelden publications, both educational and inspirational, support and strengthen lifelong recovery. In 1954, Hazelden published *Twenty-Four Hours a Day,* the first daily meditation book for recovering alcoholics, and Hazelden continues to publish works to inspire and guide individuals in treatment and recovery, and their loved ones. Professionals who work to prevent and treat addiction also turn to Hazelden for evidence-based curricula, informational materials, and videos for use in schools, treatment programs, and correctional programs.

Through published works, Hazelden extends the reach of hope, encouragement, help, and support to individuals, families, and communities affected by addiction and related issues.

For questions about Hazelden publications, please call **800-328-9000** or visit us online at **hazelden.org/bookstore.**